Leisure, Activism, and the Animation of the Urban Environment

This book brings together chapters that address questions of leisure, activism, and the animation of urban environments. The authors share research that explores the meaning and making of activist practices, events of dissent, and the arts in everyday life.

Situated in a growing body of activist scholarship and social justice research, within the field of leisure studies, the contributions spotlight understandings and disruptions of public spaces in cities. These range from overtly political practices such as protest marches to recreational practices such as skateboarding and bicycling that remake cities through their contestations of space. Across the collection the chapters raise broader questions of civil society, whether it is research on youth activism, historical uses of public spaces by right-wing or racist groups, or interrogating the absence of leisure and closure of public spaces for people experiencing homelessness. Some chapters explore events, such as festivals as sites of resistance and social change. In others, grassroots neighbourhood activism through arts is centralised, or mega-events are framed through protest campaigns against bids to host the Summer Olympic Games. A central thread running through the chapters is the question of whose voices count and whose remain unheard in events of dissent in the city.

The chapters in this book were originally published as a special issue of *Leisure Studies*.

Ian R. Lamond is Senior Lecturer in Event Studies at Leeds Beckett University, UK. Ian's primary research interests are in events of dissent, leisure activism, and creative forms of protest, though he has also worked in the fields of fandom studies, death studies, and political communication. His most recent book, *Death and Events: International Perspectives on Events that Mark the End of Life* (Routledge, 2022) considers the intersection between event studies and death studies, and he was a guest editor, with Karl Spracklen, of a recent issue of the *Journal of Fandom Studies* (2020).

Brett Lashua is Lecturer in Sociology of the Media and Education at University College London, UK. Brett's interdisciplinary research spans cultural sociology, youth leisure, popular culture, and media studies, underpinned by interests in cultural histories and cultural geographies.

Chelsea Reid is Part-Time Lecturer in the Leeds School of Arts at Leeds Beckett University, UK, who currently teaches across postgraduate music courses in skills development and research. Chelsea has previously taught in the broad areas of media and journalism at an undergraduate level. Her research interests include political communication, mediatisation, and the portrayal of North Korea within Western media.

Leisure, Activism, and the Animation of the Urban Environment

Edited by
Ian R. Lamond, Brett Lashua and Chelsea Reid

LONDON AND NEW YORK

First published 2023
by Routledge
4 Park Square, Milton Park, Abingdon, Oxon, OX14 4RN

and by Routledge
605 Third Avenue, New York, NY 10158

Routledge is an imprint of the Taylor & Francis Group, an informa business

British Library Cataloguing-in-Publication Data
A catalogue record for this book is available from the British Library

ISBN13: 978-1-032-35809-3 (hbk)
ISBN13: 978-1-032-35810-9 (pbk)
ISBN13: 978-1-003-32870-4 (ebk)

DOI: 10.4324/9781003328704

Typeset in Minion Pro
by codeMantra

Publisher's Note
The publisher accepts responsibility for any inconsistencies that may have arisen during the conversion of this book from journal articles to book chapters, namely the inclusion of journal terminology.

Disclaimer
Every effort has been made to contact copyright holders for their permission to reprint material in this book. The publishers would be grateful to hear from any copyright holder who is not here acknowledged and will undertake to rectify any errors or omissions in future editions of this book.

Contents

Citation Information

The following chapters were originally published in *Leisure Studies*, volume 40, issue 1 (2021). When citing this material, please use the original page numbering for each article, as follows:

Introduction

Leisure, activism, and the animation of the urban environment
Ian R. Lamond and Brett Lashua
Leisure Studies, volume 40, issue 1 (2021) pp. 1–12

Chapter 1

A People's History of Leisure Studies: Where the White Nationalists Are
Rasul A. Mowatt
Leisure Studies, volume 40, issue 1 (2021) pp. 13–30

Chapter 2

The right to exist: homelessness and the paradox of leisure
Justin Harmon
Leisure Studies, volume 40, issue 1 (2021) pp. 31–41

Chapter 3

Skateboarding, gentle activism, and the animation of public space: CITE – A Celebration of Skateboard Arts and Culture at The Bentway
Troy D. Glover, Sarah Munro, Immony Men, Wes Loates and Ilana Altman
Leisure Studies, volume 40, issue 1 (2021) pp. 42–56

Chapter 4

The transgressive festival imagination and the idealisation of reversal
Kirstie Jamieson and Louise Todd
Leisure Studies, volume 40, issue 1 (2021) pp. 57–68

Chapter 5

Event bidding and new media activism
David McGillivray, John Lauermann and Daniel Turner
Leisure Studies, volume 40, issue 1 (2021) pp. 69–81

Chapter 6

Experiences of urban cycling: emotional geographies of people and place
Rudy Dunlap, Jeff Rose, Sarah H. Standridge and Courtney L. Pruitt
Leisure Studies, volume 40, issue 1 (2021) pp. 82–95

Chapter 7

Leisure activism and engaged ethnography: *heterogeneous voices and the urban palimpsest*
Ian R. Lamond, Esther Solano and Vitor Blotta
Leisure Studies, volume 40, issue 1 (2021) pp. 96–108

Chapter 8

Young activists in political squats. Mixing engagement and leisure
Carlo Genova
Leisure Studies, volume 40, issue 1 (2021) pp. 109–120

Chapter 9

The emerging civil society. Governing through leisure activism in Milan
Sebastiano Citroni and Alessandro Coppola
Leisure Studies, volume 40, issue 1 (2021) pp. 121–133

Notes on Contributors

Ilana Altman is Co-Executive Director at The Bentway, a non-profit organisation in Toronto, Canada. She is Cultural Planner and Designer who has a background in art and architecture. In her role as Co-Executive Director, she works with the community to implement innovative and engaging programming, revealing new possibilities for public space, and cultivates the best visitor experience possible.

Vitor Blotta is Professor of Journalism and Media Law at the School of Communications and Arts at the University of Sao Paulo, Brazil, and Vice-Coordinator of the Centre for the Study of Violence at the same university. His research involves topics such as critical theory; the public sphere; human rights; media and communications policies; social movements; and culture.

Sebastiano Citroni teaches Sociology of Cultures and Sociology of Communication & Tourism at the Department of Law, Economics and Cultures at the University of Insubria, Como, Italy. His research interests include civil society, ethnography, social theory, events, and group styles.

Alessandro Coppola teaches Urban Planning and Urban Policy at the Department of Architecture and Urban Studies at Politecnico di Milano, Italy. His research interests include urban shrinkage, urban informality, neighbourhood policies and politics, and international urban networks.

Rudy Dunlap is Associate Professor at the Department of Health and Human Performance at Middle Tennessee State University, Murfreesboro, USA. His research has generally addressed leisure as a socio-cultural context in which community development and social changes take place.

Carlo Genova is Associate Professor at the University of Turin, Italy, where he teaches Sociology of Culture and Lifestyles and Urban Spaces. His main study interests focus on youth cultures, lifestyles and subcultures theories, and social space dynamics. In recent years, his main fields of empirical research have been youth cultures in urban space, youth political activism, and forms of religious participation.

Troy D. Glover is Professor and Chair at the Department of Recreation and Leisure Studies and Director of the Healthy Communities Research Network at the University of Waterloo, Canada. His research is focused on what he refers to as transformative placemaking, the creation of positive change for people and communities through the (re)shaping, (re) territorialising, and (re)making of community spaces.

Justin Harmon is Assistant Professor at the Department of Community and Therapeutic Recreation at the University of North Carolina Greensboro, USA. His research includes exploring the use of music for life course development, recreation interventions, post-diagnosis of cancer (nature immersion and music making), and community development through leisure.

Kirstie Jamieson co-leads an MFA in Design for Heritage and Culture at Edinburgh Napier University, UK. Her research explores festival space, cultural planning, urban heritage, and minority cultures. Kirstie is currently leading a Deaf Heritage project that brings together critical design and critical heritage to imagine BSL in public life. She is most interested in the critical potential of festivals to serve as platforms for excluded communities.

Ian R. Lamond is Senior Lecturer in Event Studies at Leeds Beckett University, UK. Ian's primary research interests are in events of dissent, leisure activism, and creative forms of protest, though he has also worked in the fields of fandom studies, death studies, and political communication. His most recent book, *Death and Events: International Perspectives on Events that Mark the End of Life* (Routledge, 2022) considers the intersection between event studies and death studies, and he was aGuest Editor, with Karl Spracklen, of a recent issue of the *Journal of Fandom Studies* (2020).

John Lauermann is Assistant Professor of Geography and Deputy Chair of the Social & Behavioral Sciences Department at Medgar Evers College at the City University of New York, USA. He is Urban Geographer who researches the planning and spatial impacts of large-scale real estate projects. His current project uses GIS to analyse the impact of luxury housing development on gentrification in New York City.

Brett Lashua is Lecturer in Sociology of the Media and Education at University College London, UK. Brett's interdisciplinary research spans cultural sociology, youth leisure, popular culture, and media studies, underpinned by interests in cultural histories and cultural geographies.

Wes Loates is Activist, Skateboarder, and Member of Build for Bokma, a Toronto-based not-for-profit organisation. The group's mandate is to produce multifunctional skateable structures within public space, and their long-term goal is to create a memorial DIY skate park that commemorates the life of pro-skateboarder Justin Bokma.

David McGillivray is Professor at the School of Business and Creative Studies at the University of the West of Scotland, UK. He is Co-Investigator on a major UK/Canadian collaborative project, exploring the role of sport events for persons with a disability in influencing community accessibility and community perceptions of disability.

Immony Men is Assistant Professor in the Digital Futures program at OCAD University, Toronto, Canada, and Co-Director of the Public Visualization Lab. His research focuses on developing a theoretical framework for understanding (specifically Khmer/Cambodian) diasporic experience through media praxis, critical race theory, and various forms of community engagement.

Rasul A. Mowatt is Head and Professor of the Department of Parks, Recreation, and Tourism Management at North Carolina State University, USA. He is President of The Academy of Leisure Sciences, Co-Editor of *Leisure Sciences*, and Founding Editor of *Recreation, Parks and Tourism in Public Health*. His areas of interest are social justice and the geographies of race.

Sarah Munro is Senior Manager of Programming at The Bentway Conservancy. Sarah has a background in the fine arts and museum collections management and has worked with a wide range of arts and cultural heritage organisations, including the Genocide Archive of Rwanda, the UK's National Holocaust Centre and Museum, and the Canadian Lesbian and Gay Archives, to name a few. At The Bentway, Sarah facilitates meaningful interactions between the city's diverse communities, within a gathering space of layered historical significance.

Courtney L. Pruitt is Instructor at Rutherford County Schools, Tennessee. She holds a Doctor of Philosophy (Ph.D.) focused on Parks, Recreation and Leisure Studies from Middle Tennessee State University, Murfreesboro, USA. She is Experienced Certified Athletic Trainer with a history of working in the hospital and health care industry.

Chelsea Reid is Part-Time Lecturer in the Leeds School of Arts at Leeds Beckett University, UK, who currently teaches across postgraduate music courses in skills development and research. Chelsea has previously taught in the broad areas of media and journalism at an undergraduate level. Her research interests include political communication, mediatisation, and the portrayal of North Korea within Western media.

Jeff Rose is Assistant Professor-Lecturer at the Department of Parks, Recreation, and Tourism and Affiliate Faculty with the Global Change and Sustainability Center at the University of Utah, USA. Jeff's research agenda uses political ecology to take a social and environmental justice approach to nature-society relations. His research tends to leverage qualitative and spatial methods to examine systemic inequities expressed through class, race, political economy, and relationships to nature.

Esther Solano is Adjunct Professor of International Relations at the Federal University of São Paulo, Brazil, and Professor of the International Interuniversity Master of Contemporary Studies in Latin America at the Universidad Complutense de Madrid, Spain. She is also Member of the Brazilian Forum of Public Security and focuses on social movements and urban conflicts in her research.

Sarah H. Standridge is Assistant Professor in the Department of Sport, Exercise, Recreation, and Kinesiology at East Tennessee State University, USA. Her research revolves around leisure.

Louise Todd is Programme Leader of the MSc International Festival and Event Management at Edinburgh Napier University, UK. Her research interests lie in arts and cultural tourism, and festivals. She is concerned with stakeholder engagement, visual culture, visual research methods, art, and design in these settings. Louise's background is in visual art, and she continues to practise art.

Daniel Turner is Deputy Dean of the School of Business and Creative Industries at the University of the West of Scotland (UWS), UK. His research interests focus on the socio-cultural exploration of events and sport and the use of such activity to generate economic, social, and cultural impacts. He is the co-author of *Lifestyle Sports and Public Policy* (2017) and *Event Bidding: Politics, Persuasion and Resistance* (2017).

INTRODUCTION

Leisure, activism, and the animation of the urban environment

Ian R. Lamond and Brett Lashua

ABSTRACT

This editorial sets the conceptual frame of reference for the special issue. It examines key themes at the intersection of activist leisure and critical event studies. Drawing on a wide range of social and leisure theory, we establish the critical lens of the Disrupt! project. Funded by Leeds Beckett University, Disrupt! used a variety of innovative methods to interrogate how activism could animate urban spaces.

Introduction to the special issue

While writing this Introduction many people around the world have experienced enforced physical distancing and lockdown due to the Covid-19 pandemic. In this context, considering the themes of our Special Issue (leisure, activism, and the animation of the urban environment) has seemed surreal, whilst also curiously appropriate. During spring and early summer of 2020, news coverage of major cities around the world offered scenes almost completely devoid of people, with eerily silent streets that reminded us of the missing immediacy and absent vibrancy of what animates a city. When the pandemic hit, it was those familiar spaces of leisure and hospitality that were among the first to be made silent. Covid-19 has highlighted, through many absences, the importance of leisure, particularly in the animation of public spaces.

Recent events have demonstrated that activism remains a vital component in the animation of urban space, too. On 18 May 2020, Extinction Rebellion lined Trafalgar Square, in London, with 2,000 pairs of children's shoes (Campbell, 2020), its banner ('COVID today > Climate tomorrow > Act now') echoing the UK government's then recommendation of 'Stay home > Stay safe > Save lives.' Such creative forms of dissent emphasised the emptiness of this typically busy space to make a point about the risks of climate change to children, while complying with guidelines to avoid mass gatherings during the pandemic[1]; however, not all activism has followed that approach.

Following the 25 May 2020 killing of George Floyd, who was suffocated whilst held to the ground by police officers in Minneapolis (USA), protests erupted across the United States focused on the injustice of Floyd's death and similar incidents of police brutality, and the persistence of systemic racism within many organisations at multiple levels of contemporary society. Anti-racism social justice protesters also took to the streets in cities around the world. These demonstrations, and those connected directly or indirectly to the Black Lives Matter movement, opted for direct action via mass rallies in public spaces. Protesters (and in turn, counter-protesters) also clashed over civic memorials, especially where these memorials (e.g., statues) connected with racist oppression and historic slavery. Some public spaces were dramatically re-made, such as the creation of Black Lives Matter plaza in Washington D.C., while in others (such as Bristol, UK), statues deemed controversial due to their association with the slave trade were removed (Wall, 2020). In many cities, protests became violent in clashes between citizens, and between protesters and police, and lead to physical damage to the city itself. These examples indicate that, as well as seeking social change, activism often has consequences for the material fabric of the city. Drawn in sharp relief during a global pandemic, such events of dissent bring to the fore numerous and complex questions around the relationships between leisure, activism, and the animation of urban spaces. To set the stage for the nine papers that follow, in this introductory essay we map out some of these questions. First, we ask: 'What constitutes "activist leisure"?' to consider theoretical links between leisure, activism and critical events. Second, we question 'public space' and its centrality in leisure and the animation (and disruption) of cities. We briefly turn to the project that served as the catalyst for this Special Issue, '*disrupt! Creativity, Protest and the City*' (2016–2017), before concluding with brief synopses of the nine papers that comprise this collection.

Leisure, activism, and critical events

If we are serious about exploring the relationships between leisure, activism and the animation of the urban environment then some consideration must be given to where those concerns are currently situated within leisure studies. Within the field, activist leisure/leisure activism is arguably underexplored and warrants greater attention.

In his 1982 paper 'Serious Leisure: A Conceptual Statement' Stebbins, was among the first to consider a connection between leisure and activism through a discussion of 'career volunteering'. In setting out a conceptual framework for serious leisure, Stebbins stated: 'In the *political and civic* sphere, volunteers get involved in citizens' movements, social advocacy, social action, and political functions' (Stebbins, 1982, p. 264). Indicating, if not directly stating, a connection between participation in activist activity and leisure, Stebbins differed from prevailing positions which, whilst acknowledging that leisure was of political significance (Wilson, 1980), suggested that activism was not itself considered to be a leisure activity. The tension between leisure as a politically significant area of human activity and activist leisure as an aspect of volunteering persists.

In some of his earlier work, Rojek seems drawn to the former position. Seeking to ground leisure studies philosophically in a radical rethinking of the field (Rojek, 1995), activism is mentioned; however, it is a tangent to the main thrust of the book, whose trajectory ran towards grappling with the political significance of our use of free time. Similarly, in Colin Rochester's literature review for Volunteering England (Rochester, 2006), activism is not ignored; however, in this instance the line of argument was that, as volunteering is a form of leisure and some forms of volunteering can be construed as a kind of activism, then some leisure can be understood in terms of activism. The route is circuitous and, consequently, its impact diluted. Mair's (2002) paper, 'Civil Leisure? Exploring the Relationship between Leisure, Activism and Social Change', provided a different and direct perspective in which Mair asked 'Why are people using their non-work time to attend political demonstrations? [...] Is it leisure? If so, what does this mean for the development of leisure theory more generally?' (Mair, 2002, p. 214).

Developed from foundations in Rojek's idea of *deviant leisure* (Rojek, 1995), though moving beyond it, Mair (2002) argues that 'social activism, particularly protests, cannot adequately be described by current leisure theory' (p. 213). Instead, Mair introduced the concept of *civil leisure* – understood as 'leisure that resists the hegemonic tendencies towards consumerization and commodification, and most importantly, attempts to generate open discussion about issues that are important to society' (Mair, 2002, p. 215). Whilst recognition of the political significance of leisure is essential for a critical dissection and analysis of policy, and for policy development, Mair argues that the pathway that considers leisure and activism from a perspective of volunteerism is an essential step, but one that is also insufficient. She contends that 'investigating leisure within the context of social and political activism from within labour, environmental and other social movements [requires] ... a new understanding' (p. 217). Mair (2002) also argues that Stebbins' conceptualisation of *serious leisure* is not up to the task. Whilst acknowledging that the characteristic of commitment is important in his construal of *serious leisure* '[t]he risks that [are] ... taken to meet this goal' (i.e. the goal of the activist) 'are arguably beyond the scope of serious leisure's sense of commitment' (p. 227). Engaging in activism in one's *discretionary time* is to take significant personal risk in the reclaiming of discursive spaces: to investigate such leisure practices, she concludes, requires greater theoretical strength than prevailing leisure theory affords. Mair (2002) concludes with a call for further research into the relationship between activism and leisure across five broad themes as the basis for future lines of inquiry into what she calls *civil leisure*. These themes include: (1) who is out there?; (2) what are they doing?; (3) where are they doing it?; (4) why?; and (5) have their activities changed?

All of Mair's identified themes are relevant to this special issue, as we will explore later, but perhaps most important to this special issue are questions of what people are doing as activist leisure, and where they are doing it. Along with others (e.g., Lashua, 2005; Rojek, 2010), Gilchrist and Ravenscroft (2013) have asked similar questions in order to explore 'how the relationship between leisure and politics can be understood' (p. 51). Following a detailed reflection of Mair's position, and others that have followed (Glover et al., 2005; Sharpe, 2008), Gilchrist and Ravenscroft argue: 'what is not clear is how these forms of political participation and their occupation of space through practices such as guerrilla gardening, or the regulated occupation of space for events such as music festivals, really confront political authority' (Gilchrist & Ravenscroft, 2013, p. 57). Adopting a case study approach, they examined the activities of a self-styled 'anarchitect' group, Space Hijackers (Space Hijackers, ND), particularly the group's tactics as politically-overt leisure interventions (such as *Midnight Cricket*[2]) 'to challenge the governance of urban space' (p. 61). Gilchrist and Ravenscroft's interest in (re)animating and disrupting urban space also connects leisure to the politics of *events*.

Spracklen and Lamond (2016) argue that a critical approach to the study of events must seek out the essentially contested nature of the *event*, where the referent 'event' is something that is, itself, ontologically and epistemologically problematic. It is only through problematising the referent 'event' that we can confront the regimes of truth and the political logics that seek to structure the 'event' to be analysed. Fundamentally this means that events are open to interpretation through more than a singular narrative; they are multiple. Some will cohere around event management, others around dissent, space, concepts of economic growth etc., and some may bridge more than one other narrative. It is this complexity that lies at the root of suggesting all 'events' are contested, and that by seeking out these contestations we may find richer and deeper understandings of the 'event' being scrutinised. Such a construct of *events* and *event* also embraces narratives of leisure and leisure activities, with which it becomes entwined. One core thread that connects all of this together is that of space. Event landscapes require a spatial component (that is, rather, they comprise spatial and *event-al* components), whether that be a material, digital, emotional, cognitive, or imaginary space. To conceive of 'event' without a consideration of space is to remove something crucial to understandings of the study of events. It is to a consideration of the spatial that we now turn.

In 'The production of space', Lefebvre (1991) considers spatial relationships through three interconnected fields – space as it is conceived (le conçu), lived (le vécu), and perceived (le perçu): activism encompasses each of these fields. Through the animation of urban space, activism and acts of dissent challenge the ways space is produced through the routines of daily life, demonstrating how space can be lived differently, whilst exposing the underlying relationships of power that frame spatial relations. A strong element in his later work, such as 'La Présence et l'Absence' (Lefebvre, 1980) and 'Éléments de Rythmanalyse' (Lefebvre, 1992), is the manifestation of relational spatialities through rhythm and repetition, difference and dissonance.

If we extend the metaphor suggested in the lines from Tennyson cited earlier, then it can be argued that Lefebvre provides a strong motif for the musicality of the city. As a theme, its variations reverberate through the work of critical geographers such as Edward Soja (1989); Andrea Huyssen (2003); Doreen Massey (1994) and David Harvey (2012). The concentration on the relationality of the spatial in the investigations and theoretical explorations of their enquiries draws heavily on the foundations of Lefebvre's three field dialectic of the production of space. It is, however, through the incorporation of his dynamics of the spatial with the *tactics* of De Certeau (1986), that we begin to see the dance and the drama of the city more clearly. It is through the fugue of their intersection that Lefebvre's construal of presence, absence and rhythm can come to the fore.

In 'The practice of everyday life' Michel de Certeau wrote: 'There is no place that is not haunted by many different spirits hidden there in silence, spirits one can "invoke" or not' (De Certeau, 1988, p. 108). It is the invocation of some of those hidden spirits, hidden through hegemonic power and articulated by repressive regimes of truth (Foucault, 2014), that animates urban spaces. Those invoked spirits, haunting an urban spatiality through the disruptive action of dissent, that are manifest through activist leisure as a 'rift [that] presents itself as an event [...] more fundamental than the continuity [of] the surface' (De Certeau, 1986, p. 178). The ideas of surfaces, rifts and events bring us to Deleuze (1968[2015]), underlining the significance of 'event' and approaching that concept critically, when examining leisure activism. It is through Deleuze that event and space converge, and activist leisure gains a potential for affective and effective change. It is the striations of space, its patterns of repetition and difference, that 'event' interrupts, exposing the multiple potentialities of moments and spaces, which Deleuze refers to as the virtual, with power seeking to coalesce that potentiality into an actuality, i.e. as something that can be framed, interpreted, and managed. To grasp the nuances of activist leisure, therefore, we must consider both the *evental* and spatial. Having dug into the *evental* in the previous section we turn to concepts of public space and leisure.

Public space and leisure

On its surface, for Campos (2017, p. 236) 'urban public space is everyone's, a democratic territory for the circulation (or hanging around) of its inhabitants.' Yet, critiquing its apparent superficiality, the architect Helen Stratford (in press) offers, 'public space is a term that is everywhere and nowhere.' Digging deeper, Stratford argues that although public space aspires towards a democratic ideal that is open for all, 'it can never be assumed that public space is democratic or, for that matter, public.' Equally ambivalent, the sociologist Mark Kingwell has conceptualised public space as both a gift (Kingwell, 2009) and a prison (Kingwell, 2014). Kingwell (2014) described public space as 'the age's master signifier', an elusive concept 'variously deployed to defend (or attack) architecture, to decry (or celebrate) civic squares, to promote (or denounce) graffiti artists, skateboarders, jaywalkers, parkour aficionados, pie-in-the-face guerrillas, underground capture-the-flag enthusiasts, flash-mob surveillance busters and other grid-resistant everyday anarchists' (p. 212). Hou (2010) noted similar contradictions and complexities of the term, celebrating the freedoms afforded by public leisure spaces as 'an important facet of cities and urban culture ... [providing] opportunities for gathering, socializing, recreation, festivals, as well as protests and demonstrations' (p. 2). Conversely, some public spaces such as large urban parks or plazas have become synonymous with displays of State control and power (Hou, 2010). Hou (2010., p. 7) concludes that public spaces are always contested, never static, and in a 'continual state of emergence.'

To help navigate this contested and emergent terrain, Johnson and Glover (2013, pp. 193–194) outlined a typology of public spaces, dependent on ownership (private or public) and perceptions of access. They noted four categories:

(1) *Public-private (or quasi-public) spaces* are privately owned and access may be denied but are generally viewed as public by users, e.g., a shopping mall, a café or pub;
(2) *Commons*, such as easements, footpaths and walking trails, and some community gardens, are privately owned but it is difficult to deny access;
(3) *Club spaces* are government-owned, but are designed for controlled access (e.g., municipal swimming pools, lawn bowling greens, or a municipal ice rink);

(4) *Outwardly public spaces* are publicly owned and access cannot be denied, such as an urban park, and as such are the 'least contested type of public space' (p. 194). Nonetheless, there are debates about access and 'improper' users, such the homeless, or sex workers, as well as debates over creeping privatisation, commodification and commercialisation of outwardly public spaces.

This typology offers a useful starting point for definitions, and further questions, of public spaces, and what it is that may be said to 'animate' them. As Kingwell cautions, public space 'also means something larger and looser: the right to gather and discuss, to interact with and debate with one's fellow [sic] citizens' (Kingwell, 2014, p. 213). For Hou (2010, p. 9), such gatherings and interactions in public spaces often take the form of 'spontaneous events, unintended uses, and a variety of activities that defy or escape existing rules and regulations.' These practices animate urban spaces into what Watson (2006, p. 19) calls sites of 'potentiality, difference, and delightful encounters.'

Such encounters are key for Iris Marion Young (2014), for whom the ideal of city life is 'the being together of strangers' (p. 249). Young explained:

> by definition a public space is a place accessible to anyone, where anyone can participate and witness, in entering the public one always risks encountering those who are different, those who identify with different groups and have different opinions or different forms of life. The group diversity of the city is most often apparent in public spaces. This helps account for their vitality and excitement. Cities provide important public spaces - streets, parks, and plazas - where people stand and sit together, interact and mingle, or simply witness one another, without becoming unified in a community of 'shared final ends.' (pp. 250-251).

This being together, in a 'collective culture' (Amin, 2008), or 'throwntogetherness' (Massey, 2005, p. 151) in public space, is a conceptual focus of the animation of public space. Glover (2015) defines the animation of public space as a means to bring people together through 'the deliberate, usually temporary employment of festivals, events, programmed activities, or pop-up leisure to transform, enliven, and/or alter public spaces and stage urban life' (p. 96).

Yet, as Kingwell (2014) cautions, the ideal of urban public spaces, and also varying ways to animate (or re-animate) it, have been widely co-opted by private corporate and commercial interests (see also Hoskyns, 2013; Massey, 2005); once-innovative interventions such as pop-up events (Harris, 2020; Lashua, 2013) and impromptu gatherings such as flash mobs (Hou, 2010) have become standard in the arsenal for advertising, marketing and selling major brands. These are characteristic hallmarks of neoliberalism. In this, we are left with what Carmona (2010) has named 'pseudo public space' (p. 134), suspect in Kingwell's view too, as a 'public good' that is now regulated, as well as competed for, consumed, and even traded. In one recent example of neoliberal encroachment in pseudo public spaces, the technology giant Apple sought to create a new store in the Kungsträdgården (the King's Garden), a historic public park in the heart of Stockholm, Sweden. The Kungsträdgården is 'one of the city's oldest parks, the venue for public events from Pride parades to election debates, political protests to winter ice-skating' (Orange, 2018, para. 10). Apple's plans blurred public and private space by referring to its stores as 'gathering places', which would see a large chunk of the surrounding public park rezoned for retail. Following citizen protests, the local government blocked Apple's plans. Similar plans and concomitant civic protests have taken place in Melbourne, Australia (Alcorn, 2018), Berlin, Germany (Lock, 2018) and London, UK (Hunt, 2018). Through 'creeping privatisation' (Hunt, 2018), many such plans for pseudo public space aim to rezone city parks into commercial or retail spaces; most have been fiercely opposed by local interest groups.

Some scholar-activists have turned to the arts (Duncombe, 2002; Gielen, 2015; Hou, 2010; MacDonald & Wiens, 2019; Sharpe, 2008; Yuen & Fortune, 2019) to re-animate and reclaim public spaces. The cultural sociologist Pascal Gielen (2015, p. 278) embraced art as a means of interrupting the city, as a way to introduce 'dismeasure' into the everyday 'measure' that is regarded as normal. This approach is particularly interesting given that much of the neoliberal commercialisation of civic spaces appears 'normal', unchallenged and inevitable. For Yuen and Fortune (2019, p. 1), the combination of leisure and art allows unique affordances for activism and engaged protest to stand out:

> traditional methods of protest (e.g., marches, chants, civic disobedience) have become outdated and ineffective, and they tend to result in messages that are easily ignored and discounted. In contrast, leisure in politics is useful because it is "participatory and productive" and ultimately increases the efficacy of disrupting the status quo.

Here Gielen's (2015, p. 278) idea of 'dismeasure' may become something more than momentary interruptions in struggles over public spaces. In this sense, '*interrupting* the city is one way of forcing the public sphere to renew itself; or if not renew then at least to rehash itself' (Bax et al., 2015, p. 11). Here the idea of animated urban space and leisure intersect via creative disruptions. Hou's edited volume, *Insurgent Public Space* (Hou, 2010) celebrated many examples of these kinds of disruptive acts of renewal, ranging from unsanctioned sidewalk sculptures, street intersections repainted in bright colours, 'sleep-in" protests in expensive city residential districts, installing 'guerrilla' benches in empty parks, and reusing residual and derelict industrial urban land: 'From Seattle to Shanghai, citizen actions ranging from gardening to dancing have permanently and temporarily taken over existing urban sites and injected them with new functions and meanings' (Hou, 2010, p. 2). In other words, they have injected a spirit of *dismeasure* into public space discourse and leisure practice. Such *dismeasure* also sat at the heart of our research cluster project, *disrupt!* (2015–2017), which brought together a group of scholar-activists at Leeds Beckett University, and served as the impetus for this Special Issue.

disrupt! creativity, protest and the city

In 2016, through the support of a research cluster award made by Leeds Beckett University (UK), colleagues from event studies, leisure studies and cultural studies collaborated to explore methodologies appropriate to researching how activist leisure can animate urban spaces. Its purpose was intentionally disruptive, both around more familiar frameworks of what constitutes academic collaboration, and how methodologies examining activism in the urban environment can emerge through negotiations with non-academic collaborators and research participants. Consequently, the project concentrated on relationship building and developing networks. In place of working from a pre-set agenda the *disrupt!* project (2016–2017) incorporated a range of cultural and social interventions that emerged from discussions with non-academic collaborators, making use of public spaces, and with elements of the publics that occupy or frequented those spaces. One intervention, which offered an urban walking tour, was developed in association with local residents in Leeds, using their individual lived histories and memories of space to peel back hidden stories that collectively challenged the anonymity and commercial homogenisation of the city through the heterogenous voices of the walkers. In another intervention, a collaboration with postgraduate architectural students, a freight-carrying bicycle was adapted to serve as a mobile cinema and used to disrupt the city through cinematic projections (Lashua & Baker, 2018). A further set of interventions involved a programme of film screenings that were disrupted through the incorporation of a live choir, a free banquet of 'rescued food' (food that was still fit for consumption but discarded by some of the larger food retailers), a demonstration for an unknown cause, or requiring the film's audience to navigate a crowd attending a music gig in a room adjacent to the one used for the screening. As a series of disruptions, these events and activities were intended to highlight and create openings for re-imagining and re-making the city, and the kinds of leisure events that might animate urban 'public' spaces. So too, alongside these re-imaginings and re-makings were questions of who may inhabit these spaces and disrupt the conception of who does or does not belong in them. Similarly, a range of re-imaginings, re-makings, and disruptive questionings were the focal points of the nine papers which were selected for inclusion in this Special Issue.

About this special issue

In their own ways, the nine papers that comprise this Special Issue address the thematic areas raised by Mair (2002) in her call for further research on activism and civil leisure. To recap, these include: (1) who is out there?; (2) what are they doing?; (3) where are they doing it?; (4) why?; and (5) have their activities changed? To this frame, we add that the contributions cut across the conceptual areas and ideas we have introduced above (e.g., leisure and politics, critical events, public spaces, arts, and disruption) while also expanding upon them and offering further theorisations. The papers also differ, with some foregrounding overtly activist leisure practices, whereas some centralise leisure activities (such as bicycling) rather than activism. Similarly, some of the papers focus on animated public spaces such as a skatepark, whereas others view the spatiality of activist leisure from more oblique angles, such as homelessness. Nonetheless, all of the papers raise critical questions that relate to the three core Special Issue themes of leisure, activism, and the animation of the urban environment.

The Special Issue opens with papers that centralise questions of leisure and urban public spaces. Leading off, Glover et al. (2019) present a case study of CITE, a celebration of skateboarding, arts and culture, located in a new public space created beneath an elevated highway in Toronto, Canada. Featuring art installations and a pop-up skate park alongside skateable sculptures, Glover et al., ask how skateboarding at CITE served as a form of 'gentle activism', providing creative ways to provoke the public to think about public spaces and inviting passers-by to imagine cities differently. Through a range of qualitative materials and fieldwork, including interviews, video and social media, promotional materials, press releases, and observational analysis, Glover et al., argued that, as a meaningful way to animate the city, skateboarding could be engaged and *designed into* city spaces, rather than deterred and bracketed out in isolated skateparks. They also highlighted the need for a mix of arts programming to complement skating. This helps to make public spaces that are more inclusive and welcoming, not only animating the urban environment but also transforming it.

Several papers question the relations of leisure and public spaces as 'civil leisure' (Mair, 2002) and what this may 'mean for the development of leisure theory more generally' (Mair, 2002, p. 214). The second paper by Rasul Mowatt (2019) asks 'where the White Nationalists are' and issues a direct call for leisure scholars to confront the discomfort of leisure spaces used for ideologically racist events. Mowatt traces four historical cases linked to White Nationalist and White Separatist activities staged in public spaces, parks and national monuments in the USA. These include mass Ku Klux Klan marches in Washington DC in 1925; tens of thousands of White Nationalists gathered at the 1939 German-American Bund rally in Madison Square Gardens in New York City; a series of demonstrations by the American Neo-Nazi movement, the National Socialist Party of America (NSPA), in public parks in Skokie, Illinois; and the 2017 'Unite the Right' rally in Charlottesville (Virginia), a response to plans for the removal of a statue of Confederate General Robert E. Lee in Emancipation Park. By adopting a longer historical overview, these gatherings can be seen not as isolated anomalies but as common, and frequent, occurrences. As such they also sharply show that hateful political ideologies such as White Nationalism also animate urban environments, offering a kind of malign 'activism' in public leisure spaces.

Addressing Johnson and Glover's call for researchers "to consider who is excluded from 'public' space (Johnson & Glover, 2013, p. 195), in the third paper of the collection Justin Harmon (2019) explores questions of leisure, public space and homelessness. Through a duoethnographic combination of the researcher's stories with those of 'Dancing Bear', a person experiencing long-term homelessness, the paper focuses on tensions between the right to the city and the right to leisure. Harmon also frames conflicts between leisure and increasingly privatised and sanitised public spaces, and the homeless who are stigmatised and viewed as 'out of place' and made to feel that they do not belong in public leisure spaces. In sharing these entwined accounts, Harmon presents a portrait of public leisure spaces that, especially for Dancing Bear, are neither public nor animated with leisure. In doing so, Harmon identifies the need to recognise leisure's absences or silences, and to do so with critical humility and ethical care. In this, Harmon demonstrates a kind of scholar-activism that begins, perhaps, from what the sociologist Les Back (2007) referred to as the art of listening.

The collection of papers next turns more fully towards questions of the animation of public spaces. Taking urban bicycling as their focus, Dunlap et al. (2020) raise questions of 'emotional geographies' to better understand cyclist's movements through urban landscapes as affective leisure experiences. Rather than position cycling as an overtly activist or transgressive leisure practice, they present pragmatic, physical, restorative, and emotional rationales for urban cycling practices. Through interviews with sixteen residents, Dunlap, et al, trace participants' journeys (in Nashville, USA) towards 'becoming a cyclist' through a process of ideation and experimentation that developed into routine practice. As a consequence of their growing commitment to cycling, participants articulated the desire to confront the hostility of urban environments, to reclaim spaces (i.e., bike lanes), and to contest the automobile-centrism of the city more broadly.

In contrast to Dunlap et al., the next paper, by Carlo Genova (2020), raises overt considerations of leisure and activism through a focus on young people's political engagement in Italian cities. Against a perceived lack of youth participation in political groups, Genova re-frames political participation as a leisure activity by exploring the context of young people living in 'political squats', i.e., the intentional occupation of abandoned public buildings. Through interviews with activist squatters, Genova identified the challenges of partial alignments, fragmented worldviews, weakly-shared values and a lack of trust in political institutions among young Italians. The paper argues that the complex facets of political engagement made more sense when understood not as formal politics, but instead as a mix of leisure and activism. For the participants in Genova's research, this mix takes into consideration individuals' tastes, lifestyle choices and personal satisfactions, as young citizens attempt to (re)position themselves, vis-à-vis leisure and activism, within Italian civil society.

Turning to critical events and festivals as sites of resistance and social change, Jamieson and Todd (2019) explore the festival and activist processes of 'reversal.' Such festive forms challenge widely held instrumental views (e.g., within events and creative industries) of festivals as consumeristic and touristic (pseudo-)public celebrations. Exploring festivals at intersections 'of both revolution and consumerism' (Jamieson & Todd, 2019, p. 2), Jamieson and Todd seek to develop a conceptual framework for analysis of a transgressive festival imagination. Drawing together Bakhtin's conceptualisation of the carnivalesque (as authorised transgression) and the notion of play, as developed by the developmental psychologist and psychoanalyst D. W. Winnicott (as central to establishing a sense of being-in-the-world), they challenge mainstream formulations of the festival experience. With play as a space of rebellious exploration they develop a more transgressive perspective on the transformative potential of the festival, one that can provide tools and routines – the *techne* – of resistance. Through the processes of reversal, and their novel conceptual framework, events and leisure practices are able to manifest an imagery of playgrounds for dissent.

While all of the papers connect questions of leisure and activism, the final three papers in the collection do so in ways that illustrate the complex relations between leisure and public protest, particularly in view of policy and governance. David McGillivray et al. (2019) offer critical case studies of protests against bids to host Summer Olympic Games in three American cities. In the context of mega sports events (MSEs), protesters often share concerns where MSEs are seen to violate human rights, distort fiscal spending, sanction corruption and exacerbate social inequities. Like several contributions to this collection, the paper draws from interviews with activists and analyses of social media campaigns in opposition to MSE boosterism. It differs, however, in questioning the role of new media, particularly where it intersects with mainstream media (i.e., broadcast and print media) and physical protests in cities including Chicago, Boston and Los Angeles. In their analyses, McGillivray, et al highlight where protest campaigners were adept in using new media in ways that promoted the core messages of opposition activists. Nevertheless, anti-Olympic protests appeared more effective where campaigners were able to also influence legacy media, and most successful when engaged with broader urban debates, working within political parties and social movements, and by amplifying wider concerns about social equity. The paper shows the potency of leisure activism, especially when connected to debates about broader urban politics.

In the penultimate paper, a richly detailed and fascinating account of civil society in the 'NoLo' (North of Piazzale Loreto) area of Milan (Italy), Citroni and Coppola (2020) investigate leisure and activism in local public policy-making processes. They focus on a range of arts, leisure and cultural initiatives, originating from grassroots neighbourhood activism, as these initiatives encountered and became part of the neoliberal governance of the city. Through participant observation during local events, interviews with residents and key stakeholders and analyses of social media, the authors develop two in-depth case studies that trace subtle forms of power in neighbourhood events, not as protest, but as part of transforming local policies towards uses of NoLo's public spaces. In echoes of Mair (2002), Citroni and Coppola (2020) consider leisure, activism and the animation of urban environments as vital components in an 'emerging civil society' in Milan.

Finally, exploring the theme of whose voices are excluded from 'public' space, the paper by Lamond et al. (2020) sets out to develop a research approach that can embrace the diversity of voices associated with leisure activism, and the animating of the city. Acknowledging the challenges that researchers face when trying to grasp the multiplicity of voices associated with leisure activism, the authors confront some of the many difficulties in investigating events of dissent within the city. Pursuing Latour's (2007) call to seek out the controversy, and drawing on prior research on activism in the UK and Brazil, they propose an approach that brings contested voices together. In doing so they consider how such a multivocal and polyphonic research approach creates both opportunities for dialogue between voices more commonly raised in opposition, whilst also challenging the researchers' presuppositions and pre-conceptions around how leisure activism animates the city.

Concluding thoughts and future directions: Leisure, activism, and the animation of the urban environment

This special issue has been co-edited by two colleagues (Lamond and Lashua) who worked on the previously mentioned *disrupt!* project. In concluding we return, briefly, to where we opened, and the disruptions of the Covid-19 pandemic. The pandemic has drawn our attention, from extraordinary absences and silences to the importance of leisure in the animation of urban environments. For one of the guest editors, an enduring impression has been the stillness and emptiness of the public leisure spaces of his home town (a popular visitor destination in the UK); for the other, what stood out were the acts of collective music-making that took place in cities around the world, from residents' balconies and across rooftops (and also laptops). These creative interventions – forms of disrupting the disruption of Covid-19 and enforced lockdowns – showcased not only the 'musicality' of the city, but also the creation of new social rhythms and public connections (Lefebvre, 1992). Also, against the backcloth of overbearing silences and stillnesses, came the mass public outcries for social justice following the death of George Floyd, and so many others, due to racism, systemic violence, and enduring institutional inequalities. In this moment, the importance of leisure as activism, protest, dissent and resistance – that is, *civil leisure* (Mair, 2002) – and the role of public spaces (and subsequent closures of them) have resonated through Black Lives Matter rallies and marches around the world. Other movements, such as anti-climate change protests, and anti-war activism (e.g., against ongoing conflict in Yemen), have also shown that, even in an age of 'social' distancing and worrying silences, collective voices can make wonderfully disruptive and much-needed noises.

These voices and noises, moments and movements, and absences and silences are resonant across the nine papers included in this collection. Yet, with only nine papers, there are of course numerous gaps and many further absences: for instance, we did not receive submissions regarding protest and gender politics, or activism against sexual violence, or in regard to leisure and LGBTQIA+ activist spaces. So too, we did not receive papers in other crucial areas such as disability rights campaigns. We recognise that these activist concerns, and many others, will appear in the 'regular' course of *Leisure Studies'* (and other leisure journals') published research articles. In this, we acknowledge the growing body of activist scholarship, and social justice research in particular, within the field. Yet, as often noted in other introductions for special issues (e.g., Sharpe & Lashua, 2008), there is always more work to do, and research gaps remain at the interstices of leisure, activism, and the animation of urban environments. We welcome and look forward to seeing, and hearing, more scholarly *noise* in these important spaces.

Notes

1. Another example is the increased use of the performance art piece Mirror Casket as part of the activism undertaken by Black Lives Matter. Initially created in 2014, following the murder of Michael Brown, the Mirror Casket is a coffin covered in mirrors, with a cracked mirror on top. The surfaces of the funeral casket reflect back the gaze of the police as they seek to contain the protest action (Yoganathan, 2020).
2. In Midnight Cricket, the game of cricket is played in symbolically significant and highly surveilled urban sites, at night, as a 'means to defetishise the exclusionary infrastructure of urban space' (Gilchrist & Ravenscroft, 2013, p. 61).

Acknowledgments

We are grateful to the *Leisure Studies* editors who have generously and patiently supported us in the preparation of the Special Issue. It was a pleasure to work with all of the authors who contributed to the Special Issue, and we extend our heartfelt thanks for everyone's hard work and perseverance. We would also like to acknowledge the research cluster award funding we received for the *disrupt!* project from Leeds Beckett University. Thanks are due to our colleagues in *disrupt!* including project partners Lynne Hibbard and Zoë Tew-Thompson. Finally, we must acknowledge the immeasurable contributions of Chelsea Reid, who capably served as project coordinator during *disrupt!* and provided invaluable support during all phases of co-editing this Special Issue.

Funding

This work was supported by the Leeds Beckett University [Research Cluster Award].

References

Alcorn, G. (2018, April 9). *The struggle for Melbourne: Has the world's 'most liveable' city lost its way? The Guardian.* https://www.theguardian.com/cities/2018/apr/09/the-struggle-for-melbourne-has-the-worlds-most-liveable-city-lost-its-way

Amin, A. (2008). Collective culture and urban public space. *City*, *12*(1), 5–24. https://doi.org/10.1080/13604810801933495
Back, L. (2007). *The art of listening*. Berg.
Bax, S., Gielen, P., & Ieven, B. (2015). Introduction: A public sphere, for example. In P. Gielen, S. Bax, & B. Ieven (Eds.), *Interrupting the city: Artistic Constitutions of the Public Sphere* (pp. 9–27). Valiz Publishing.
Campbell, M. (2020 November 25th) *Thousands of kids' shoes appear in London square as a form of protest. Euronews.* https://www.euronews.com/living/2020/05/19/thousands-of-kids-shoes-appear-in-london-square-as-a-form-of-protest
Campos, R. (2017). On urban (In)Visibilities. In J. Hannigan & G. Richards (Eds.), *The SAGE handbook of new urban studies* (pp. 232–249). Sage.
Carmona, M. (2010). Contemporary Public Space: Critique and Classification. Part One: Critique. *Journal of Urban Design*, *15*(1), 123–148.
Citroni, S., & Coppola, A. (2020). The emerging civil society. Governing through leisure activism in Milan. *Leisure Studies*, 1–13. https://doi.org/10.1080/02614367.2020.1795228
De Certeau, M. (1986). *Heterologies: Discourse on the other* (Trans. B. Masumi.). University of Minnesota Press.
De Certeau, M. (1988). *The practice of everyday life* (Trans. S. Rendall). University of California Press.
Deleuze, G. (1968 [2015]). *Différence and Répétition.* Presses Universitaires de France.
Duncombe, S. (2002). Introduction. In S. Duncombe (Ed.), *Cultural resistance reader* (pp. 1–15). Verso.
Dunlap, R., Rose, J., Standridge, S. H., & Pruitt, C. L. (2020). Experiences of urban cycling: Emotional geographies of people and place. *Leisure Studies*, 1–14. https://doi.org/10.1080/02614367.2020.1720787
Foucault, M. (2014). *On the government of the living: Lectures at the Collège de France, 1979 - 1980* (Trans. G. Burchell). Palgrave Macmillan.
Genova, C. (2020). Young activists in political squats: Mixing engagement and leisure. *Leisure Studies*, 1–12. https://doi.org/10.1080/02614367.2020.1791936
Gielen, P. (2015). Performing the common city: On the crossroads of art, politics and public life. In P. Gielen, S. Bax, & B. Ieven (Eds.), *Interrupting the city: Artistic constitutions of the public sphere* (pp. 275–298). Valiz Publishing.
Gilchrist, P., & Ravenscroft, N. (2013). Space hijacking and the anarcho-politics of leisure. *Leisure Studies*, *32*(1), 49–68. https://doi.org/10.1080/02614367.2012.680069
Glover, T. D. (2015). Animating public space. In S. Gammon & S. Elkington (Eds.), *Landscapes of Leisure* (pp. 96–109). Palgrave Macmillan.
Glover, T. D., Munro, S., Men, I., Loates, W., & Altman, I. (2019). Skateboarding, gentle activism, and the animation of public space: CITE – A celebration of skateboard arts and culture at The Bentway. *Leisure Studies*, 1–15. https://doi.org/10.1080/02614367.2019.1684980
Glover, T. D., Shinew, K. J., & Parry, D. C. (2005). Association, sociability, and civic culture: The democratic effect of community gardening. *Leisure Sciences*, *27*(1), 75–92. https://doi.org/10.1080/01490400590886060
Harmon, J. (2019). The right to exist: Homelessness and the paradox of leisure. *Leisure Studies*, 1–11. https://doi.org/10.1080/02614367.2019.1640775
Harris, E. (2020). *Rebranding precarity: Pop-up culture as the seductive new normal.* Zed Books.
Harvey, D. (2012). *Rebel cities: From the right to the city to the urban revolution.* Verso.
Hoskyns, T. (2013). *The empty place: Democracy and public space.* Routledge.
Hou, J. (2010). (Not) your everyday public space. In J. Hou (Ed.), *Insurgent public space: Guerrilla urbanism and the remaking of contemporary cities* (pp. 1–17). Routledge.
Hunt, E. (2018, August 31). *London's parks accused of 'creeping privatisation' of public spaces.* The Guardian. https://www.theguardian.com/cities/2018/aug/31/londons-parks-accused-of-creeping-privatisation-of-public-spaces
Huyssen, A. (2003). *Present pasts: Urban palimpsests and the politics of memory.* Stanford University Press.
Jamieson, K., & Todd, L. (2019). The transgressive festival imagination and the idealisation of reversal. *Leisure Studies*, 1–12. https://doi.org/10.1080/02614367.2019.1693090
Johnson, A. J., & Glover, T. D. (2013). Understanding urban public space in a leisure context. *Leisure Sciences*, *35*(2), 190–197. https://doi.org/10.1080/01490400.2013.761922
Kingwell, M. (2009). Masters of chancery: The gift of public space. In M. Kingwell & P. Turmel (Eds.), *Rites of way: The politics and poetics of public space* (pp. 3–22). Wilfrid Laurier Press.
Kingwell, M. (2014). The prison of "public space". In J. J. Gieseking, W. Mangold, C. Katz, S. Low, & S. Saegert (Eds.), *The people, place, and space reader* (pp. 212–215). Routledge.
Lamond, I. R., Solano, E., & Blotta, V. (2020). Leisure activism and engaged ethnography : Heterogeneous voices and the urban palimpsest. *Leisure Studies*, 1–13. https://doi.org/10.1080/02614367.2020.1724318
Lashua, B. D. (2005). Leisure, civil disobedience, and the history of low power FM (LPFM) radio. *Leisure/Loisir*, *29*(1), 27–48. https://doi.org/10.1080/14927713.2005.9651322
Lashua, B. D. (2013). Pop-up cinema and place-shaping: Urban cultural heritage at Marshall's Mill. *Journal of Policy Research in Tourism, Leisure and Events*, *5*(2), 123–138. https://doi.org/10.1080/19407963.2013.789728
Lashua, B. D., & Baker, S. (2018). Urban subversion and mobile cinema: Leisure, architecture and the "Kino-Cine-Bomber". *Leisure Sciences*, *40*(7), 697–710. https://doi.org/10.1080/01490400.2018.1534624

Latour, B. (2007). *Reassembling the Social: An Introduction to Actor-Network Theory.* Oxford: Oxford University Press.
Lefebvre, H. (1980). *La Présence et l'Absence': Contribution à la Théorie des Représentations.* Casterman.
Lefebvre, H. (1991). *The production of space* (Trans. D Nicholson-Smith). Oxford.
Lefebvre, H. (1992). *Éléments de Rythmanalyse: à la Introduction Connaissance des Rythmes.* Syllepse.
Lock, H. (2018, May 9). *'Google go home': The Berlin neighbourhood fighting off a tech giant.* The Guardian. https://www.theguardian.com/cities/2018/may/09/fuck-off-google-the-berlin-neighbourhood-fighting-off-a-tech-giant-kreuzberg
MacDonald, S., & Wiens, B. I. (2019). Mobilizing the "Multimangle": Why new materialist research methods in public participatory art matter. *Leisure Sciences, 41*(5), 366–384. https://doi.org/10.1080/01490400.2019.1627960
Mair, H. (2002). Civil leisure? Exploring the relationship between leisure, activism and social change. *Leisure/Loisir, 27*(2–3), 213–237. https://doi.org/10.1080/14927713.2002.9651304
Massey, D. (1994). *Space, place and gender.* Polity Press.
Massey, D. (2005). *For space.* Sage.
McGillivray, D., Lauermann, J., & Turner, D. (2019). Event bidding and new media activism. *Leisure Studies,* 1–13. https://doi.org/10.1080/02614367.2019.1698648
Mowatt, R. A. (2019). A people's history of leisure studies: Where the white nationalists are. *Leisure Studies,* 1–18. https://doi.org/10.1080/02614367.2019.1624809
Orange, R. (2018, November 1). *Stockholm says no to Apple 'town square' in its oldest park.* The Guardian. https://www.theguardian.com/cities/2018/nov/01/stockholm-apple-town-square-park-kings-garden-kungstradgarden
Rochester, C. (2006). *Making SENSE OF VOLUNTEEring: A literature review.* Volunteering England.
Rojek, C. (1995). *Decentring leisure: Rethinking leisure theory.* Sage.
Rojek, C. (2010). *The labour of leisure.* Sage.
Sharpe, E. K. (2008). Festivals and social change: Intersections of pleasure and politics at a community music festival. *Leisure Sciences, 30*(3), 217–234. https://doi.org/10.1080/01490400802017324
Sharpe, E. K., & Lashua, B. D. (2008). Introduction to the special issue: Tuning in to popular leisure. *Leisure/Loisir, 32* (2), 245–258. https://doi.org/10.1080/14927713.2008.9651409
Soja, E. (1989). *Postmodern geographies: Reassertion Of space in critical social theory.* Verso.
Space Hijackers (ND) space hijackers: Introduction. https://www.spacehijackers.org/html/history.html
Spracklen, K., & Lamond, I. R. (2016). *Critical event studies.* Routledge.
Stebbins, R. (1982). Serious leisure: A conceptual statement. *Sociolological Perspectives, 25*(2), 251–272. https://doi.org/10.2307/1388726
Wall, T. (2020, 14 June) *The day Bristol dumped its hated slave trader in the docks and a nation began to search for its soul. The Guardian.* https://www.theguardian.com/uk-news/2020/jun/14/the-day-bristol-dumped-its-hated-slave-trader-in-the-docks-and-a-nation-began-to-search-its-soul
Watson, S. (2006). *City publics: The (Dis)enchantments of urban encounters.* Routledge.
Wilson, J. (1980). Sociology of Leisure. *The Annual Review of Sociology, 6*(1), 21–40. https://doi.org/10.1146/annurev.so.06.080180.000321
Yoganathan, N. (2020) *Black lives matters movement use creative tactics to confront systemic racism. The Conversation.* https://theconversation.com/black-lives-matter-movement-uses-creative-tactics-to-confront-systemic-racism-143273
Young, I. M. (2014). City life and difference. In J. J. Gieseking, W. Mangold, C. Katz, S. Low, & S. Saegert (Eds.), *The people, place, and space reader* (pp. 247–251). Routledge.
Yuen, F., & Fortune, D. (2019). Leisure, art, and advocacy: Opportunities for conscientizaçao, contentious dialogue, and social justice. *Leisure Sciences.* https://doi.org/10.1080/01490400.2019.1604276

A People's History of Leisure Studies: Where the White Nationalists Are

Rasul A. Mowatt

ABSTRACT

What we are witnessing in these contemporary times isn't just the interplay of a racialised-populist sentiment in the political sphere through the amassing of political influence (political parties, campaigns, and policies). What we are also witnessing is the increasing performance of racialised-populist political sentiments in the very physical, and public spaces of society. The aim of this manuscript is to discuss this performance within the United States at four historical junctures of animation of leisure space and White Nationalist activity in public and private-public spaces: 1) 1925 Ku Klux Klan March; 2) the 1939 German-American Bund Rally; 3) the 1977 National Socialist Party of America Rally; and, 4) the 2017 Unite the Right Rally. There is a complexity to the contestation of meanings and values ascribed to spaces. The political act of protesting is highlighted in its violation of the sanctum of these public and private-public spaces within the theoretical lenses of the White Genocide Conspiracy Theory or the Great Replacement Theory. Each highlights the impact of this growing White populism, and serves as a cautionary tale for appeals of counter activities and expressions of resistance with the animation, through protest and dissent, of public and private-public spaces.

What we are witnessing in these contemporary times isn't the interplay of generalised populism intertwined with a tinge of racialised-populist sentiment in the political sphere through the amassing of political influence (political parties, campaigns, and policies). What we are also witnessing is an increasing performance of a clear and directed White racialised-populist and political sentiment within the very physical, and public spaces of society. The performance of these political acts of protesting is highlighted in their violation of the sanctum of these public and private-public spaces within the theoretical lenses of the White Genocide Conspiracy Theory or the Great Replacement Theory (Bergmann, 2018). The aim of this manuscript is to discuss such performances within the United States at four historical junctures of leisure space and White Nationalist and White Separatist activity in public and private-public spaces, in which each serves as a cautionary tale for appeals of counter activities and expressions of resistance. As Johnson and Glover (2013) argued that these spaces warrant far more attention from researchers, because an 'understanding the complexity of space as a construct, we believe, allows for a greater appreciation for the relevance and contested nature of urban public space' (p. 191). It is with an emphasis on the contested nature of urban public space that the work of this manuscript serves the field by situating a discussion of the uncomfortable into an academic forum for further intellectual discourse.

White Nationalism, not Whiteness

In initiating this task a defining, and in some cases, a re-defining of terms, concepts, and ideologies needs to be presented. White, Whiteness, White Privilege, White Supremacy, White Nationalism, and White Separatism are each respectively important for advancing the field of leisure studies' understanding of Race in a critical leisure studies context. But how do they fundamentally differ? And why is this relevant for this manuscript and for any future study?

White, as a distinct racial identity and one of superiority is concretised in two tomes, Arthur de Gobineau's ((1915)[1853])*An Essay on The Inequality of Human Races* (that was originally published in 1853) and Madison Grant's (1916) *The Passing of the Great Race: Or, The Racial Basis of European History*. Up to the 1800s, many scholars in a range of fields postulated their definitions of Race (environmental, behavioural, genetic, biological, psychological, evolutionary, and sociological). de Gobineau ((1915)[1853])and Grant (1916) simply summarised and congealed these prior works into two coherent articulations and warnings. Besides racialising the world's populations, both racialised the populations of Europe that would otherwise be considered White, elevating the Nordic, Aryan stock from Eastern and Southern European. They both described a dual warning, the fear of Race-mixing and fear of invasion of the racial 'Other'. But what is most important is that Race should not be respected as an apolitical identifier in society much less for the purposes of research as a demographic identification and potential independent variable for understanding behaviour. Race is solely an indicator of the presence of superiority and inferiority, and only serves the project of Race-making (Stanfield, 1985).

Du Bois (1935) on White identity and the emergence of Whiteness is situated in a specific historical context, and for the purposes of those in power to prevent interracial class-based solidarity,

> It must be remembered that the White group of laborers, while they received a low wage, were compensated in part by a sort of public and psychological wage. They were given public deference and titles of courtesy because they were White. They were admitted freely with all classes of White people to public functions, public parks, and the best schools. The police were drawn from their ranks, and the courts, dependent on their votes, treated them with such leniency as to encourage lawlessness. Their vote selected public officials, and while this had small effect upon the economic situation, it had great effect upon their personal treatment and the deference shown them ... The newspapers specialized on news that flattered the poor Whites and almost utterly ignored the Negro except in crime and ridicule. (p. 700-701)

Racism, and by extension, White privilege is then, just the 'structuration' of Race in society (Guess, 2006). This structuration is the way in which ideas of Race as a concept become institutionalised, and certain forms of racism are officially and unofficially approved by a populace. Adopting Giddens (1984) three structural dimensions of a racialised social system, Guess (2006) expanded an understanding of 1) signification (the discourse of Race becoming biological and normalised, rather historical); 2) domination (the representation of Race in decision-making and resource allocation); and, 3) legitimation (the rewarding and penalising of Race based on policies and legislation). Race becomes a social fact, that can be fixed or not, and can benefit or constrain a segment of a population by their designation at any given point. White privilege determines who will and will not face the brunt of the machine of White Supremacy.

In regards to defining White Supremacy, Ansley (1997) stated that,

> I do not mean to allude only to the self-conscious racism of ... hate groups. I refer instead to a ... system in which Whites overwhelmingly control power and material resources, conscious and unconscious ideas of White superiority and entitlement are widespread, and relations of White dominance and non-White subordination are daily reenacted across a broad array of institutions and social settings. (p. 1024)

Further, in creating an understanding of the difference between Whiteness and White Nationalism, and more specifically, White Separatism, George Lincoln Rockwell in *White Power* (Rockwell, 1966/2016) proclaimed that,

> We must have an all-White America, an American which our children and our grandchildren will play and go to school with other White children ... We must have an America without swarming Black filth ... an America ... free of alien, Jewish influence; and America in which White people are the sole masters of our own destiny. (p. 345)

This articulation of a White Nationalist and Separatist ideologies distances itself from an articulation of Whiteness in the leisure studies literature as solely expressions of socio-political privilege (Arai & Kivel, 2009; Carrington, 2010; McDonald, 2009) or even from larger systems of dominance (Hylton & Long, 2016; Mowatt, 2009; Spracklen, 2013). What this manuscript posits is that White Nationalism and Separatism are not the ideologies or work of White people in power but of those who have been denied the full expanse of privileges assigned to Whiteness and a prevention of the fulfilment of a reality of White Supremacy. And in response, White Nationalism and Separatism have created two theoretical lenses to function, White Genocide Conspiracy Theory or the Great Replacement Theory. As previously mentioned, de Gorbinaeu (de Gobineau, (1915) [1853]) and Grant (1916) both warned of the desolation of the White Race through 'Race-mixing' and immigration. This was further articulated by von Coudenhove-Kalergi (1925) in *Practical Idealism* inevitable terms for the future of Europe and the West, and laid the seeds of White Genocide articulated by David Lane, former member of the Ku Klux Klan and founder of The Order, in his 'Fourteen Words': 'We must secure the existence of our people and a future for white children' (Michael, 2009). This lens dictated the behaviours of members of White Nationalist and Separatist organisation to be both visible to prevent erasure and to engage in activities that could grow membership.

Leisure literature & White Nationalism

With the exception of Spracklen's (2013) 'Nazi Punks off: Leisure, Nationalism, Cultural Identity and the Consumption of Metal and Folk Music' there has not been an overt, direct discussions of a connection between leisure and White Nationalism in leisure-based text and literature. However, there have brief mentions in a range of texts. Virden and Walker (1999) quoted Harris, a Black outdoorsman,

> The point, of course, is that historically bad things have happened to Black people in the outdoors. If we choose to conjure them up, our associations with the woods can easily run in the direction of bloodhounds, swinging hemp ropes, and cracker Wizards in Klan bedsheets. (p. 233)

While Silk (2007) posited in a discussion on the reconstitution of urban space that

> Somewhat butting against Martin Luther King Boulevard, semantically, ideologically, if not physically, 'Confederate Park' (which commemorates the Confederate soldiers who died in the 1st Battle of Memphis in the Civil War) and 'Nathan Bedford Forrest Park' (named after, and indeed the burial site of, the General who led the Confederacy during the second battle of Memphis and was the first 'Grand Wizard' of the Ku Klux Klan after the war) create a topographic web of glorification and memorialization of an 'Old South' based on slave labor, White supremacy, the Confederate 'cause'. Indeed, these two names, along with Jefferson Davis Park (commemorating the only President of the Confederate States in America), are sites of local contestation. (p. 262)

Riordan (1988) and Horna (1988) both referenced the rising tide of a fascination and allure of Nazism in youth culture and among youth gangs post-Cold War. Rose and Spencer (2016) mentioned Nazism in their literature review of biopolitics involved in (virtual) spaces. And there was a brief mention of Nazi symbolism and sentiments in conjunction with displays of masculinity and homophobia (Cauldwell, 2011) and with Black footballers being threatened in their experiences (Holland, 1997) in football culture in the U.K.

Beckers (1990) and Parry (1983) provided an understanding that Nazi Germany played a fundamental part in establishing a segment of sociology that examined society, capitalism, and democracy and how each are inexplicably producers of leisure. Stephenson and Hughes (2005) highlighted the dangers in travelling to and within European destinations due to the rising popularity of Neo-Nazi groups. While Chambers (1983) made mention of the use Nazi helmets and leather boots in the attire of the Viking (biker) Gang in an overall discussion of symbolism and imagery in leisure.

Leisure history & White Nationalist ideologies

While Mowatt (2009) presented some measure of visual evidence at the 1955 meeting of the American Institute of Park Executives in Louisville, KY in which a large Confederate flag was prominently displayed on the walls of a potential association with White Nationalist Ideals there are far greater associations (see Figure 1). Mobily (2018) extensively discussed the imbedded ideals and ideology of the eugenics movement within the playground movement. Leaders of various eugenics societies, specifically the National Conference of Race Betterment, regularly intermingled intellectually with key individuals within the Playground Association of America.

While the influence of Gifford Pinchot, first Chief of the United States Forest Reserve, and Madison Grant, key founder of the environmental movement, on the conservation movement is not as significant as the eugenics movement's influence on them. Pinchot, in particularly, served as a United States delegate to the first and second International Eugenics Congress, in 1912 and 1921, and a member of the advisory council of the American Eugenics Society, from 1925 to 1935 (Allen, 2013). And for the aforementioned Grant (1916), not only was the preservation and sanctity of the Nordic stock of the utmost importance for Grant, the preservation of land and wildlife were extensions of his environmentalism. His tome, *The Passing of the Great Race*, was so influential that it was used as evidence in the Nuremberg Trials (Spiro, 2009).

Leisure (spaces) & White Nationalism

Power has been a contested tool and sociopolitical expression not just in contemporary politics but also within the long history of Western civilisation. The location of its contestation is embedded in the halls of major social institutions of various Western societies. Additionally, the location of its contestation can also be found in the physical space of Western society, in the public and private-public space. Public parks, public malls, streetscapes, stadia, and arena and other leisure spaces all exert a power over the less powerful to restrict bodies and regulate

Figure 1. American Institute of Park Executives Annual Conference, 1955, Louisville, KY.

behaviours. But in the vein of Stuart Hall conceptions of power, power does not only subside in the grips of the dominant elites and governments of the Western world, but also in the act of resistance and within the location of contestations of those less powerful (Osborne & Segal, 1997).

It is within this context that on one hand, we view racialised populism as the struggle for power by the disenfranchised labourers and economically impoverished of society, but from those who have not fully benefited from the promises of a greater conception of White Supremacy. These disenfranchised White groups seek to usurp power from the elites despite sharing an underscored racialised similarity with those White elites. With this as a working understanding, it can be inferred that not all White people control power and material resources, thus the basis of struggle or fight of the American racialised populist.

While on the other hand, racialised populism seems like the doubling down, through the power of social control, by the White disenfranchised and impoverished against the racial and ethnic 'Other'. The racial and ethnic 'Other' are attacked by members of White populist groups while also facing historical and perpetual forms of discrimination from White elites. The impact of this doubling down is much to the pleasure of the White elites and governments that seemingly condone the actions of these White populist actors, as they unbeknownst to them and the 'Other' served the interests of those same authorities. Rentals and permits were granted, and city services were given to protect expressions of free speech. In this respect, leisure served as simply a site, a venue, and a location for such actions of a racialised populism.

Through these four junctures in history: 1) the 1925 Ku Klux Klan March on Washington; 2) the 1939 German-American Bund Rally in New York City's Madison Square Garden; 3) the 1977 National Socialist Party of America planned rally in Skokie, IL; and, 4) the 2017 Unite the Right Rally on the University of Virginia's campus and in Emancipation Park in Charlottesville, VA.; this manuscript does not seek to define or operationalise power but to simply highlight the exertion of it as an ideology within leisure spaces. Each of these historical junctures was selected for discussion as they all occur in locations of leisure and recreation within the United States. Each centres the activities of White Nationalists and Separatists (specifically those more aligned with the Ku Klux Klan and the Neo-Nazi Party) that for intents and purposes function at the populist level inside and beyond the borders the United States.

Utilising historical documents (newspapers, photographs, and speeches) as primary sources and secondary sources of books and articles on the various White Nationalist and Separatist organisations, the four junctures in history serve as historical cases in which a leisure setting was used for their purposes, and that the formation of a White nationalist organisation was assisted in its development by use of the leisure setting. Other gatherings have occurred, but not with crowds of a 1000 or more people or three or more organisation as a part of the planning. In all cases, White Nationalism was displayed in a publically significant way in the United States, rather than in clandestine and privates spaces. This manuscript seeks to understand how the contest for power that were situated in leisure spaces significantly highlighted how Race-based populist politics imagined power in response to conceptions of White Genocide Conspiracy Theory and The Great Replacement Theory and have formulated into a movement that seemed to be quite resistant to elimination from government forces and counter movements.

White Nationalists on the mall: the 1925 Ku Klux Klan March on Washington

After a personal viewing of D. W. Griffith's *The Birth of a Nation* in the White House in 1915, then President Woodrow Wilson proclaimed that, 'it's like writing history with lightening. My only regret is that it is so terribly true' (Benbow, 2010, p. 509). And with that statement and the popularity of the movie the Second Ku Klux Klan (the Klan) was formed. While the First Klan operated between 1865 and 1900, the second Klan began in 1915 and lasted until the 1940s. The Second Klan maintained the anti-Black stance of the First Klan but broadened their views to include anti-immigration (of Italians, and Eastern Europeans), anti-Catholicism (anti-Irish), and anti-Communist (anti-Jewish) (Gordon, 2017). Its membership swelled and eventually resulted in a 30,000 person march on Washington on 8 August 1925. *The Washington Post* placed the march on the front page with a picture entitled, 'Pennsylvania Avenue Mass of White During Klansmen's Parade' (see Figure 2).

The Washington Post.

NO. 17,951. WASHINGTON: SUNDAY, AUGUST 9, 1925.—EIGHTY-SIX PAGES FIVE CENTS.

BROWNING IN TEARS AS HE SURRENDERS YOUNG CINDERELLA

Decision Follows Girl's Attempt to End Her Life With Poison.

SURROGATE TO WRITE LAST CHAPTER MONDAY

Mary Spas Keeps Her Gowns; Deceived Rich Man, His Attorney Asserts.

French Fliers Still Aloft After 24 Hours

Chicago's Criminals Threatened by Ads

Buried Miner Saved After 10-Hour Ordeal

CITY GROUPS URGE TELLING NATION OF ADVANTAGES HERE

Million In Population Soon Predicted From Publicity Drive.

COMFORT AND BEAUTY OF HOMES NOTABLE

Bringing Conventions Especially Favored to Advance City's Unique Feature.

PENNSYLVANIA AVENUE MASS OF WHITE DURING KLANSMEN'S PARADE.

6 ARMED MEN IN AUTO GET AIR MAIL IN HOLDUP

Family, Church and School To Share in Bryan's Estate

SECRET OF BETTER AUTO FUEL REPORTED FOUND

WHITE-ROBED KLAN CHEERED ON MARCH IN NATION'S CAPITAL

Police Estimate 30,000 to 35,000 Take Part in Demonstration.

PRAYER FAILS TO HALT RAIN AS PARADE ENDS

Thousands at Monument Rush to Shelter; Some Remain Through Downpour.

AIR OF TENSITY MARKS START OF PROCESSION

Friendly Reception, However, Given to Klansmen of East, South and West.

Figure 2. 'White-Robed Klan Cheered on March in Nation's Capital', The Washington Post, 9 August 1925.

The Post's account described the 'parade' in somewhat majestic fashion, as 'phantom-like hosts of the Klan spread their white robe over the most historic thoroughfare yesterday in one of the greatest demonstrations this city has ever known' ('White Robbed Klan', 1925, p. 1). The banal labelling of the march and of such an organisation with the legacy like the Klan, as a simple parade spoke to the perceived mainstream nature of their presence even in their second incarnation.

White Nationalism as mainstream

Quite startling in the after-effects of both marches, the Klan became so mainstream that in various parts of the United States they outright 'sponsored, in public, baseball teams, father–son outings, beautiful baby contests, weddings, baby christenings, junior leagues, road rallies, festivals', according to Kathleen Blee. A familial culture within the Klan was key, as they established youth groups, a Tri-K Klub for young girls, and a Klan University for older youth. According to Blee (1991), the Klan,

> As early as 1921 ... presented Lanier University in Atlanta with a substantial endowment, citing its full agreement with principles of the university ... Lanier University advertised itself as an institution dedicated to the teachings of 'pure Americanism' ... two years later, [the Klan] tried to purchase Valparaiso University in northern Indiana to become a Klan University but failed. (p. 160)

White Nationalism membership

The second Klan made an increased effort to be gender inclusive in membership and leadership (Blee, 2002). According to McWhirter (2011), the second Klan had far more strident directive and purpose. The Klan, although reflecting a populist tinge, also embraced all sectors and classes of American society under the purpose of,

> To shield the sanctity of the home and the chastity of womanhood; to maintain White supremacy … and by a practical devotedness to conserve, protect and maintain the distinctive institutions, rights, privileges, principles and ideals of a pure Americanism. (McWhirter, 2011, p. 65)

The day after the August 1925 march, a smaller contingency of the Klan travelled to Arlington to place wreaths on the Tomb of the Unknown Soldier and the grave of William Jennings Bryan, famed American populist orator and alleged supporter of the Klan who died that year. Later in the evening, an initiation ceremony of 200 new members was conducted ('200 Join', 1925). With nearly 75,000 people present, all witnessed the burning of an electrically lit 80-foot cross at the Arlington Park horse grounds, in the spirit of what was depicted in *The Birth of Nation* and was not a tradition of the Klan until its depiction. On 13 September 1926, the Klan returned to march on Washington once more; however, this time only 15,000 attended and participated (see Figure 3). D.C. area resident and rider with the First Klan, Alfred B. Williams (1925) wrote in a letter to the editor on the 1925 and future marches of the Klan,

> The wise course for all the people of Washington is to allow the emasculated, distorted, perverted sham of the Ku Klux Klan to come here, like any other burlesque show, or circus, and do its stuff, look at it, laugh at it and let it go in perfect peace and quiet. Very likely the organization is on its last legs and is staging the performance to revive waning interest … Like everything else of its kind, it depends for life on persecution and publicity … the more the K. K. K. is ignored, laughed at and left to go its way undisturbed, the more quickly it will vanish, like other playthings … . (p. 6)

Figure 3. Bird's eye vied ow Ku Klux Klan parade down Pennsylvania Avenue with the Capitol building in the background on September 13, 1926 in Washington, D.C. (Photo courtesy Library of Congress/Getty Images)

White nationalists in the bleachers: the 1939 German-American bund rally in Madison square garden

A total number of 22,000 attendees were packed into Madison Square Garden on 20 February 1939 (See Figure 4) ('22,000', 1939). The German-American Bund (the Bund), the name for the American Nazi party, were the sole organisers of this event which not only celebrated the actions that were occurring in Nazi Germany but also ironically George Washington's 207th Birthday (amongst members of the Bund, George Washington was the first true Fascist overseeing an 'unmongrelised' America). The rally was billed as the 'Mass Demonstration for True Americanism', and as an op-ed stated, 'for so large a meeting of so insolent a character the occasion passed off pretty peaceably' with crowds yelling 'Free America!' ('The Bund Meeting', 1939). A total of 100,000 anti-rally demonstrators stood in vicinity of the Garden shouting their dismay, while another estimated 10,000 were not able to make it inside and yet stood in support of the rally shouting, 'blut und boden' (Race and land).

Fritz Kuhn, *Bundesführer*, the national Fuehrer of the Bund came to the lectern and said that followers of the Bund must be ready, 'to protect themselves, their children and their homes against those who would turn the United States into a Bolshevik paradise ... the Jew is the driving force of communism' ('The Bund Meeting', 1939). For nearly six hours, audience members took in the various propagandised speeches from Bund leadership while sitting in what had already become a key sports landmark for basketball and boxing. The only restriction in the Bunds' rental of the amphitheatre was no anti-Semitic displays, banners, or speeches be made.

White Nationalism as free speech

As it was clear in Kuhn's speech, adherence and enforcement of this restriction did not occur. Ironically, the American Jewish Committee were in support of the rally as they indicated that the Committee,

Figure 4. US flags, swastikas and a portrait of George Washington at a meeting of the German American Bund held at Madison Square Garden, New York City, 20th February 1939. The American Nazi organization attracted twenty thousand people to the meeting, which was addressed by its leader Fritz Julius Kuhn. Among the banners is one which reads 'Stop Jewish Domination Of Christian Americans'. (Photo by FPG/Archive Photos/Getty Images)

> Had considered the question raised by the protests ... in connection with the leasing of Madison Square Garden ... [the Bund] is, in our opinion, completely anti-American and anti-democratic. Nevertheless, because we believe that the basic rights of free speech and free assembly must never be tampered with ... we are opposed to any action to prevent the Bund from airing its views. It is natural today, when our American system is being attached from many sides, that people should seek to suppress their enemies. We are confident, however, that citizens of the United States will reject all un-American propaganda. ("22,000", 1939)

However, the Bund rally was just the outcome of a couple years of work by Kuhn and his associates. Camp Siegfried and Camp Nordland were two summer campsites of nearly 20 others that were established to train youth and young adults in doctrine and philosophy (See Figure 5).

White Nationalism and the need for White ethnostate

The Bund divided the country into regions and districts for administration of newsletters but also recruitment and training. In essence, the Bund operated as an independent ethnostate within the United States, growing in size and scope and in opposition to the Klan, as the inevitable world war was looming greatly on the minds of many.

But despite the incredible show of numbers which would imply continued growth as one poster stated, 'ONE MILLION BUND MEMBERS BY 1940', the Bund rally marked the downfall of the movement on three fronts: 1) The growing animus among American citizens towards the Bund as impending war with Germany became a reality; 2) the Bund's public embrace of violence and hatred towards Jews in Germany that harmed Germany's hopes for the U.S. to not take a side in the War; and, 3) the embezzling of $14,000 by Fritz Kuhn, leader, and his 2.5 year sentence to prison for tax evasion in which Germany declared war and the U.S. became an ally (Bernstein, 2013). The month after the Bund Rally, the final game of the National Invitational Tournament (NIT) annual collegiate basketball game was played in the same space.

Figure 5. American Bund Camp: Nazi Youth Salute Hindenburg 1934, Location: Griggstown, New Jersey. (Getty Images)

White Nationalists in the park: the 1977 National Socialist Party of America & Skokie, IL

In an effort to preserve history, facilitate awareness, and provide educational leisure opportunities, the 65,000 square foot Illinois Holocaust Museum and Education Center opened in 2009 in the Chicago suburb of Skokie, containing numerous displays, exhibits on genocide (the Jewish Holocaust and other genocides), and thousands of video/audio testimonials and artefacts attesting to the atrocities inflicted on those of the Jewish faith both in Nazi-controlled Germany (Levine, 2009). The grand opening of the Museum and Centre drew thousands of supporters but also members of the neo-Nazi movement that displayed imagery from World War II Nazi Germany; they chanted and played music to affirm a Neo-Nazi identity in opposition of a distinct Jewish identity (see Figure 6).

A similar sentiment and set of actions impacted the Holocaust Museum in Washington, D.C. in the summer of 2009. The Museum and the people within it were the target of a shooting that left one guard dead and resulted in the Skokie, Illinois Museum adding to their security ("Illinois Museum Adding," 2009). But this was not the first time that an issue of anger towards Jewish identity arose in Skokie. Skokie, nearly 50% Jewish, uniquely became a suburb that attracted a high percentage of Jewish immigrants, specifically a high number of Jewish death camp survivors outside of Israel. This highly visible Jewish identity garnered the attention of the resurgent American Neo-Nazi movement, the National Socialist Party of America (NSPA) under the leadership of Frank Collin. (Levine, 2009)

White Nationalism in public space

In 1977, the NSPA chose a little known public park in Skokie (presumably named Birch Park) as the second site for their planned demonstration primarily to show their growing strength. The NSPA initially chose Marquette Park in Chicago, based on the negative response that Martin Luther King received in 1966 (when he was struck by a rock) as the site for the demonstration. George Lincoln Rockwell, leader of the American Nazi Party (the National Socialist White People's Party – NSWPP, a precursor to the NSPA), organised a 'White People's March' in neighbouring Gage Park to recruit members. NSPA continued the efforts of the American Nazi Party in Marquette Park, purchasing a building as an office; years after a former member of the American Nazi Party murdered Rockwell (Downs, 1985; Strum, 1999).

However, City of Chicago officials required the NSPA to take out a large summed public-safety insurance bond and approved a policy banning political demonstrations. Skokie, was then selected

Figure 6. A Neo-Nazi protest, organized by the National Socialist Movement, demonstrates near the Illinois Holocaust Museum & Education Center 19 April 2009 in Skokie, Illinois. Photo Credit: Nicole Cohen.

by the NSPA, a permit was requested, but was turned down by the Village government because of their concern and sensitivity to the numerous Jewish residents of the Village (Skokie Park District, 1976a). Specifically, in two meetings of the Board of Commissioners of the Skokie Park District, the Board first directed Daniel Brown, director of the Skokie Park District at the time, to inform Frank Collin that the district did not have a 'Birch Park', and second, passed an ordinance on public assemblies and parades that required at least 30 days of notice and an insurance bond over $300,000 (Skokie Park District, 1976b).

However, after this second refusal, the NSPA chose to take the Village of Skokie to court for violating their basic rights to demonstrate on public property. Over the span of three years and with the American Civil Liberties Union (ACLU) providing defence, the NSPA won the Supreme Court ruling that overturned the Village's decision (Dubey, 1977). The Village granted the NSPA permission to use the space in front of the Village Hall with the restriction that swastikas (symbols that affirm neo-Nazi identity) could not be worn or present. The legal battle became a landmark case on Freedom of Speech in the United States (National Socialist Party of America v. the Village of Skokie, 1977).

NSPA organisers chose to hold three demonstrations in Chicago's Marquette Park, whose officials chose to eliminate the insurance requirement and political demonstration ban out of fear of legal liability (Berlet, 2001). The first rally of 25 members was on 9 July 1978 and was organised as an anti-integration rally (Black families were moving into the 'White ethnic' neighbourhood) with roughly 2,000 counter protestors (Kneeland, 1978). The second on 28 June 1986 was a joint rally with the American First Committee, with 75 counter protestors, and thousands of White residents, and were spurned on by the second term of then-Mayor Harold Washington, Chicago's first Black mayor (Gibson & Zambrano, 1986) (See Figure 7).

Figure 7. KKK and White Power rally in Marquette Park, Chicago, Illinois, USA, September, 1986. Photo Credit: Mark Reinstein (Alamy).

The last rally on 28 August 1988 attracted 500 White Nationalists of various organisations, another 300 counter protestors, and hundreds of resident onlookers ("Mob Attacks", 1988). Furthermore, the attempts of the NSPA and 'White Ethnic' residents of the Marquette Park were not successful to preventing housing integration as Census trends in 2000 showed Black and Latinx populations at 53% and 35%, respectively (in the 1980 Census, they were at 5.3% and 11%) (U.S. Census 1981, 2001). Frank Collin in 1979 was also convicted for child molestation and sentenced to seven years in prison, which resulted in the NSPA moving from Illinois to North Carolina under new leadership and desolation of the organisation (Kaplan, 2000).

White Nationalists on the streets: the 2017 Unite the Right Rally in Charlottesville

Yet in Emanuel African Methodist Episcopal Church on the evening of 17 June 2015, Dylann Roof proceeded to kill nine people (Cynthia Hurd, Susie Jackson, Ethel Lee Lance, Depayne Middleton-Doctor, Clementa Pinckney, Tywanza Sanders, Daniel Simmons, Sharonda Coleman-Singleton, and Myra Thompson) as they attended a prayer service. Roof hoped that his attack would be a call to arms, 'worsen race relations, increase racial tensions that would lead to a Race war' (Cobb, 2017). The Charleston shooting became a touch point for the question of White Nationalism and its symbolism. The presence of Confederate Monuments in public parks began to be in question and their removal was the answer for some.

White Nationalism as organiszation

In response, a wide range of White Nationalists from various organisations sought to protect them: Identity Evropa and Traditionalist Youth Network, two campus-based groups; the League of the South, a neo-Confederate organization; the National Policy Institute represented heavily by Richard Spencer; Traditionalist Worker Party, a political campaign and candidacy focused group; the Ku Klux Klan; the National Socialist Movement inheritors of the National Socialist Party of America; and, the American Nazi Party. The Unite the Right Rally on August 11th and 12th was planned as one of those responses to protect the statue of Robert E. Lee, the Confederate General, that was located in Emancipation Park in Charlottesville, VA (see Figure 8).

Prior to major rally in August, there were preceding activities that the diligence and persistence of White nationalist organising abilities to respond to the removal of the statue. The National Policy Institute was the earliest to respond to the city council vote to remove the statue and to rename Lee Park, Emancipation Park in May 2017 (another park named after another Confederate General Thomas 'Stonewall' Jackson was also up for renaming) (Griggs, 2017). This smaller rally was followed by another Klan-led rally after a permit was secured by members but was moved by the City to another park (McKenize, 2017).

White Nationalism organsied

Similar to the 1977 NSPA Rally, the city was sued by the lead organiser Jason Kessler with support by the ACLU that resulted in an injunction and the Kessler and the groups were able to hold the rally within the intended location. Other similarities to past gatherings of White Nationalism: the chanting and use of the slogan, 'blut und boden' – the Bund Rally; and the invoking anti-Jewish sentiments – the Klan March in Washington; and, the invocation of free speech from an outside actor (this case, Virginia Senator, Tim Kaine), as the first rally on the evening of August 11th occurred on the University of Virginia's campus.

However, it was the rally on the next day that represented ultimately the tragedy as a cautionary commentary of what can ensue from this animation of public space. Law enforcement officers nor counter-protestors were prepared for the number of White Nationalist

Figure 8. Emancipation Park just prior to The Unite the Right rally in Charlottesville, Va. on Saturday, August 12, 2017. Photo Credit: Andrew Shurtleff.

representatives that attended the second day nor their readiness for direct action and provocation. The White Nationalists that appeared initiated agitation with counter protestors while armed, as Virginia is an open carry state. Additionally, in virtual spaces, several digital platforms and social media sites were utilised to enable White Nationalists in attending and gathering resources for their actions, such as Google and GoDaddy (for general searching of information for event logistics) ("Google Cancels", 2017), AirBnB (for lodging needs of visiting White Nationalists from other states) (Bromwich, 2017), and, PayPal (for raising money for travel and the purchase of supplies) (Berr, 2017).

The ACLU also faced criticism for once again protecting White Nationalists use of free speech and assembly; however, they did issue a statement indicating that they will no longer engage in cases where free speech is coupled with the presence or use of guns and ammunition. The public outrage of both rallies and the subsequent vehicular killing of Heather D. Hayer, a counter-protestor may be perceived as a detriment to the White Nationalist organization that were involved, but this is far from the case. Nathan Domigo, founder of Identity Evropa, indicated, 'this is a huge victory for us ... we are going to get national attention' (Stapley, 2017). And the words of David Duke, long-standing White Nationalist political candidate and party member, provide a further emphasis of such a caution in understanding the outcomes of the rally, 'a turning point for the people of this country. We are determined to take our country back' (Cohen, 2017).

National populism, leisure, & race: a conclusion

Duke's words are only lessons taught by George Lincoln Rockwell and the aforementioned *White Power* (Rockwell, 1966/2016), leader of the NSWPP and the American Nazi Party until his murder. The 49 listed and active White Nationalist groups by the Southern Poverty Law Center (2018) within the United States all reflect a different interpretation and articulation of Rockwell's points.

But preceding Rockwell, William Joseph Simmons, Imperial Wizard of the Second Klan, in *Klan Unmasked* (1923), presented the basis for these groups' activity and selective use of leisure spaces,

> We Americans are barely reproducing our numbers on our own soil. In comparison with the colored and foreign elements our percentage is every year being reduced ... the new America, if the present tendencies continue, will be a nation composed of a majority of American white farmers only in the Middle Western and plains states. Black farmers ... the coastal regions of the South and the Mississippi Delta, and Japanese farmers will rapidly multiply their numbers on the Pacific coast. (p. 104)

These four historic junctures of leisure and White Nationalism and Separatism: 1) 1925 Ku Klux Klan March on Washington; 2) 1939 German-American Bund Rally in New York City's Madison Square Garden; 3) 1977 National Socialist Party of America planned rally; and, 4) the 2017 Unite the Right Rally, also reflect the intent to animate leisure spaces with the use of political ideologies of White Supremacy that further related agendas.

If examined in isolation they appear as momentary points of concern that have been easily dispersed into forgotten annals of history. However, within each case White Nationalism and Separatism grew and adapted by becoming more mainstream than fringe; more savvy in its use of the protections of free speech than exclaiming a rhetoric of violence; more concerned with claiming and occupying space than being reclusive; and, more organised in activities than aggressively haphazard. The manner that national populism made use of leisure spaces only seemed to enable the growth and sophistication of a stridently racialised White identity than hinder or diffuse it. As Mowatt (2019) articulated on the concept of racecrafting, the public use of leisure spaces was articulations of their power, demarcations of their intolerance of erasure, and reifications of who and what the White Race ought to be.

The site of this contestation between identities was a location for recreation that was administered by leisure service entities. The social construction of racialised identities is at the very heart of societies' production of national populism (McKean, 2016). Identity is confusingly exacerbated by its meiosis into social identity, cultural identity, and ethnic identity. Monuments of historic figures of the Confederacy and of nativist, populist, and eugenic histories are being protected by the 'flawed' human beings myth, yet these human beings were enemies to humanity in their ideology and actions (Gilbert, 2017). There is a tension between racecrafted media representations of White Nationalist as simple, general, or ordinary populists and their truer or grander schemes of White dominance. These racialised populist, regardless of their domestic and international location have a dubious relationship with either anti-government, White purity, or neo-Fascist sentiment. Thus, it is troubling when a member of a Missouri militia stated that, '... some of the places we train are public parks where you can find all sorts of people frequenting the area' (Donovan, 2010).

And train for what? David Copeland on April 17–30, a Neo-Nazi placed nail bombs in three distinct public locations in London, one of which was the Admiral Duncan Pub in SoHo, which is in the centre of gay community of London ("Profile: Copeland the Killer", 2000). Anders Behring Breivik on 22 July 2011 in Norway, detonating a van bomb killing eight people, and then opening fire on 65 children at a nearby youth summer camp of the Workers' Youth league (Hartman, 2011). Amanda and Jerad Miller, avid cosplayers, on 8 June 2014, who posted on FaceBook that 'the dawn of a new day. May all our coming sacrifices be worth it' as they killed two police officers eating at a pizzeria in Las Vegas and then proceeded to drape a 'DON'T TREAD ON ME' and Swastika flags on their bodies (Warren, 2014). Or, Jared Taylor's killing of 50 and injuring of others on 15 March 2019 in New Zealand (Barrouquerre, 2019).

There is a complexity to the contestation of meanings and values ascribed to public and private-public space. As Glover (2015) indicated, research can 'expose the routine appropriation of "animation" of public space to legitimise claims to urban space and serve the public good' (p. 96). It is not, then, surprising that the Klan marched on Washington; the Bund rented Madison Square Garden; the NSPA chose to demonstrate in a public park; or the various White nationalists organizations signed a permit to use campus areas, city streets, and a public park. The political act of protesting is highlighted in its violation of the sanctum of these public and private-public spaces. To protest where children may play and find entertainment, families may eat and choose to vacation to, and adults may engage in sports, changes the personalised simplicity of these settings with the complications of political, cultural, and ideological difference.

A recreation centre then became a point of contention, not just significant representation of the 'Other' in a community. Each case in this manuscript is not only an affirmation of racialised White identities that have been marginalised but also the persistent presence of

White Nationalism in America and the protection of free speech. As American National populism turns to calls of fascism it is far more important to see the relevance of leisure spaces in obscuring those calls with either benign displays of free speech rallies or violent protections of the first amendment. The true magnitude of White Supremacy is still elusive in many of our discussions that favour a focus on White privilege. Rowan (1996) warned while tuning into early interview-styled AM radio shows, hearing of law enforcement officers receiving unofficial summer training at ranches, and witnessing gatherings in public spaces such as park that, 'the sprouting up of highly armed militias and paramilitary groups across America ... pressing to create a constitutional crisis by promoting a ghastly Race war are going underground' (p. 8).

This turn to fascism by perceived White Nationalist and Separatist populism underscored a tension with the fundamentals of populism, anti-elitism in individuals or government. If populism can be seen as resistance to elitism, then this persistent embracing of White Nationalism could be seen as a form co-option of the fundamentals of populism, a co-option of resistance that is being further commodified in the present day with red-coloured baseball hats and green avatars (Butsch, 2001). As Caplan (2016) stated 'not just the big bang of mass rallies and extreme violence; it is also the creeping fog that incrementally occupies power while obscuring its motives, its moves and its goals'. Not unlike the history that preceded White nationalisms coupling with national populism where alliances across Race challenged the social order (Horton, 2004), what is being called for is a change in society that will further exclude the racially and religiously marginalised while not fulfilling the full wishes of the economically White marginalised in hopes for a White society. Leisure is the site, and animation thereof, for either making America great again or it can be the site for just making America what it could've been all along.

Disclosure statement

No potential conflict of interest was reported by the author.

ORCID

Rasul A. Mowatt http://orcid.org/0000-0003-4177-0725

References

(1925, August 10). 200 join as fiery cross lights capital. *The New York Herald*. Amsterdam, NE: JAI/Elsevier.
(1939, February 21). 22,000 Nazis hold rally in Garden; Police check foes. *The New York Times*. Retrieved from https://timesmachine.nytimes.com/timesmachine/1939/02/21/94680980.html?emc=eta1&pageNumber=1
Allen, G. E. (2013). "Culling the herd": Eugenics and the conservation movement in the United States, 1900–1940. *Journal of the History of Biology*, *46*(1), 31–72.
Ansley, F. L. (1997). White supremacy (and what we should do about it). In R. Delgado & J. Stefancic (Eds.), *Critical white studies: Looking behind the mirror* (pp. 592–595). Philadelphia: Temple University Press.
Arai, S., & Kivel, B. D. (2009). Critical race theory and social justice perspectives on Whiteness, difference(s) and (anti) racism: A fourth wave of race research in leisure studies. *Journal of Leisure Research*, *41*(4), 459–470.
Barrouquere, B. (2019, March 15). After New Zealand shooting, far-right, racists claim victimhood, hail killer as hero. *The Southern Poverty Law Center*. Retrieved from https://www.splcenter.org/hatewatch/2019/03/15/after-new-zealand-shooting-far-right-racists-claim-victimhood-hail-killer-hero

Beckers, T. (1990). Andries Sternheim and the study of leisure in the early critical theory. *Leisure Studies, 9*(3), 197–212.

Benbow, M. E. (2010). Birth of a quotation: Woodrow Wilson and "like writing history with lightning". *The Journal of the Gilded Age and Progressive Era, 9*(4), 509–533. Retrieved from: http://www.jstor.org/stable/2079940

Bergmann, E. (2018). *Conspiracy & populism: The politics of misinformation.* Cham, CH: Palgrave Macmillan.

Berlet, C. (2001). Hate groups, racial tension and ethnoviolence in an integrating Chicago Neighborhood, 1976–1988. In B. A. Dobratz, L. K. Walder, & T. Buzzell (Eds.), *Research in political sociology, vol.9: The politics of social inequality* (pp. 117–163). Amsterdam, NE: JAI/Elsevier.

Bernstein, A. (2013). *Swastika nation: Fritz Kuhn and the rise and fall of the German-American Bund.* New York, NY: St. Martin's Press.

Berr, J. (2017, August 17). PayPal cuts off payments to right-wing extremist. *CBS News.* Retrieved from https://www.cbsnews.com/news/paypal-suspends-dozens-of-racist-groups-sites-altright-com/

Blee, K. M. (1991). *Women of the Klan: Racism and gender in the 1920s.* Berkeley, CA: University of California Press.

Blee, K. M. (2002). *Inside organized racism: Women in the hate movement.* Berkeley, CA: University of California Press.

Bromwich, J. E. (2017, August 9). Airbnb cancels accounts inked to White Nationalists rally in Charlottesville. *The New York Times.* Retrieved from https://www.nytimes.com/2017/08/09/us/airbnb-white-nationalists-supremacists.html

(1939, February 22). The Bund meeting. *The New York Times.* Retrieved from https://timesmachine.nytimes.com/timesmachine/1939/02/22/96020197.html?pageNumber=17

Butsch, R. (2001). Considering resistance and incorporation. *Leisure Sciences, 23*(2), 71–79.

Caplan, J. (2016, November 17). Trump and fascism. A view from the past. *History Workshop.* Retrieved from http://www.historyworkshop.org.uk/trump-and-fascism-a-view-from-the-past/

Carrington, B. (2010). *Race, sport and politics: The sporting black diaspora.* London, UK: Sage Publication.

Caudwell, J. (2011). 'Does your boyfriend know you're here?' The spatiality of homophobia in men's football culture in the UK. *Leisure Studies, 30*(2), 123–138.

Chambers, D. A. (1983). Symbolic equipment and the objects of leisure images. *Leisure Studies, 2*(3), 301–315.

Cobb, J. (2017, February 6). Inside the trial of Dylann Roof. *The New Yorker.* Retrieved from http://www.newyorker.com/magazine/2017/02/06/inside-the-trial-of-dylann-roof/amp

Cohen, Z. (2017, August 19). Trump's mixed messaging sparks concerns of 'emboldened' White supremacists. *CNN.* Retrieved from http://www.cnn.com/2017/08/19/politics/trump-remarks-alt-right/index.html

de Gobineau, A. ((1915)[1853]). *An essay on the inequality of human races.* [trans. A. Collins]. New York, NY: G.P. Putnam's Sons.

Donovan, D. (2010, September 12). Voices of reason: An open response to the Kansas City Star article "the new militia". *Ad Astrum.* Retrieved from http://adastrum.kansascity.com/?q=node/1026.

Downs, D. A. (1985). *Nazis in Skokie: Freedom, community and the First Amendment.* South Bend, IN: University of Notre Dame Press.

Du Bois, W. E. B. (1935). *Black reconstruction.* New York, NY: Harcourt Brace.

Dubey, D. (1977). *No swastikas allowed: Lift march injunction. The Skokie Life.* Chicago, IL: Chicago Historical Museum Archives. July 14.

Gibson, R., & Zambrano, M. (1986, June 29). Marquette hostilities boil. *The Chicago Tribune.* Retrieved from http://articles.chicagotribune.com/1986-06-29/news/8602160298_1_klan-rally-ku-klux-klan-supremacist-group

Giddens, A. (1984). *The constitution of society.* Berkeley, CA: University of California Press.

Gilbert, P. (2017, October). A monumental decision: What to with Confederate monuments? *Parks & Recreation Magazine,* 36–39. Retrieved from http://www.nrpa.org/parks-recreation-magazine/2017/october/a-monumental-decision/

Glover, T. D. (2015). Animating public space. In S. Gammon & S. Elkington (Eds.), *Landscapes of leisure: Space, place and identities* (pp. 96–109). Basingstoke: Palgrave Macmillan.

(2017, August 14). Google cancels Neo-Nazi site registration soon after it was dumped by GoDaddy. *Reuters.* Retrieved from https://www.cnbc.com/2017/08/14/godaddy-boots-the-daily-stormer-because-of-what-it-wrote-about-charlottesville-victim.html

Gordon, L. (2017). *The second coming of the KKK: The Ku Klux Klan of the 1920s and the American political tradition.* New York, NY: Liveright Publishing Corporation.

Grant, M. (1916). *The passing of the Great Race: Or, the racial basis of European History.* New York, NY: Charles Scribner's Sons.

Griggs, B. (2017, May 15). Protests over Confederate statue shake Charlottesville Virginia. *CNN.* Retrieved from http://www.cnn.com/2017/05/15/us/charlottesville-lee-monument-spencer-protests-trnd/index.html

Guess, T. J. (2006). The social construction of Whiteness: Racism by intent, racism by consequence. *Critical Sociology, 32*(4), 649–673.

Hartman, B. (2011, July 24). Norway attack suspect had anti-Muslim, pro-Israel views. *Jerusalem Post*. Retrieved from http://www.jpost.com/International/Norway-attack-suspect-had-anti-Muslim-pro-Israel-views
Holland, B. L. (1997). Surviving leisure time racism: The burden of racial harassment on Britain's black footballers. *Leisure Studies*, *16*(4), 261–277.
Horna, J. L. A. (1988). Leisure studies in Czechoslovakia: Some east-west parallels and divergences. *Leisure Sciences*, *10*(2), 79–94.
Horton, J. O. (2004). Urban alliances: The emergence of Race-based Populism in the age of Jackson. In J. W. Trotter, E. Lewis, & T. W. Hunter (Eds.), *African American urban experience: Perspectives from the Colonial period to the present* (pp. 23–34). New York, NY: Palgrave Macmillan.
Hylton, K., & Long, J. (2016). Confronting 'Race' and policy: How can you research something you say does not exist? *Journal of Policy Research in Tourism, Leisure and Events*, *8*(2), 202–208.
(2009, April 19). Illinois Holocaust Museum opens in Skokie: Bill Clinton, Elie Wiesel address crowd of thousands. *The Huffington Post*. Retrieved from http://www.huffingtonpost.com/2009/04/19/illinois-holocaustmuseum_n_188750.html
(2009, July 11). Illinois Museum adding armed cops to security detail after DC shooting. *The Huffington Post*. Retrieved from http://www.huffingtonpost.com/2009/06/11/illinois-holocaust-museum_n_214378.html
Johnson, A. J., & Glover, T. D. (2013). Understanding urban public space in a leisure context. *Leisure Sciences*, *35* (2), 190–197.
Kaplan, J. S. (Ed.). (2000). *Encyclopedia of White power: A sourcebook on the radical racist right*. Walnut Creek, CA: AltaMira Press.
Kneeland, D. E. (1978, July 10). 72 seized at rally of Nazis in Chicago. *The New York Times*. Retrieved from http://www.nytimes.com/1978/07/10/archives/72-seized-at-rally-of-nazis-in-chicago-police-keep-2000-under.html
Levine, L. (2009, April 17). Skokie to open new Holocaust museum: Site of neo-Nazi march that launched Shoah education. *The Jewish Daily Forward*. Retrieved from http://www.forward.com/articles/104682/
McDonald, M. G. (2009). Dialogues on Whiteness, leisure, and (anti)racism. *Journal of Leisure Research*, *41*(1), 5–21.
McKean, B. (2016). Toward an inclusive populism? On the role of Race and difference in Laclau's politics. *Political Theory*, *44*(6), 797–820.
McKenzie, B. (2017, August 7). City says permit will only be ok'd if rally is moved to McIntire Park. *The Daily Progress*. Retrieved from http://www.dailyprogress.com/news/local/city-says-permit-will-only-be-ok-d-if-rally/article_29f8e566-7baa-11e7-906d-63c9ea503128.html
McWhirter, C. (2011). *Red Summer: The Summer of 1919 and the Awakening of Black America*. New York: Henry Holt and Company.
Michael, G. (2009). David Lane and the Fourteen Words. *Totalitarian Movements and Political Religions*, *10*(1), 43–61.
(1988, August 29). Mob attacks black man at Klan rally. *The Washington Post*. Retrieved from https://www.washingtonpost.com/archive/politics/1988/08/29/mob-attacks-black-man-at-klan-rally/6fa6c25b-076a-4d1d-8c4a-adfa91450039/?utm_term=.d63a94153312
Mobily, K. E. (2018). Eugenics and the playgrouud movement. *Annals of Leisure Research*, *21*(2), 145–160.
Mowatt, R. A. (2009). Notes from a leisure son: Expanding an understanding of Whiteness in leisure. *Journal of Leisure Research*, *41*(4), 509–526.
Mowatt, R. A. (2019). A people's history of leisure studies: Leisure, the tool of racecraft. *Leisure Sciences*. doi:10.1080/01490400.2018.1534622
National Socialist Party of America v. Village of Skokie on petition for writ of certiorari to the supreme court of Illinois citations, 432 U.S. 43 97 S. Ct. 2205; 53 L. Ed. 2d 96; 1977 U.S. Lexis 113, 2 Media L. Rep. 1993. docket no. 76-1786 (June 14, 1977).
Osborne, P., & Segal, L. (1997). Culture and power: Interview with Stuart Hall. *Radical Philosophy*, *86*, 24–41.
Parry, N. C. A. (1983). Sociological contributions to the study of leisure. *Leisure Studies*, *2*(1), 570–581.
(2000, June 30). *Profile: Copeland the killer. BBC News*. Retrieved from http://news.bbc.co.uk/2/hi/uk_news/781755.stm
Riordan, J. (1988). Problems of leisure and Glasnost. *Leisure Studies*, *7*(2), 173–185.
Rockwell, G. L. (1966/2016). *White power*. Newtown, Powys, UK: Sandycroft Publishing Limited.
Rose, J., & Spencer, C. (2016). Immaterial labour in spaces of leisure: Producing biopolitical subjectivities through Facebook. *Leisure Studies*, *35*(6), 809–826.
Rowan, C. T. (1996). *The coming race war in American: A wake up call*. Boston: Little, Brown, and Company.
Silk, M. L. (2007). Come downtown & play. *Leisure Studies*, *26*(3), 253–277.
Simmons, W. J. (1923). *The Klan unmasked*. Atlanta, GA: W. E. Thompson Publishing Co.
Skokie Park District. (1976a, October 4). Letter from Frank Collin to Skokie Park District. *Skokie Park District/ Minutes of the Board Meeting of October 25, 1976, Skokie Park District Board of Park Commissioners Archives*.

Skokie Park District. (1976b, October 25). Skokie Park District Board of Park Commissioners (Ordinance Attached). *Skokie Park District/Minutes of the Board Meeting of October 25, 1976, Skokie Park District Board of Park Commissioners Archives.*

Southern Poverty Law Center. (2018). *In 2018, we tracked 1,020 hate groups across the U.S.* Retrieved from https://www.splcenter.org/hate-map

Spiro, J. P. (2009). *Defending the master race: Conservation, eugenics, and the legacy of Madison Grant.* Burlington, VT: University of Vermont Press.

Spracklen, K. (2013). Nazi punks folk off: Leisure, nationalism, cultural identity and the consumption of metal and folk music. *Leisure Studies, 32*(4), 415–428.

Stanfield, J. H. (1985). Theoretical and ideological barriers to the study of race-making. *Research in Race and Ethnic Relations, 4*, 161–181.

Stapley, G. (2017, August 14). 'This is a huge victory.' Oakdale White Supremacist revels after deadly Virginia clash. *The Modesto Bee.* Retrieved from http://www.modbee.com/news/article167213427.html

Stephenson, M. L., & Hughes, H. L. (2005). Racialised boundaries in tourism and travel: A case study of the UK Black Caribbean community. *Leisure Studies, 24*(2), 137–160.

Strum, P. (1999). *When the Nazis came to Skokie: Freedom for speech we hate.* Lawrence, Kansas: University Press of Kansas.

U.S. Census Bureau. (1981). *1980 Census Report.* U.S. Census Population Division. Retrieved from https://www2.census.gov/prod2/statcomp/documents/1981-02.pdf

U.S. Census Bureau. (2001). *2000 Census Report.* U.S. Census Population Division. Retrieved from https://www2.census.gov/prod2/statcomp/documents/1981-02.pdf

Virden, R. J., & Walker, G. J. (1999). Ethnic/racial and gender variations among meanings given to, and preferences for, the natural environment. *Leisure Sciences, 21*, 219–299.

von Coudenhove-Kalergi, R. N. (1925). *Praktischer idealismus (Practical idealism).* Leipzig, GA: Paneuropa Wien.

Warren, L. (2014, June 9). 'The dawn of a new day … may all out sacrifices be worth it' Chilling online messages of white supremacists couple. *Daily Mail.* Retrieved from http://www.dailymail.co.uk/news/article-2653139/Online-messages-white-supremacist-couple-Amanda-Jerad-Miller-gunned-two-police-officers-shopper-Walmart-taking-lives.html

(1925, August 9). White-robbed Klan cheered on march in nation's capital. *The Washington Post.* Retrieved from https://www.washingtonpost.com/news/retropolis/wp/2017/08/17/the-day-30000-white-supremacists-in-kkk-robes-marched-in-the-nations-capital/?utm_term=.b3330f23a90c

Williams, A. B. (1925, June 29). Welcome the K. K. K. parade. *The Washington Post.*

The right to exist: homelessness and the paradox of leisure

Justin Harmon

ABSTRACT
This essay explores one man's life as a person experiencing homelessness and the societal impositions (stigma) and barriers (criminal ordinances) that shape his sense of self and perceived ability to transcend homelessness. The focus is on trying to understand what leisure is – or if it can even exist – for someone experiencing homelessness. As will be demonstrated, much of the societally available resources are lacking (shelters, legal help, access to water and hygiene needs) for those who need them; yet still others are wary of using anything in the 'system' because it saps whatever sense of agency they may have left. Still others prefer to stay on the periphery of society and focus solely on their daily survival. As public space is contested and evermore privatized, how do those without spaces of their own fight for their right to exist?

'Free time is an interesting concept for me. I guess the way I live now, without a permanent place to stay or a permanent job, some would say all of my time is free. But the reality is, most of my time is spent simply surviving. That isn't to say that every minute of my life is a struggle, because it's definitely not, but that every day of my life has some degree of uncertainty. That can be troubling. Honestly, it often is.' – Dancing Deer[1] (58, 'homeless' for seven years)

Introduction

Just what exactly *leisure* is from a definitional standpoint has been pondered for years. Most are willing to accept, at a bare minimum, that leisure involves a degree of intrinsic motivation with some growth or edifying properties, and that there is some element of freedom in its undertaking (Blackshaw, 2017). But as Blackshaw further considered the meaning of this quixotic idea, leisure also implies, at least etymologically, a degree of license or permission. That is, there are external, structural forces that guide our ability to partake in leisure, just as we are limited by the extent of our internal interests and capabilities. A question worth considering, then, is, what societal barriers are there to being able to engage in leisure for a marginalized population? As Johnson and Glover (2013) indicated, 'it is incumbent upon leisure researchers to consider who is excluded from "public" spaces, for no space is fully accessible to everyone at all times' (p. 195). One group that is consistently pushed out of public spaces and marginalized are those experiencing homelessness.

People experiencing homelessness have been called 'the strongest symbol of disenfranchisement' in a city (Mitchell, 2003, p. 168). The homeless have a unique, if not imperiled, relationship with the cities they reside in due to the extent the environment structures their survival needs, identities, and the opportunities available to them to attend to their personal goals (Wolch & Rowe, 1992). That homeless people are at the mercy of the city in most situations, yet not really seen as part of the cities in which they reside, creates a problem of agency and a lack of respect for those experiencing homelessness (Langegger & Koester, 2016; Somerville, 1992). Frequently, and quite unfortunately, the homeless are viewed as 'failures' (Rose & Johnson, 2017), and perhaps more accurately, as seen through the lens of western capitalist societies, the homeless are simply 'flawed consumers' (Casey, Goudie, & Reeve, 2008, p. 903). Amster (2003) said that 'homeless people embody the social fear of privileged consumers' (p. 198), forcing us to consider the polis and the public sphere – who is it really for? Only those who can afford to opt in?

Johnson and Glover (2013) put forth the notion that as public spaces have become ever more privatized, the communal locations that formerly 'belonged' to the masses have evolved into spaces explicitly for consumption; preference is given to those with purchasing power (Casey et al., 2008). In tandem with this is the increased efforts at policing these 'public' spaces which results in the criminalization of poverty for those experiencing homelessness (Wilking, Roll, Philhour, Hansen, & Nevarez, 2018). When one stops to consider the reality of life for those who are homeless, they are dependent on public space to live (Mitchell, 2017); the privatization of public space, then, usurps their *right to exist.* This study sought to address how homelessness affects one's ability to have leisure in light of the daily struggle simply to survive (Langegger & Koester, 2017).

Literature review

People experiencing homelessness and the spaces they spend their time in – the public forum, typically – have been a contentious pairing, seemingly since time immemorial. As public spaces have become increasingly more privatized and policed (Amster, 2003; Johnson & Glover, 2013; Mitchell, 2017), there has been an increased focus on criminalizing acts typically committed by those without stable homes and/or jobs. These trespasses include vagrancy, sleeping in public, loitering, and panhandling, thus leading to the criminalization of poverty (Adcock et al., n.d.; Wilking et al., 2018). Foucault (1967/1984) indicated that society and our lives are governed by a number of oppositions that remain 'inviolable,' such as the false dichotomies of public-private space, and the work-leisure divide. However, some dualities are more pronounced, such as whether one is housed or unhoused (Somerville, 1992). Others remain culturally contrived, such as the distinction between who is respectable member of society and who is a deviant outsider (Amster, 2003); the latter often being a classification where the homeless are relegated. It is troubling to see a group of people ostracized and stigmatized in such a manner. The emphasis of future explorations needs to explicitly focus on the social problem of homelessness (Fitzpatrick, 2005) – a need to transform the rules of inclusion for those who have been excluded (Martin, 2005) – with less emphasis on the homeless people themselves as the problem to be addressed (Clapham, 2003).

Homelessness and leisure

Several scholars have made significant contributions to the exploration of homelessness and leisure, though there remains greater need for further investigations in this area. Researchers inside the field of leisure studies have focused on coping, stress, and mental health issues as it relates to the homeless and their pursuit of leisure (Klitzing, 2003, 2004a, 2004b; Knestaut, Devine, & Verlezza, 2010), and as a resource for social integration into communities (Dawson & Harrington, 1996; Trussell & Mair, 2010). Rose (2014, 2017) has explored the intersection of placemaking, nature, and homelessness, and Rose and Johnson (2017) have investigated masculine identities in homeless men. Scholars outside the field have used leisure as a lens to understand personal choice in leisure decisions for the homeless (Borchard, 2010), as well as integration into the urban social landscape (Hodgetts & Stolte, 2016).

Due to the perceived excess of 'free time' often attributed to those experiencing homelessness, studies such as those done by Borchard (2010) that seek to emphasize the agency of the homeless in parallel with their personal characteristics and daily survival regimens are beneficial in understanding the fluidity of leisure in the lives of the homeless. Related, Hodgetts and Stolte (2016) sought to delineate that leisure, for the homeless, can be both an escape from adversity but also an 'escape into society' (p. 912), thus reinforcing that extreme poverty does not reduce the need for leisure, nor differentiate the less-fortunate from the well-off in terms of their desire to be part of the broader community. Building on the latter, Trussell and Mair (2010) endeavor focused on access to community services for the homeless and how they might be improved in order to be the most effective for those who need them. That being said, not all homeless people seek out assistance from the community (Zimmerman, Singleton, & Welch, 2010); and in many cases, the community simply does not welcome the homeless into leisure spaces (Harvey, 1992).

One area that remains underexplored in the leisure literature is the fluidity and ephemerality of leisure for those experiencing homelessness. Can leisure ever really be a given when most other aspects of life are not? Taking into consideration the various hardships and responsibilities that the homeless must endure on a daily basis, we are well-advised to return to Blackshaw's (2017) reminder that leisure never has to 'look a certain way or be of a certain style' (p. 16). However, when societal stigma and the imposition of segregation and criminalization efforts become the foreground of life for the homeless, what, then, really is leisure?

Societal stigma

Those experiencing homelessness are placed in a double-bind, often simultaneously being viewed as unable to contribute to society – and more often than not are seen as detracting from it – and in many instances, they come to view themselves as failures in their own lives as well (Mitchell, 2003; Rose, 2014; Rose & Johnson, 2017; Takahashi, 1996). W.E.B. Du Bois (1903/1994) first explored this juxtaposition in a concept he described as 'double-consciousness,' or the ability to embody two distinct views of the self: how society sees the individual (often in a negative light), and how the individual sees themselves (typically in a more positive light). And while society habitually views the homeless as 'flawed consumers' with 'spoiled identities' (Casey et al., 2008, p. 909), the unfortunate accompanying, subjective identity for many homeless is that due to their dependence on social resources and inability to provide for themselves consistently, they have failed in their existential personal responsibilities to care for themselves and contribute to society (Paccaro, 1996). This relegates one's double consciousness to the double-bind through the lesser likelihood of a positive self-image, thus making the potential to transcend homelessness all the more difficult (Amster, 2003; Langegger & Koester, 2016; Snow & Anderson, 1987; Somerville, 1992). When society has pre-determined the worth of those experiencing homelessness, it renders their voice speechless in the public sphere (Johnsen, Cloke, & May, 2005).

The right to the city

In Henri Lefebvre's (1968/1996) classic work, 'The right to the city,' he illustrates the contradiction between 'the socialization of society and generalized segregation,' (p. 157), highlighting the inadequacy of the 'working class' to overcome the 'segregation directed essentially against it' (p. 154). For Lefebvre (1991), the 'social space' that comprise our cities serves as a means of domination for the marginalized and disaffected, such that the powerholders (e.g. municipal governments, police) seek to control the agency, visibility, and patterns of mobility that make 'public' the problem of homelessness (Langegger & Koester, 2016). Lefebvre saw the 'right to the city' as a struggle to 'de-alienate urban space' through political struggle (Purcell, 2013, p. 149). The problem is, however, all residents in a city do not share equal political or social capital to engage in that struggle, especially the homeless (Herring, Yarbrough, & Alatorre, 2019).

In a sense, then, people experiencing homelessness embody Foucault's (1967/1984) heterotopias of deviation, in that they are 'deviant' in relation to the societal norms, and that aberration is essentially compulsory due to the inadequacy, or unavailability, of the requisite resources needed to transcend their station in life (Herring et al., 2019). Public space, then, remains a 'locus of exploitation and oppression' for the homeless (Harvey, 1992, p. 590), where those that 'have' operate by an 'accumulation by dispossession' over those who 'have not' (Harvey, 2008, p. 33). The homeless, in effect, are put through 'material and psychological harm' through 'pervasive penality' due to constant harassment for living in extreme poverty (Herring et al., 2019, p. 16).

Mitchell (2003) stated that, 'anti-homeless legislation helps institutionalize the fact that [the] homeless are not really citizens by assuring that the homeless have no place in public to be sovereign' (p. 183). Pawson (2007) felt that citizenship is embodied with indelible rights, however, this is not something we often see extended to the homeless (Mitchell, 2017; Takahashi, 1996). Therefore, the dialog over what rights individuals truly have, and whose rights are favored more in the public sphere remains contentious (Casey et al., 2008). Because of this, there needs to be a greater embrace of strategies looking at how society reifies the institutional barriers that hold the homeless in abeyance (Clapham, 2003). The supposed 'civil' efforts that focus on criminalization of life-sustaining activities typically undertaken by the homeless (i.e. sleeping, elimination of bodily waste, securing food), when accompanied by the perpetuation of the status quo in regards to provision of homeless services, will solely result in people continually being trapped in endless cycles of poverty with few options out (Fitzpatrick & Jones, 2005).

Writing more than a quarter of a century ago, Somerville (1992) stated that there is a need to 'place home and homelessness in the context of the economic and political system' in order to understand how societal decisions and civil ordinances disenfranchise the poor (p. 536). What has instead been the case is that the focus has been heightened to improve the private, commercial, and privileged interests in the public sphere (Adcock et al., n.d.; Wilking et al., 2018). Holding out a glimmer of hope, Amster (2003) intimated that the homeless may be the last best chance at preserving 'public spaces as democratic, spontaneous, and inclusive' (p. 206); while aspirational, it will require a coordinated effort, and improved understanding of what it means to build social cohesion for all. For as Mitchell (2003) indicated, the homeless are an 'indicator species' (p. 136) – the proverbial canary in the coalmine letting us know the health of social relationships in society and our willingness to help the homeless simply *exist*. Currently, measured this way, our collective health is not good.

Methods

Background of study

A homelessness advocacy organization, Homeless Awareness Group[2] (HAG), was established in February, 2018 as an offshoot of a larger political activism group in a mid-sized, Southern city in the United States. Its establishment was deemed necessary in order to be able to adequately respond to pressing issues regarding homelessness in the community which included access to resources and recent criminalization efforts initiated by the city council (CC) and the local business improvement district (BID).

The founder of HAG, John,[3] has worked with the homeless population for more than a decade in two cities. He was previously homeless himself starting at the age of 15 when he was a victim of domestic abuse. He is a frequent speaker at CC meetings and I met him through our participation in a political activism group in town. He had conducted research on homelessness and homeless rights in his prior city of residence with researchers from a university there, and he was seeking support from those conversant in data collection and analysis skills in his new hometown. I offered to help because his plight aligned with a project I was then involved in, exploring the allocation of public resources in our city. Several other faculty members from two academic institutions collaborated to improve a survey instrument he was using and coordinated a plan for collecting data in three parts: short surveys, smaller focus groups ('lunch n' learns'), and more in-depth semi-structured interviews with individuals experiencing homelessness.

The goal was to create a store of data that will be used to present to the CC and challenge aspects of their criminal ordinances that target the poor, thus leading to the criminalization of poverty, as well as to make reasoned arguments for improving the resources and services available to help combat homelessness and improve the lives of those experiencing homelessness in the city. Additionally, all data will ultimately be housed in a repository for the faculty of these two institutions to analyze through their respective disciplinary lenses.

The effort at hand focuses on the lived experiences of one homeless man in town in order to tell *his* story about how homelessness has impacted his life, taking into consideration how currently available resources and criminal ordinances affect his right to exist, and his (in)ability to have leisure.

Duoethnographic approach

Autoethnography as method draws from the personalized accounts of an individual's experiences to tell the story of what transpired in/with the phenomenon of interest (Denzin, 2006). Ellis (2004) said that autoethnography is often deeply personal and that its emotional components are comprised of introspection that result in a narrative style of representation. Because this essay is the story of one man's (Dancing Deer) experiences of homelessness, it is more accurately duoethnographic in nature. While duoethnography is conceptually understood as two researchers working together to build a narrative, in this instance, my understanding of what took place is an interpretation of Dancing Deer's experiences and story (Breault, 2016).

In duoethnography, 'the journey is mutual and reciprocal' (Norris & Sawyer, 2012, p. 13), thus suggesting that what is read here was ultimately reached through my interactions with Dancing Deer. He is a late-50s, Native American, retired Army veteran with some serious health conditions (kidney and spinal issues). He has never been married, has no children, and has minimal contact with his family, though he considers many of the people he 'camps' with to be as close as family. At the time of writing he has been homeless for approximately seven years. I spent about twenty-five hours with him over the course of three months (roughly two hours per week, most weeks), and this is where trustworthiness was established (Tracy, 2013).

Because of my desire to accurately present his story, this manuscript is a co-constructed effort. As an auto/ethnographer, I saw it as my charge to provide adequate detail in order to create an opportunity for the reader to transfer the relevant aspects of the essay to their lives and their work (Ellis, 1998). The narrative ethnographic method of this essay attempts to emphasize the reality of one person's ongoing experience of homelessness and how his reality is constructed, and then presented, through my writing (Gubrium & Holstein, 2008). As the author, and as someone who has never experienced homelessness, I have approached this essay delicately and respectfully due to the simple fact that I am choosing to use another's perspective to understand a systemic, societal problem.

Results and discussion

Introducing dancing deer

'I spend a lot of time out on that corner you first met me on. On an average week, I might be out there 30 hours, maybe less. All I need to do is earn enough to get the essentials for camp. But sometimes that takes a little longer than I'd hope – but I understand I'm at the mercy of strangers. Though some of these people, like you, well, some of 'em are more like friends now, at least a little. I do feel I'm working out there though; it ain't easy standing at the on-ramp all day, especially when it's beating down sun or cold and rainy.' – Dancing Deer

Dancing Deer was not a user of any of the amenities or services provided for the homeless in town. While he had briefly used some when he first came into town about five years earlier, he found that many of the patrons of the day centers and shelters to be volatile and they often made him uncomfortable (Johnsen et al., 2005). He felt that through an explicit reliance on community-provided services, he would be forfeiting his dignity, and therefore, he was better able to hold on to some semblance of agency and control by living outside 'the system' as he called it (Rose & Johnson, 2017; Zimmerman et al., 2010). Because of this, he stayed on the periphery of town when he panhandled, which is where I met him, and retreated to his camp after he had collected enough money or supplies to return 'home.' Dancing Deer was wary of the potential for violence, abuse, and getting caught up with law enforcement, something he knew to be a problem, especially in the downtown area. Due to the increased enforcement of criminal ordinances, he felt downtown was simply not a place he was welcome (Casey et al., 2008; Wilking et al., 2018).

Dancing deer's path to homelessness

'Once I got into the military, I thought I'd left behind all the problems from my childhood. Man, I tell you, that sure wasn't the case. They just got put on a shelf for a little while, I guess, but I pulled 'em off once I got out. Throw a bunch of other life shit in the mix to follow, and well, it wouldn't be a lie to say my life now is not what I expected – or what I hoped for.' – Dancing Deer

After he left the military in his late-20s, Dancing Deer never felt he had established a firm footing, something he viewed as, at least in part, a consequence of his unstable upbringing. While he did not have abusive parents, his home-life was scattered and often void of support. His mother was an alcoholic, something he had had problems with over the years as well, and his father was in and out of the picture for the duration of his youth. Both his parents, he believed, were deceased now, and he had lost touch with a sister years ago.

In Clapham's (2003) work on homelessness pathways, he stressed the need to evaluate the intersection of both structural forces and individual choices in understanding the trajectory of those experiencing homelessness. For Dancing Deer, his upbringing held many of the ingredients for instability in his transition to adulthood, and when he left the regimented structure of the military, he lacked a positive framework to guide him into the future. He had one bout of homelessness in his mid-30s, something he attributed to his problems with alcohol, but he was able to find stability for almost fifteen years before a run of bad luck forced him into his current situation, including health problems and the loss of a job that prevented him from being able to afford his rent. As Greer, Shinn, Kwon, and Zuiderveen (2016) suggest, those who have experienced homelessness in the past are far more likely to experience it again in the future, signaling the need to better understand the inadequacies in social support systems to help people cope through their socioeconomic struggles and be resigned to homeless recidivism (Shinn et al., 2017).

Identity, stigma, and homelessness

'I don't know, man. I know I've made some poor choices in life, but I also know I've been a good person more than I haven't, at least, I hope. While I've come to accept my life as someone without a fixed address, that doesn't mean I wouldn't like a permanent roof over my head, and it certainly doesn't mean others should view me as lesser than them. I've had people tell me to "get a job," or just give me the look that reeks of disgust. I try not to let it get me down, but it does, sometimes.' – Dancing Deer

Casey et al. (2008) put forth the notion of 'spoiled identities' for 'those who are unable to conform to standards that society regards as normal' (p. 909). This was a topic that I broached with Dancing Deer: whether or not he felt either societal stigmatization because he was homeless, or if he felt any sense of shame because he was not housed or living within the confines of a more 'traditional' way of life. He said that he had come to find comfort in his life, and that camp had become something that was stable for him, giving him some sense of continuity in an otherwise uncertain life. Dancing Deer stated that, 'I guess I can't control what others say or think about me, so I sort of have to be the one who's got to view my life positively, because not many others are. That can be tough at times, most certainly, but it's something I try to hold onto.' Rose (2014) echoed this sentiment in his work on the intersection of social and environmental justice, suggesting that a 'politics of justice' needs to be established to redirect the narrative of the homeless as unproductive or less-than-valuable members of society.

Unfortunately, the policies and preferences of many city's decision makers, business owners, and by default, by proxy support from voters (or simply apathy), favor cutting off access to life-sustaining necessities for those in extreme poverty and a strategy of extradition from the city center as the preferred method of 'fixing' the homeless problem (Langegger & Koester, 2017; Wilking et al., 2018). Those who are reliant on shelters to provide some modicum of normalcy in their lives also face issues. This points to the extreme inadequacy in much of the societally provided support mechanisms (Herring et al., 2019; Langegger & Koester, 2016).

As Mitchell (2003) and other have pointed out, municipal efforts at creating and enforcing anti-homeless legislation seeks to 'institutionalize the fact that homeless are not really citizens' (p. 183) and this then gets perpetuated by constituents writ large as the master narrative, and in many cases gets embodied by those experiencing homelessness (Amster, 2003; Takahashi, 1996). As the cultural dialog of self- and social-worth becomes engrained into the fabric of society, the homeless are relegated to either invisibility or problem-status, more often both (Somerville, 1992). The conflicting social identities (what others attribute to an individual) and personal identities (what one ascribes to the self) of the homeless become the base ingredient for the self-concept, or the overarching view of one's value as a human in light of their social position (Snow & Anderson, 1987). For Dancing Deer, he said that,

> My place in society isn't really my decision to make any longer. At this point, my sole focus has to be on existence, survival, and that doesn't leave me enough time to fight others about how they should view me. It wouldn't be worth my time to try, anyways.

The amount of stress that befalls a homeless individual's life is staggering, and in some cases can be insurmountable (Klitzing, 2003). Unfortunately, in addition to a lack of, or inadequate, facilities and support resources, issues of mental health and substance abuse, and the societal disposition to stigmatize the homeless, there are not many options other than street life – and now that is being challenged by municipalities (Adcock et al., n.d.; Langegger & Koester, 2017; Wilking et al., 2018).

Who belongs in a city?

'I'm plenty comfortable on the outskirts of town. I'm in an area that doesn't get much traffic, no one bothers us out there, really. It's quite a commute for me to come in to work (panhandle) and get supplies, go to the veterans' center, you know, but out there, at least there's some consistency. I'm not bothering anyone and most (the housed) are probably happy I'm out at the camp more often than not anyways.' – Dancing Deer

As mentioned, Dancing Deer had little interest in spending much time in the city center. While he used many of the resources in town out of necessity, like grocery stores, thrift shops, and libraries, he rarely spent any more of his 'free time' there than was necessary. His time spent in commercial space was for just that, commercial transactions, but he did not feel that the public space was truly public, at least not for him or others experiencing homelessness. Waldron (1991) asserted that the homeless can only exist to the extent that they have access to public space, something that Dancing Deer was clearly reliant on – just not in the city center.

This notion that he was left alone and out-of-sight, and therefore out-of-mind to most people, was somewhat comforting to Dancing Deer. However, as Mitchell (2017) reminds us, 'the ideology of public space is problematic because it can be easily co-opted by those who seek to exclude undesirable people' (p. 503). This is something Rose (2014, 2017) found in his work with the homeless population at 'the Hillside' – those reliant on public spaces to live are 'safe' until someone more powerful finds them and decides they do not approve of how they live their lives (Langegger & Koester, 2017). This is something quite commonly found in the literature on homelessness: that the privileged, even in their leisure pursuits, often seek to privatize their personal experiences to cater to their wants and needs (Langegger & Koester, 2016). As Rose (2014, p. 266) asked, 'How can a single activity – camping – be both a necessity of life and recreational pursuit?' The concern then becomes how society and its privileged inhabitants feel empowered to determine how those less fortunate get to exist at all (Johnson & Glover, 2013).

Homelessness, free time, and the sticky problem of leisure[4]

'For fun? Oh, I read a lot. Back at the camp we chat, play cards, shoot the shit, you know, typical stuff people do. I guess I don't really have any hobbies. I used to play guitar years ago, but I don't have one anymore. I really have to keep my possessions to a minimum. There are some things I'd love to own, things I'd love to do, sure, but I guess in some way I'm better off not having so much stuff. A simple life is really the only one that works when you don't have a roof, I figure.' – Dancing Deer

While Dancing Deer had no formal education beyond high school (which he could not remember if he had finished 'properly'), he was a very intelligent and well-read individual, thus making our discussions very enjoyable. I asked him directly to put in order the priorities in his life on a daily basis and he said, 'Stay dry so I don't get sick; earn enough money to get food; get to the doctor to make sure my kidney issues don't get worse; and try not to bother nobody so I don't get myself in trouble. Oh, and eat. I guess those'd be the most important ones.' Since I wanted to learn more about what he did for intrinsic enjoyment and personal growth, I pried a little further asking him, 'Is that it?' Since he knew about my job as a professor in a recreation department, that triggered his response a little, to which he replied, 'Well, if you're trying to get at what I do for fun, for improving myself and whatnot, not much. Like I said, when the focus is on staying alive and safe, that doesn't leave a whole lot of time or concern for recreating. Sorry, professor.'

Dancing Deer was largely averse to receiving help from any social services for the homeless. The only agency in town he frequented was the veterans' health system, something he felt he had earned through his time in the military. Because of his reluctance to use social support services, and his wariness of being in the city center, he also never attempted to use any of the public recreation offerings because he simply felt they were 'not intended' for him. This echoes Trussell and Mair (2010) findings that the overriding stigma that pervades society permeates the self-perception of the homeless, and that in absence of 'judgment free zones,' many potential opportunities for leisure for this population would not be successful. While Knestaut et al. (2010) found that recreation programs targeting the homeless could have some existential benefit, even if only in the moment, it still remains that the unhoused who do not feel a part of the community are going to be far less receptive to those types of programs.

Dancing Deer, while he believed that taking care of himself needed to include rest, mental stimulation (e.g.from reading), exercise (walking from camp to 'work'), and personal growth (i.e. as in a preferred hobby), the simple fact any extraneous activity could divert from his ability to simply exist could prove detrimental, especially in light of his health conditions. For him, the multiple society-wide *structural* failures, as well as some of his self-admitted poor decisions along the way, relegated him to a position where his personal choices, his *agency*, had to be streamlined to focus on mere survival. What was leftover, the *culture* of stigmatization and the privileging of the consumer society (Casey et al., 2008) over the health of the community writ large that views the homeless as 'social waste' (Rose, 2017, p. 18), left him wondering whether or not leisure was something that could really be 'understood, or taken part in, for those of us without a roof.'

Conclusion

I asked Dancing Deer if there was anything that I could do to help him, and he simply said, 'Just keep doing what you're doing. I don't need any help, at least not right now. But the people who need help, those are the people that view us (the homeless) as failures, or as the dregs of society. I mean, it's surprising the stories of how people end up without a home. A lot of times a whole lot has to go wrong to get here. Even if some of us are at fault along the way, we shouldn't be thrown out [of society]. Although, I guess broadly speaking, I've kind of accepted that I have.'

What is leisure when the bulk of one's time and focus is spent merely on survival? This question cannot be definitively answered in this essay if for no other reason than the deeply engrained systems of power in many Western cities have dictated that the homeless will not be the executors of their lives; only the forces that uphold the system of power currently in place will determine that (Amster, 2003; Wolch & Rowe, 1992).

This study sought to address how homelessness affects one's ability to have leisure in light of the daily struggle to exist, and while the emphasis was on one man's cumulative story of seven years of homelessness, it is evocative of countless others in its sentiment (Borchard, 2010; Hodgetts & Stolte, 2016; Klitzing, 2003, 2004a, 2004b; Rose, 2014, 2017; Trussell & Mair, 2010) in that failures in society have largely paved the road to a system that suppresses the potential for transformation for those experiencing homelessness (Mitchell, 2003).

Hodgetts and Stolte (2016) and others (e.g. Knestaut et al., 2010) found that 'leisure is foundational' to a homeless person's identity and 'offers opportunities for being something more' (p. 911) – this is not in contest. For Dancing Deer, and numerous others, however, leisure is largely inaccessible to those society has deemed undesirable and chosen to prohibit from public space (Mitchell, 2017). The pervasive reality is that, while many homeless people may find time for recreational or leisurely activities, those activities are often relegated to the fringes of their existence due to the simple fact that the struggle for many, life-sustaining activities have been criminalized, thus criminalizing poverty and the right to exist (Mitchell, 2003); there is simply no time, nor space, for leisure.

Notes

1. A pseudonym.
2. A pseudonym.
3. A pseudonym.
4. See: Hays, S. (1994). Structure and agency and the sticky problem of culture. *Sociological Theory, 12*(1), 57–72.

Disclosure statement

No potential conflict of interest was reported by the author.

References

Adcock, R. A., Butler-Dines, R., Chamber, D. W., Lagarde, M. J., Moore, A. M., Nutting, C. F., … Zwiebel, E. M. (n. d.). *Too high a price: What criminalizing homelessness costs Colorado*. University of Denver Sturm College of Law, Homeless Advocacy Policy Project. Denver, CO.

Amster, R. (2003). Patterns of exclusion: Sanitizing space, criminalizing homelessness. *Social Justice, 30*(1), 195–221.

Blackshaw, T. (2017). *Re-imagining leisure studies*. New York: Routledge.

Borchard, K. (2010). Between poverty and a lifestyle: The leisure activities of homeless people in Las Vegas. *Journal of Contemporary Ethnography, 39*(4), 441–466.

Breault, R. A. (2016). Emerging issues in duoethnography. *International Journal of Qualitative Studies in Education, 29*(6), 777–794.

Casey, R., Goudie, R., & Reeve, K. (2008). Homeless women in public spaces: Strategies of resistance. *Housing Studies, 23*(6), 899–916.

Clapham, D. (2003). Pathways approach to homelessness research. *Journal of Community & Applied Social Psychology, 13*, 119–127.

Dawson, D., & Harrington, M. (1996). "For the most part, it's not fun and games." Homelessness and recreation. *Loisir Et Société/Leisure and Society, 19*(2), 415–435.

Denzin, N. (2006). Analytic autoethnography, or déjà vu all over again. *Journal of Contemporary Ethnography, 35*, 419–428.

Du Bois, W. E. B. (1903/1994). *The souls of black folks*. Mineola, NY: Dover Publications.

Ellis, C. (1998). Exploring loss through autoethnographic inquiry: Autoethnographic stories, co-constructed narratives, and interactive interviews. In J. Harvey (Ed.), *Perspectives on loss: A sourcebook* (pp. 49–62). Philadelphia: Brunner/Mazel.

Ellis, C. (2004). *The ethnographic I: A methodological novel about teaching and doing autoethnography*. Walnut Creek, CA: AltaMira.

Fitzpatrick, S. (2005). Explaining homelessness: A critical realist perspective. *Housing, Theory and Society, 22*(1), 1–17.

Fitzpatrick, S., & Jones, A. (2005). Pursuing social justice or social cohesion?: Coercion in street homelessness policies in England. *Journal of Social Policy, 34*(3), 389–406.

Foucault, M. (1967/1984). Of other spaces: Utopias and heterotopias. *Architecture/Mouvement/Continuité, 10*, 1–9.

Greer, A. L., Shinn, M., Kwon, J., & Zuiderveen, S. (2016). Targeting services to individuals most likely to enter shelter: Evaluating the efficiency of homelessness prevention. *Social Service Review, 90*(1), 130–155.

Gubrium, J. F., & Holstein, J. A. (2008). Narrative ethnography. In S. N. Hesse-Biber & P. Leavy (Eds.), *Handbook of emergent methods* (pp. 241–264). New York: Guilford Press.

Harvey, D. (1992). Social justice, postmodernism, and the city. *International Journal Of Urban and Regional Research, 16*(4), 588-601. doi:10.1111/ijur.1992.16.issue-4

Harvey, D. (2008). The right to the city. *New Left Review, 53*, 23–40.

Herring, C., Yarbrough, D., & Alatorre, L. M. (2019). Pervasive penality: How the criminalization of poverty perpetuates homelessness. *Social Problems*, 1–19.

Hodgetts, D., & Stolte, O. (2016). Homeless people's leisure practices within and beyond urban socio-scapes. *Urban Studies, 53*(5), 899–914.

Johnsen, S., Cloke, P., & May, J. (2005). Day centres for homeless people: Spaces of care or fear? *Social & Cultural Geography, 6*(6), 787–811.

Johnson, A. F., & Glover, T. D. (2013). Understanding urban public space in a leisure context. *Leisure Sciences, 35*, 190–197.

Klitzing, S. W. (2003). Coping with chronic stress: Leisure and women who are homeless. *Leisure Sciences, 25* (2–3), 163–181.

Klitzing, S. W. (2004a). Women living in a homeless shelter: Stress, coping and leisure. *Journal of Leisure Research, 36*(4), 483–512.

Klitzing, S. W. (2004b). Women who are homeless: Leisure and affiliation. *Therapeutic Recreation Journal, 38*(4), 348–365.

Knestaut, M., Devine, M. A., & Verlezza, B. (2010). "It gives me purpose": The use of dance with people experiencing homelessness. *Therapeutic Recreation Journal, 44*(4), 289–301.

Langegger, S., & Koester, S. (2016). Invisible homelessness: Anonymity, exposure, and the right to the city. *Urban Geography, 37*(7), 1030–1048.

Langegger, S., & Koester, S. (2017). Moving on, finding shelter: The spatiotemporal camp. *International Sociology, 32*(4), 454–473.

Lefebvre, H. (1968/1996). *Writing on cities*. Oxford: Blackwell.

Lefebvre, H. (1991). *The production of space*. Malden, MA: Blackwell.

Martin, S. (2005). Culs-de-sac: Review of the politics of aesthetics: The distribution of the sensible. *Radical Philosophy, 131*, 39–44.

Mitchell, D. (2003). *The right to the city: Social justice and the fight for public space*. New York: The Guilford Press.

Mitchell, D. (2017). People's park again: On the end and ends of public space. *Environment and Planning A, 49*(3), 503–518.

Norris, J., & Sawyer, R. (2012). Toward a dialogic method. In J. Norris, R. Sawyer, & D. Lund (Eds.), *Duoethnography: Dialogic methods for social, health, and educational research (pp. 9-39)*. Walnut Creek, CA: Left Coast Press.

Paccaro, J. (1996). *The unequal homeless: Men on the streets, women in their place*. New York: Routledge.

Pawson, H. (2007). Local authority homelessness prevention in England: Empowering consumers or denying rights? *Housing Studies, 22*(6), 867–883.

Purcell, M. (2013). Possible worlds: Henri Lefebvre and the right to the city. *Journal of Urban Affairs, 36*(1), 141–154.

Rose, J. (2014). Ontologies of socioenvironmental justice: Homelessness and the production of social natures. *Journal of Leisure Research, 46*(3), 252–271.

Rose, J. (2017). Cleansing public nature: Landscapes of homelessness, health, and displacement. *Journal of Political Ecology, 24*, 11–23.

Rose, J., & Johnson, C. (2017). Homelessness, nature, and health: Toward a feminist political ecology of masculinities. *Gender, Place & Culture, 24*(7), 991–1010.

Shinn, M., Brown, S. R., Spellman, B. E., Wood, M., Gubits, D., & Khadduri, J. (2017). Mismatch between homeless families and the homelessness service system. *Cityscape, 19*(3), 293–307.

Snow, D. A., & Anderson, L. (1987). Identity work among the homeless: The verbal construction and avowal of personal identities. *American Journal of Sociology*, *92*(6), 1336–1371.

Somerville, P. (1992). Homelessness and the meaning of home: Rooflessness or rootlessness? *International Journal of Urban and Regional Research*, *16*(4), 529–539.

Takahashi, L. M. (1996). A decade of understanding homelessness in the USA: From characterization to representation. *Progress in Human Geography*, *20*, 291–310.

Tracy, S. (2013). *Qualitative research methods: Collecting evidence, crafting analysis, communicating impact.* Hoboken, NJ: Wiley-Blackwell.

Trussell, D. E., & Mair, H. (2010). Seeking judgment free spaces: Poverty, leisure, and social inclusion. *Journal of Leisure Research*, *42*(4), 513–533.

Waldron, J. (1991). Homelessness and the issue of freedom. *UCLA Law Review*, *39*, 295–324.

Wilking, J., Roll, S., Philhour, D., Hansen, P., & Nevarez, H. (2018). Understanding the implications of a punitive approach to homelessness: A local case study. *Poverty & Public Policy: A Global Journal of Social Security, Income, Aid, and Welfare*, *10*(2), 159–176.

Wolch, J. R., & Rowe, S. (1992). On the streets: Mobility paths of the urban homeless. *City & Society*, *6*(2), 115–140.

Zimmerman, L. J., Singleton, C., & Welch, J. (2010). Activism and creating a transnational archaeology of homelessness. *World Archaeology*, *42*(3), 443–454.

Skateboarding, gentle activism, and the animation of public space: CITE – A Celebration of Skateboard Arts and Culture at The Bentway

Troy D. Glover, Sarah Munro, Immony Men, Wes Loates and Ilana Altman

ABSTRACT

This paper examines the interplay of leisure, activism and the animation of public space by exploring CITE – A Celebration of Skateboard Arts and Culture, an art installation and pop-up skate park featuring skateable sculptures constructed in commemoration of Toronto skateboarder Justin Bokma. CITE, which took place in the summer of 2018, deliberately transformed The Bentway, a new public space and programming platform in Toronto which has transformed the underside of the Gardiner Expressway into a gathering place for city inhabitants, into a temporary destination where skateboarders engaged in activist, educational, and arts and cultural practices to situate the act of skateboarding within the broader context of urban placemaking. Drawing on a variety of empirical materials (e.g., interviews, videos, social media, promotional materials, press releases, observations), this case study seeks to understand how so-called 'gentle activism' animates public space and advances inclusive placemaking. Findings show that, through gentle activism, CITE underscored (1) the salience of arts and aesthetics in advocating for skateboarding, (2) inclusivity of programming to facilitate interaction between skateboarders and the non-skateboarding public, (3) the utilisation of programming to amplify the activist message, and (4) intentional efforts to change perceptions of skateboarders. The case reveals a successful alternative to defensive placemaking efforts.

Introduction

Skateboarders show an uncommon dedication to their activity in spite of abundant messages that aim to discourage their presence in public space. Public spaces attractive to skateboarders are so replete with 'No Skateboarding' signs and architectural designs intended to dissuade skateboarding that the presence of these intentional deterrents has become a routine part of skating. Moreover, attempts to find places to skate in the city often lead to confrontations with authorities (e.g., police, security guards, shopkeepers). All of these measures combine to persuade skateboarders to view potential spaces to skate as temporary skatespots until removed.

Hostility toward stakeboarders in public spaces is nothing new, but the use of defensive architecture to discourage skateboarding appears to be rising. Defensive architecture constitutes a deliberate placemaking strategy to deter undesirable behaviours and people through architectural design features. The approach, which surprisingly receives no attention in the leisure literature despite its ubiquitous usage across the globe, includes modifying existing infrastructure to make it impossible to use in certain ways and/or adding elements to a public space to discourage possible uses (e.g., bolting metal pieces to curbs to prevent stakeboarders from grinding) (de Fine Licht, 2017). In this article, we use the broader term *defensive placemaking* to recognise the breadth of tactics employed intentionally by placemaking officials and entities to shape a public space into a particular place for its preferred users. Additional strategies may include removing or displacing objects from public space so that certain functions disappear or relocate to more desirable areas (e.g., removing ramps, building skateparks away from downtown cores), using off-putting nudges (e.g., colours or sounds) to encourage unwanted individuals to gather elsewhere, or closing off areas to certain uses, prohibiting certain activities, or restricting access (de Fine Licht, 2017). While not always successful due to the persistence of skateboarders, these strategies position skateboarding as a subversive activity that has no place in valued city spaces.

In an age when the current generation of youth is disparaged for its lack of physical activity, discouraging activities such as skateboarding seems misplaced and hypocritical. Moreover, skateboarding can be used to animate public space for multiple publics, not just skateboarders. What if instead of using defensive placemaking approaches to deter such activity, public spaces acted deliberately to encourage it? Not just on the edges of the city or in convenient out-of-sight spaces, but in everyday public spaces intended to serve everyone. Doing so would represent a form of what Coombs (2012) described as *gentle activism*, tactics aimed to provoke the public and raise awareness about issues of public space, while seeking to help passersby or users imagine different ways of negotiating urban life. With such an initiative in mind, this article draws on a variety of empirical materials (e.g., interviews, videos, media reports, promotional materials, press releases, observations) to explore CITE – A Celebration of Skateboard Arts and Culture, an art installation and pop-up skate park featuring skateable sculptures constructed in commemoration of Toronto skateboarder Justin Bokma. CITE, which took place in the summer of 2018, deliberately converted The Bentway, a new public space and programming platform in Toronto, Canada, that transformed the underside of the elevated Gardiner Expressway into a gathering place for city inhabitants, into a temporary destination in which skateboarders engaged in activist, educational, and arts and cultural practices to situate the act of skateboarding within the broader context of urban placemaking. With CITE as its focus, this article aims to examine the interplay of leisure, activism and the animation of urban environment to understand how gentle activism can be used effectively to engage in inclusive placemaking.

Skateboarding in the city

> "We live amid surfaces, and the true art of life is to skate well on them."
>
> *Ralph Waldo* Emerson (1844, p. 65)

Skateboarders animate public spaces by defying accepted classifications and uses of public space to reshape our normative understandings of the urban environment (Borden, 2001). The creative spirit of skateboarding arises from unearthing and enjoying architecture designed for different purposes (Borden, 2001; Lundry, 2003). Skateboarders comb the city in search of thrilling terrain, finding inspiration in mundane, everyday objects for unique, fresh, and gratifying uses (Vivoni, 2009). Once found, they appropriate the space, making unsanctioned modifications to it and transforming some of the assigned purposes of its architecture to create 'temporary autonomous play zones' (Vivoni, 2009, p. 133). In this sense, skateboarders interact with public space to reveal opportunities responsive to their particular leisure needs rather than the intended design. Shirtcliff (2014, p. 4) argued, "[a skateboarder], who appropriates a space to play, produces a setting that reveals a level of environmental justice previously inaccessible. Through the creation of such settings for play, the city becomes a playground, rife with opportunities (for good or bad), for 'playing-in-the-world'. In search of the thrill of play, skateboarders persist in their use of public space, even in the face of a high degree of social control from authorities and citizens (Chiu, 2009).

Skateboarders claim their right to the city through their engagement with public space. By 'right to the city', we reference Harvey's (2008, p. 23) interpretation of it as 'a right to change ourselves by changing the city'. Street skateboarding, in many ways, stems from an aspiration of (primarily) youth who are only superficially integrated into society and constrained in their opportunities for creative activity to restructure the power relations that underlie the production of public space, shifting control away from capital and the state to themselves. By accessing, occupying, using, and modifying public space for their own purposes and gratification, skateboarders ' ... pose a direct challenge to a set of political-economic relationships that have been critical to the valorization of urban space and the accumulation of capital in the modern era' (Purcell, 2002, p. 103; see also Borden, 2001).

So, while skateboarding brings 'emotion to emotionless terrain' (Wilsey, 2015, p. 109) by making places overlooked by others (e.g., parking lots, alleyways, handrails) more meaningful (O'Connor, 2018), it regularly involves the appropriation of spaces valued by government and commercial interests (Chiu, 2009; Smith & Walters, 2018). Such behaviour is regarded as unacceptable, for as Woolley and Johns (2001, p. 1) explained, '[skateboarders] occupy urban space without engaging in economic activity, which annoys building owners and managers. Businessmen do not want skateboarders interfering with their customers and so teenagers are only accepted when they are spending money' This attitude is rooted in the workings of a system that sees public space entirely in terms of value generated through exchange, as opposed to function. In such a system, only commodities for sale in the marketplace of public space count as something of value. Street skateboarding, in short, undermines the capital interests that underpin contemporary public space. This perspective drives efforts by authorities to discourage, deter, and displace skateboarding from valued public space.

To this end, architecture found in many public spaces, not surprisingly, aims explicitly to exclude skateboarders. In an attempt to discipline urban inhabitants into primarily consumption based modes of interaction with and in public space, defensive placemaking tactics, such as the use of architectural designs that discourage skateboarding, create social and spatial exclusion, and restrict skateboarders from claiming their 'right to the city', thereby narrowing the definition of who is and who should be allowed in public space (Smith & Walters, 2018). Defensive placemaking efforts in public space, in other words, dictate who is considered a member of the 'public'. Despite these messages, skateboarders persevere in their use of public space, undermining bans, regulation, surveillance, hostile designs, and provision of skate parks.

What if instead of using defensive placemaking to dissuade activity, public spaces embraced *inclusive* placemaking strategies to encourage more play? What would such a strategy look like? These questions guided this manuscript. To explore them further, we move to our description of an innovative programme hosted by The Bentway called CITE – A Celebration of Skateboard Arts and Culture.

The Bentway

The programme described below would not be possible without the creative vision that embodied the public space in which it took place. The Bentway, a unique and innovative public space that transformed 1.75 km underneath Toronto's Gardiner Expressway into a gathering place for the city's growing population, represents an intentional city-building project financed largely by an unprecedented $25 million donation from local philanthropists, Judy and Wilmot Matthews, to the City of Toronto to transform an underutilised city space into an exciting recreational, cultural, and social landscape. Undergirded by 'bents', the enormous structures of reinforced concrete that support the elevated highway 15 m above, The Bentway includes an open-air theatre, walking and skating trails, commissioned visual and performance art, and programming both directly and in partnership with community and cultural groups of all kinds. As a member of the High Line Network, an association of infrastructure urban reuse projects across North America that aims to ensure the benefits of such projects reach the entire community, The Bentway offers accessible and participatory programming that explores the site's unique histories, features, and possibilities. In this spirit, it describes itself on its website as 'both of the city and about the city' (The Bentway Conservancy, 2019a, p. 5), therein underscoring its commitment to connect the city, in its broadest sense, to the space and vice versa. Accordingly, through the lens of culture and recreation, The Bentway explores Toronto's changing urban landscape, as well as the opportunities and issues that unite cities across the globe (Altman, 2018).

Before its current transformation, The Bentway remained a largely unused and abandoned site below the Gardiner Expressway. A few industrious skateboarders built their own DIY skatepark, including ramps and ledges, at The Bentway's current location between Strachan Avenue and Bathurst Street, but the skatepark was eventually demolished to make way for the transformation of the space. The original idea for CITE came from Build for Bokma, a not-for-profit organisation in Toronto that creates multifunctional, skateable public structures, and advocates to integrate skateboarding into developments, initiatives, and community-led activities in the city. Build for Bokma approached the Director of Programming at The Bentway about building a skate installation. The Bentway staff embraced the idea because it was '... emblematic of the goals we had set for ourselves' (TAS Design Build, 2018, p. 3). That is, '[The Bentway's] mandate is to explore the intersection between arts and urbanism'. And, of course, '[The Bentway] wanted to respect the fact that [it] had displaced this community of skateboarders' (TAS Design Build, 2018, p. 3).

CITE – A Celebration of Skateboard Arts and Culture

For six weeks beginning in June 2018, CITE – A Celebration of Skateboard Arts and Culture transformed The Bentway into a destination to hone skateboarding skills and participate in accompanying activist, educational, and arts and cultural practices that situated the act of skateboarding within the broader context of urban placemaking in Toronto. It featured *Semblance*, an art installation and pop-up skate park that included skateable sculptures conceived and constructed by Build for Bokma in commemoration of Toronto skateboarder Justin Bokma, a former pro-Canadian Skateboarder who was killed while trying to disarm a gunman outside a Toronto Club in 2016. The sculptures built for *Semblance* utilised forms and materials that referenced iconic skateboarding destinations within Toronto, New York, Barcelona, and other major urban centres. Together, they created what Build for Bokma called a 'moveable destination', a temporary gathering place for local and international skate communities alike. In addition to *Semblance*, CITE incorporated a variety of interdisciplinary programming, including workshops, performances, a marketplace, and speaker series. Through its involvement as the host of CITE, The Bentway intended to 'speak to the simultaneous accessibility and inaccessibility of urban spaces, to the reclamation of the city by marginalized groups and counter-cultures, and to the potential for functional and inclusive city-building through creative collaboration' (The Bentway Conservancy, 2019b, p. 3). The program served as a response to Toronto's new skateboard strategy by modelling how to better integrate skateparks in the future development of the city.

Planning, of course, began well in advance of the programme. The Bentway had always planned to incorporate skateboarding onto its site and into its programming schedule after displacing the DIY skatepark that existed onsite before The Bentway's development. Formal planning with Build for Bokma began approximately nine months to a year in advance, though efforts became more intense four or five months before the actual event. The planning process engaged the network of skateboarders already connected to Build for Bokma. Additional groups reached out to be included, but a few withdrew because of the nature of their activities or the lack of synergy. For example, a long boarding group expressed interest in getting involved, but found the site and the planned events did not match well with long boarding activities. Initially, members of the community voiced concerns about noise and attracting undesirable users to the site, but the concerns turned out to be non-issues. The Bentway received no complaints related to these concerns during the event. In this

Figure 1. Bentway 75 – credit: Black Umbrella Photography.

Figure 2. DM_CanadaDay_01Jul2018-379 – credit: Denise Militzer.

sense, the project served to mitigate its own concerns. Internally, The Bentway staff were worried about safety of participants, given the physical nature of skateboarding and the potential for injury, but appropriate measures were taken to mitigate them (i.e., encouraging the use of safety equipment, insurance). And finally, concerns were voiced about the temporary nature of the event and the desire to see skateboarding to continue to be showcased on site. In response, The Bentway invited Build for Bokma to return to the site with skateable structures that would be onsite temporarily and later donated to other parks in Toronto.

Opening weekend included DJ sets and musical performances, live graffiti demonstrations, open skates, trick showcases, demos, meet and greets with professional skateboarders, and a marketplace featuring local skateboard retailers. In subsequent weekends, CITE offered a variety of free workshops, including learning to skateboard clinics for youth, building skate sculptures, videography, screen printing, and designing skateboards. Vans, the American manufacturer of skateboarding shoes and apparel, co-sponsored the event and offered games and giveaways on site. In addition to *Semblance*, CITE showcased *Spent*, a series of hanging banners created by artist and skateboarder Pascal Paquette, which were installed on The Bentway's columns depicting images of hand-painted skateboards decks. The CITE programme launch was deemed a success by The Bentway with a remarkable turnout of well over 2,000 visitors, spectators, and active participants throughout the day and evening festivities (The Bentway Conservancy, 2018). Attendance at both the workshops and skate clinics were also impressive, with over 300 combined attendees at the workshops and clinics (The Bentway Conservancy, 2018).

Methods

This qualitative case study involved collecting and analysing a variety of qualitative empirical materials (i.e., texts) about CITE with the intent of gaining insight into an inclusive placemaking approach that contrasted markedly with defensive placemaking. Consistent with this methodology, CITE represented the unit of analysis for the study, and so the research team involved explored and described it as a phenomenon in context using a variety of data sources (Baxter & Jack, 2008). These multiple sources allowed for greater comprehension of CITE, the players involved, its aims and intents, its characteristics, and how it unfolded (Yin, 2009).

Specifically, the data sources for this study included interviews, videos, media reports, promotional materials, press releases, and observations. Interviews focused on the two-member programme staff at The Bentway Conservancy, the not-for-profit agency that maintains, operates, and programmes at The Bentway. The programming team included Ilana Altman, the Director of Programming, and her colleague, Sarah Munro, the Manager of Programming. In addition, Immony Men, a visual artist and one of the directors of Build for Bokma, participated in an interview to discuss his experience in designing *Semblance*. These three individuals represented people in key positions associated with CITE, which afforded them extensive and detailed knowledge about the project.

Consistent with conventional qualitative interviewing, conversations with participants involved face-to-face meetings that lasted between 40 and 80 min. Transcripts of the interviews provided data for analysis. Each interview included questions about the participants' involvement with CITE (e.g., How did this project come together? How were you involved?), details about CITE (e.g., What was the purpose? What were the desired outcomes? What strategies were used to achieve the outcomes?), and the perceived results of the project (e.g., What happened? How was it a success/failure? What made it a success/failure?) All interviews were audio-recorded digitally and transcribed professionally.

In addition to interviews, the lead author analysed videos, media reports, promotional materials, and press releases for content. The Manager of Communications at The Bentway gathered these materials and shared them with the lead author for analysis. The materials included 53 media reports (2 in print, 51 online): 39 of the reports were features, nine were listings (i.e., public announcements of the programme), one was a televised segment, and four were online video features. Additionally, five promotional videos were shared, along with a produced (short) film, three press releases, 16 print materials, and one report (recap), all from The Bentway. These materials served as texts that were reviewed thoroughly, and content from them was used in the analysis similar to the transcripts from interviews (see below). Where these materials appear in the findings, they are cited in text to provide greater transparency for the reader and listed in the references.

To conduct the analysis, the lead author sorted the data, which involved reading each transcript and the texts from other data sources to create initial broad themes (i.e., 'art-based activism' and 'facilitating interactions between skateboarders and the non-skating public'). Relevant quotes from the texts were copied into a working data-sorting document to give shape to the themes in an iterative and inductive process. Ultimately, the analysis sought to understand how CITE provoked the public and raised awareness about issues of public space, while seeking to help event attendees imagine different ways of negotiating urban life. The initial groupings of data were then compared and contrasted, which led to the identification of four main thematic areas that encompassed the initial groups: (1) the salience of arts and aesthetics in advocating for skateboarding, (2) inclusivity of programming to facilitate interaction between skateboarders and the non-skateboarding public, (3) the utilisation of programming to amplify the activist message, and (4) working together to change public perceptions. In more technical language, open coding within and between data sources resulted in the identification recurrent conceptual themes. Focused or selective coding followed as a next step to compare categories both within and between data sources, and to identify emerging conceptual themes. Subsequently, patterns of relationships among themes were also examined (such as the relationship between The Bentway staff and the skateboarder activists). These patterns of relationships were developed into the major themes for this article (see below). Although individual data sources were analysed through the development of themes, the data sources were synthesised to compare and contrast developing patterns of relationships. All told, the themes were inclusive of data across the variety of sources collected to compose the case.

In the spirit of the call for papers for the special issue to which this manuscript was submitted, the lead author welcomed the main activists and organisers of CITE to join the paper as co-authors. As a result, readers should note the co-authors listed also represented key informants in the data collection process for this case study, either as interview participants or individuals cited in media reports. Arguably, the co-authors held partial views of the study, given their passion for the project under examination. However, their inclusion as co-authors benefited the manuscript tremendously insofar as they worked together with the lead author and examined multiple drafts and iterations of the paper as the writing process evolved. Once drafted, individual sections of the paper (e.g., introduction, literature review, method, findings, discussion, conclusion) were sent separately to each member along with requests for feedback. Co-authors replied with various comments, clarifications, insights, and additional observations which were incorporated into revised drafts. In short, the co-authors provided important oversight, not unlike member checks, a strategy used to ensure the credibility of the findings in qualitative research. The result, we believe, is a manuscript that accurately reflects the phenomenon under investigation and offers audiences insight into a successful programme with activist aims and intentions.

Findings

This section provides the results of the case study analysis. It does so under four headings that represent individual themes in the data. Specifically, findings show that, through gentle activism, CITE underscored (1) the salience of arts and aesthetics in advocating for skateboarding, (2) inclusivity of programming to facilitate interaction between skateboarders and the non-skateboarding public, (3) the utilisation of programming to amplify the activist message, and (4) intentional efforts to change perceptions of skateboarders.

Salience of art and aesthetics

The application of art to animate The Bentway invited participants from Build for Bokma to be imaginative in their vision for CITE. Wes Loates, a skateboarding activist and leader associated with *Semblance*, described 'the heart and ethos behind [CITE]' as 'really thinking through the lens of creativity' (as quoted by Acquisto, 2018). As a result, art and aesthetics played a meaningful role in advancing the message communicated by the medium. 'I mean, that's what's dope about this, is it doesn't look like a skatepark, traditionally. This is a skatable art sculpture garden', praised Loates (as quoted by Vice, 2018). Ultimately the aesthetic was used deliberately to convince local government officials and the non-skateboarding public to rethink the presence of skateboarders in the community and consider how to better integrate them in public space.

By targeting its activist message at local government, those involved in creating the skateable sculptures 'really want[ed] to let the city know that you do not need to box us into a grey zone of concrete'. The current designs of skateparks in the city, in other words, remain unimaginative and could use greater input from the skateboarding community. 'That's the goal for [CITE], is really to showcase the fact that you can do something that is very aesthetically pleasing welcoming to skateboarders, but also welcoming to the broader community' (Loates as quoted by Sho, 2018). Quite intentionally, CITE offered a glimpse into what could be.

While skateboarders involved in CITE acknowledged there were skateparks across the city, they felt current designs failed to reflect their input or desires. 'There's a reason why people still skate the streets', explained Loates. 'The streets aren't made for skateboarding and that's what we really want. We want to put our own creativity to creating architecture: what line you put to it, how you skate it. So we've created these [skate]spots [at The Bentway] that would be illegal. But it's legal' (as quoted by Daily Vice, 2018). Men, an artist involved in the design of the skatable sculptures, hoped that *Semblance* would encourage the city to engage in dialogue with skateboarders: 'if there's an actual dialogue, then we might be able to plan [skateboarding] into the space or design it in'. Altman, the Director of Programming at The Bentway, noted, the timing of CITE coincided with Toronto's efforts to create a plan for skateboarding in the city: 'The city had just finished a skateboard strategy that it had been working on for a couple of years, which was about integrating skateboard facilities and parks and amenities into [Toronto's Department of] Parks, Recreation and Forestry's planning going forward and how to better involve the community in that process'. By showcasing aesthetically pleasing, yet highly functional designs, CITE exhibited how things could be done to 'design *in* skating instead of designing it out' (Men, his emphasis).

As for the broader community, CITE aimed to draw non-skateboarders into the conversation through its art project, too. Specifically, the aesthetics of the sculptures beautified the space to reveal that skateboarding did not need to be 'locked into a concrete cage' (Loates as quoted in the Daily Vice, 2018). 'You know, you look at skateboard parks', said Loates, 'and it's very uninviting to everyone else that isn't skateboarding. So what [CITE] wants to do is the opposite. We want to make this an inviting space for the community as a whole. Not just skateboarding, right? So we want everyone to come here and enjoy this' (as quoted by Daily Vice, 2018). To this end, inclusivity proved to be an important value to bring to this initiative.

Inclusivity of programming to facilitate interaction

For its activist aims to be achieved, Altman felt The Bentway, and by extension CITE, had to '... create a space that's as inclusive as possible'. More specifically, she was resolute that the space needed to '... provide the right parameters for a community to make it its own. If programming is treated in a totally top-down manner, then you run the risk of making those same mistakes'. At the same time, Altman explained that '[The Bentway is] a space that attempts to work with and support as many different community organizations as possible. Support in terms of financially, in terms of execution, in terms of communications ... we're not saying drop in and create an event at your own whimsy. Ultimately, we do still have to manage the space ... So I think it's much more about a partnership model than a bottom up model'. In talking about CITE specifically, Altman discussed how The Bentway '... treated our work over the summer with the skateboard community as a partnership from the beginning. And we made sure that that was a project that was built, designed, programmed hand-in-hand with the [skateboard] community the entire way along. As a result, we saw that there was real buy-in and that people felt welcome ... Personally, it's for me the strongest example of community arts that I've ever witnessed or participated in'.

The focus on inclusivity also extended to welcoming the non-skating public to attend CITE. In this regard, inclusivity meant programming needed to be sufficiently diverse both in terms of its artistic mediums and the people who were executing it. As a result, the guiding principle was, 'If you come down to The Bentway', explained Munro, the Manager of Programming at The Bentway, 'you can recognize yourself in the programming that's happening here, and you feel that it is a space that is welcoming to you'.

And so, The Bentway insisted on free programming. 'We heard that a lot over the skateboard season, how appreciative families were to have spaces where they could bring down their kids and spend the day, and not to spend $100'. In addition, programme decisions were made with diverse audiences in mind: 'It may not be obvious, but we ran DJ nights on Friday [during CITE], and we had different types of music playing. For us, [music] was as much about animating the space, trying to welcome people who weren't necessarily interested in skateboarding but who were interested in the music'. In this sense, music was described by Altman as 'a way of ensuring that the communities, who may not necessarily be the prime demographic for skating, are welcome here'. This sort of tactic increased the accessibility of the space, argued Altman. 'I think that by virtue of the fact that it's taking place in public space, you have an obligation to ensure this is a space for the public. And the public is many things, right? The public is not a singular entity, so I think inclusivity is kind of key to making sure that it is truly a space for all of the public and not just for a few'.

Utilising programming to amplify the activist message

Despite its intent for visitors to enjoy themselves, CITE was described as a program that transcended recreation. As Altman explained it, '[CITE] intersected with our mandate, which is that this was an activity that was as much about recreation as it was about exploring the city and an attitude towards the way that we occupy and inhabit the city'. Likewise, Munro noted CITE:

> wasn't just about recreation; it was about creating these beautiful sculptural pieces that respond to architecture, that talk about built space, that talk about the connection between Toronto and other cities throughout the world, that create an opportunity for young people to engage in the process of making the work, skating the work, activating the site with marketplaces and musical programming and workshops. So it's this kind of generative process where if you open your site up to people who want to be creatively engaged, there were so many different phases that enable that engagement.

Accordingly, Munro underscored the importance of ensuring 'Programming is not an afterthought to the space'.

More than a set of activities, though, the programming staff at The Bentway understood implicitly that 'each project [at the site] will be bigger than itself'. With this in mind, they saw programming playing an important role in advancing the activist message at the crux of CITE. Specifically, programming was thought to further animate the space to encourage positive interactions among all participants, skateboarders and non-skateboarders alike. This recognition, Altman believed, focused programming on helping different communities 'find each other. And to strengthen those relationships'. From the standpoint of the agency involved in managing the public space, this perspective warranted an important shift in mindset. That is, Altman believed 'It's not about pre-determining how the space is used, but trying as much as possible to bring different communities, different partners into conversation with each other'.

Cross programming became an important strategy to achieving the goal of inclusivity and broadening the accessibility of the space. One example of it involved parallel programmes coinciding with CITE. For example, The Bentway staff 'tried to bring communities together through [their] work with The Spoke, a storytelling series, which took on DIY as a framework in which storytellers engaged. And a lot of the musical artists [they] chose in response to the skateboarding community. So [the programming staff] tried to create connections'. These connections, Munro pointed out, were furthered through '... music and food and art and all of these things that we maybe don't give as much credence to [but] are really what creates that moment. A beautiful space is a beautiful space, don't get me wrong. And it's impressive in its own way. But it's what you do within that space I think that really matters'. Indeed, the idea of 'creating a moment' mattered in meeting CITE's activist objectives. That moment '... really helps [participants] to see something', Munro argued. She described CITE as '... encroaching on this space in the best possible way to create a moment where people feel as though they are engaged and active and are a participant in that process'.

Working together to change public perceptions

In the end, CITE aimed to change the dominant cultural narrative that depicts skateboarding and skateboarders as activities and people who do not belong in public space, respectively. 'There's that stigma attached to skateboarding of, like, we're hooligans and whatever. That, you know, we're thrashing things and wrecking stuff and whatever. Yes, there is an element of truth to it, of course. I mean, we skate illegally, we build illegal spots, we get kicked out of places' (Loates as quoted in Daily Vice, 2018). Concerns stemming from these negative perceptions not surprisingly drive what Munro described as '... an aversion to inviting skateboarders onto [a public space] ... around liability perhaps'. That, and 'an aversion to a particular culture of people and what they're seen to represent.' But Munro and the programme staff at The Bentway felt CITE had the potential to challenge such perceptions and make visitors rethink them. 'If you give people an opportunity to make themselves known outside of a stereotype', she explained, 'they will rise to that. And then some. And really prove to people that actually all of the preconceptions that you have around us and what we do are completely false.'

In this sense, working with skateboarders was itself an activist effort, one that the programming staff at The Bentway embraced with enthusiasm. 'I get very excited about a project like this because my background is largely in working with marginalized or lesser represented communities to find a way to carve out space to address their own needs and tell their own stories', said Munro. In her view, 'people want a space for themselves where they can feel safe and engaged in the activities that they like to engage in and where they can tell their story and have their voices be heard. I mean, I think that's a very human quality, wanting to be recognized. I think in the context of skateboarding, it's a group that, for a variety of reasons, already feels marginalized'. This recognition led to positive outcomes:

> Altman: What was wonderful, and I think it could only truthfully happened as a result of the way the project came together and because it was community-led, was how respectful all of the skateboarders were to the site, to each other, to people who were onsite to do other things. And so it was a great example of how the site could be used for a particular purpose, while also playing host to all sorts of other activities ... things lived together quite nicely.

Giving skateboarders ownership over the project ensured they respected its overall goals.

Ultimately, CITE was deemed a success because of the positive interactions observed during its implementation. In Munro's observations:

> We saw so many people rally behind the project to physically make the work happen. We saw so many people come out of the woodwork and want to sell incredible things that they created on our site or to be a part of the musical programming. When you come here on an incredibly hot, long weekend and you don't know whether anyone's in the city and whether they want to be outside, and you have all kinds of questions about attendance and then you see on the trail guys in their forties who are teaching little girls how to skateboard. When you see people of all different kinds of cultural backgrounds in the same space. When you see people who you wouldn't associate as being a part of that demographic of skateboarders who come out to cheer people on and just spectate and to really be positive about that. I mean, I think it was such an affirmation of what is possible when you give people the space and the freedom and financial assistance. And certainly they brought a lot to the table themselves, but to create this kind of moment for everyone. I do think that it really flipped on its head, for me and for a lot of people who attended, the expectations around what skateboarding culture is all about.

In sum, CITE demonstrated how art, aesthetics, inclusivity, and intentional programming can be used as activist interventions to change perceptions of skateboarders.

Discussion

As a form of gentle activism or 'contention in disguise' (Taylor, 2015, p. 185), CITE set out to achieve a deliberate set of activist goals through inclusive programming that appealed to more than just skateboarders. In so doing, it served as a vehicle for participatory and co-operative activity that fostered social interaction, promoted a sense of community, contributed to local identity, and introduced creative ways to address social exclusion (Schuermans, Loopmans, & Vandenabeele, 2012). It also represented a partnership between Build for Bokma and The Bentway that stemmed from a recognition by both parties that The Bentway, as a high-profile public space in Toronto, provided a potentially useful space in which to engage the public in civic exchange and foster greater cosmopolitan attitudes toward skateboarders and skateboarding. As Lofland (1998) underscored, the public realm teaches civility towards diversity through interaction with others with whom an everyday social distance exists. In this sense, programming in public space, such as CITE, has the potential to create what Sennett (2017) described as necessary 'social friction', the interaction between different groups of people who would otherwise not meet. In Montgomery's (1995, p. 107) words, 'it is the public realm and associated semi-public spaces which provide the terrain for social interaction and therefore transactions'. Bringing people into physical contact within public space, therefore, matters, particularly if the desire of programming is to advance some form of meaningful change.

Clearly, CITE embodied more than recreation, and yet recreation programming served as an effective tactic to achieve its activist goals. While 'theming' of The Bentway changed how the space looked, the programming worked in tandem with the aesthetic to give cues about what types of interactions ought to take place there and between whom (Borer, 2013). In theory, CITE programming produced a period during which participants were 'betwixt and between' and therefore potentially open to change. It aimed to capture the attention of participants and observers, even if for only a brief moment, thereby affecting The Bentway in terms of 'density, accretion, durations, dispersal, and flow' (Harrison-Pepper, 1990, p. 131). For all intents and purposes, then, CITE programming as a form of thoughtful placemaking fostered community in public space by transforming the minds of participants and not simply the space itself (Silberberg, Lorah, Disbrow, & Muessig, 2013).

Animating public space through art and programming, as demonstrated by CITE, merges well with activism because it ultimately aims to 'subvert, loosen, or transform presupposed rules of social conduct' (Pinder, 2005, p. 400). That is, it introduces urban inhabitants to new spatial patterns by shifting practices and encouraging different ways of relating to others (Simpson, 2011). Indeed, CITE provided a 'moment' of social practice that attempted to break the alienating routines of everyday life (Lefebvre, 1991) by offering valuable cues about the character of The Bentway and the potential of its programming. Put differently, CITE provided a focal point or targeted activity to promote social cohesion between skateboarders and the non-skateboarding public to overcome the constraints that prevent skateboarders from being accepted for taking part in public space (Bagnall et al., 2018).

Ultimately, the art and aesthetics of CITE played a salient role in facilitating civic exchange among its different participant groups. *Semblance* and its use of skateable structures created a 'art sculpture garden' that humanised skateboarders by drawing skateboarding participants into the landscape and encouraging greater interaction between skateboarders and the non-skating public. Instead of 'boxing skateboarders into a grey zone of concrete,' CITE showed how skateboarders could be incorporated into public space in an aesthetically pleasing way. The aesthetic signified that skateboarders belonged at The Bentway and by association in other public spaces, too. It did so by 'creat[ing] scenes for living by affording people opportunities to interact in diverse modes of exchange' (Demerath & Levinger, 2003, p. 219). *Semblance*, as a form of 'artivism' (Nossel, 2016) or social art practice (Cartiere & Zebracki, 2015), offered an intentional 'common referent [to] help establish a shared orientation toward the interaction' (Demerath & Levinger, 2003, p. 221). In this regard, it embodied what Whyte (1980) called 'triangulation', the connecting influence of a third presence. More than simply 'beautifying' The Bentway, CITE aestheticised the public space ' . . . to create new senses' (Pan, 2015, p. 10). Our common desire for what Demerath and Levinger (2003, p. 227) referred to as 'aesthetic fulfilment' introduced the possibility that an aesthetic appreciation of skateboarding in public space could potentially shape our acceptance of it.

In some ways, CITE reflected an attempt to 'aestheticize everyday life' (Featherstone, 2007), yet in other important ways, as an intentionally activist endeavour, it served as a medium for the communication of symbolic meanings (Hall & Smith, 2005). More specifically, it disrupted everyday city life, questioned and explored the problems and conflicts associated with street skateboarding, and resisted the processes through which urban spaces, inclusive and exclusive of skateboarding, are currently produced to encourage more democratic alternatives (Pinder, 2008). CITE, in other words, served as a form of appropriation of public space through which the artists from Build for Bokma articulated and communicated their activist interests and identities as skateboarders and community members who desire to belong.

Belonging meant skateboarders themselves needed to direct CITE and provide leadership in its planning, organisation, and implementation. As a project that was described as 'built, designed, programmed hand-in-hand with the skateboard community', working with skateboarders was itself an activist effort. As Silberberg et al. (2013, p. 13) explained:

> The intense focus on place has caused us to miss the opportunity to discuss community, process, and the act of making. The importance of the placemaking process itself is a key factor that has often been overlooked in working toward many of these noble goals . . . The most successful placemaking initiatives transcend the 'place' to forefront the 'making'. (Silberberg et al., 2013, p. 3)

CITE, accordingly, was less about The Bentway and more about the intentional placemaking effort to partner with skateboarders to alter perceptions about their literal and figurative place in public space.

Not surprisingly, the skateboarders involved in CITE expressed their desire to 'put their own creativity to creating architecture'. In this sense, CITE provided an example of how successful placemaking efforts can, and really ought to, include activists in the 'making' process. 'While we have concentrated on defining physical characteristics of a good city fabric', wrote Jacobs and Appleyard (1987, p. 120), 'the process of creating it is crucial . . . It is through this involvement in the creation and management of their city that citizens are most likely to identify with it and, conversely, to enhance their own sense of identity and control'. To this end, the support of The Bentway programming staff warrants praise, for they 'provided the right parameters for a community to make [the space] its own'. And in so doing, they countered the popular practice of defensive placemaking to offer a viable alternative of interacting with marginalised groups in public space. As Zukin (1998, p. 1) reminded us, 'Whoever controls public space sets the "program" for representing society', an observation consistent with Lefebvre's (1991) belief that space, whether public or private, encourages and discourages certain forms of interaction and gives form to social structures and ideologies. In sum, CITE gave form to the acceptance of skateboarding in public space.

Conclusion

As a case study, CITE demonstrated a successful model of *inclusive* placemaking (in contrast to defensive placemaking). By focusing on values such as partnership, inclusivity, creativity, accessibility, and intentionality, public spaces can 'flip the script' and embrace people and behaviours regarded as so-called nuisances by seeking to engage, as opposed to deter. Skateboarders bring a vitality to public space that ought to be welcome. And programmes such as CITE at The Bentway, even if only temporary, harness that energy to the benefit of skateboarders and the non-skateboarding public alike. The benefits to all parties make the effort worthwhile.

From a research standpoint, the literature is desperate for more work on the topics of inclusive and defensive placemaking, in leisure studies and in other fields. Smith and Walters (2018, p. 2991) commented about the lack of academic critique or investigation of the integration of defensive architecture in public space. In so doing, they called for more research on what we refer to defensive placemaking and the types of social spaces produced through such efforts. We share their call and encourage researchers to examine ways activists, organisers, and agencies resist such strategies, whether through gentle or more aggressive forms of activism.

From a practical standpoint, several recommendations emerge from this case study. First, CITE revealed the non-skateboarding public's acceptance of skateboarders can be high, perhaps in this case because it held progressive views about marginalised groups or because experimentation and boundary-pushing were seen as a benefit, not a detriment, to the neighbourhood. Either way, CITE, as a case study, encourages greater risk-taking for The Bentway and other public spaces, with an earned confidence to believe that visitors will respond favourably. Second, CITE revealed skateboarders are wise to the idea of defensive placemaking. Such tactics seem to be viewed as constraints to inclusive engagement and unnecessary precautions. Future construction of public spaces would do well to acknowledge the public's growing mistrust of these defensive tactics and appreciate the growing appetite for 'space for all'. And third, the hard work done to welcome marginalised groups to a public space must continue. Public spaces that welcome skateboarders for a temporary period, like The Bentway, should avoid severing ties once completed. These relationships, once cultivated, are better to be nurtured in a longer-term manner, allowing for future collaboration that sees populations welcomed to the site, not in a token or 'one-off' way, but through efforts that suggest ongoing possibilities. All told, skateboarding ought to be more welcome in public space. Temporary, impermanent interventions like CITE offer communities effective tactics to create a greater sense of belonging among those who use public spaces, whether skateboarders or otherwise.

Disclosure statement

No potential conflict of interest was reported by the authors.

ORCID

Troy D. Glover http://orcid.org/0000-0003-1076-7523

References

Acquisto, S. (2018). *Local skateboard legend remembered*. Toronto, ON: City News.

Altman, I. (2018). *The Bentway: Creating public spaces in urban environments*. Toronto, ON: Presentation.

Bagnall, A., South, J., Di Martino, S., Southby, K., Pilkington, G., Mitchell, B., ... Corcoran, R. (2018). A systematic review of interventions to boost social relations through improvements in community infrastructure (places and spaces).

Baxter, P., & Jack, S. (2008). Qualitative case study methodology: Study design and implementation for novice researchers. *The Qualitative Report*, *13*(4), 544–559.

Borden, I. (2001). *Skateboarding, space and the city: architecture and the body*. Oxford: Berg.

Borer, M. I. (2013). Being in the city: The sociology of urban experiences. *Sociology Compass*, *7*(11), 965–983.

Cartiere, C., & Zebracki, M. (Eds.). (2015). *The everyday practice of public art: Art, space, and social inclusion*. New York: Routledge.

Chiu, C. (2009). Contestation and conformity: Street and park skateboarding in New York city public space. *Space and Culture*, *12*(1), 25–42.

Coombs, G. (2012). park(ing) day. *Contexts*, *11*(3), 64–65.

Daily Vice. (2018, Month Date). *Inside the memorial skatepark for a legendary pro skater*. Retrieved from https://video.vice.com/en_ca/video/inside-the-memorial-skatepark-for-a-legendary-pro-skater/5b734633be407758d40d3b22?latest=1

de Fine Licht, K. P. (2017). Hostile urban architecture: A critical discussion of the seemingly offensive art of keeping people away. *Etikk I praksis-Nordic Journal of Applied Ethics*, (2), 27–44.

Demerath, L., & Levinger, D. (2003). The social qualities of being on foot: A theoretical analysis of pedestrian activity, community, and culture. *City & Community*, *2*(3), 217–237.

Emerson, R. W. (1844). *Essays: Second series*. New York: Macmillan.

Featherstone, M. (2007). *Consumer culture and postmodernism*. London: Sage.

Hall, T., & Smith, C M. Miles & T. Hall (eds (2005). Public art in the city: meanings, values, attitudes and roles. In M. Miles & T. Hall (eds (eds), *Interventions. advances in art and urban futures (pp. 175-179)*. OR: Intellect Books: Portland.

Harrison-Pepper, S. (1990). *Drawing a circle in the square: Street performing in New York's Washington square park*. Jackson: University Press of Mississippi.

Harvey, D. (2008, Sept/Oct). The right to the city. *New Left Review*, *53*, 23–40.

Jacobs, A., & Appleyard, D. (1987). Toward an urban design manifesto. *Journal of the American Planning Association*, *53*(1), 112–120.

Lefebvre, H. (1991). *The production of space*. Malden, MA: Blackwell.

Lofland, L. H. (1998). *The public realm: Exploring the city's quintessential social territory*. New Brunswick, NY: Transaction Publisher.

Lundry, W. (2003). To classify ... is to control. *Thrasher*, *267*, 134–149.

Montgomery, J. (1995). Editorial: Urban vitality and the culture of cities. *Planning Practice & Research*, *10*(2), 101–110.

Nossel, S. (2016). Introduction: On "artivism," or art's utility in activism. *Social Research: An International Quarterly*, *83*(1), 103–105.

O'Connor, P. (2018). Handrails, steps and curbs: Sacred places and secular pilgrimage in skateboarding. *Sport in Society*, *21*(11), 1651–1668.

Pan, L. (2015). *Aestheticizing public space: Street visual politics in East Asian cities*. Portland, OR: Intellect Books.

Pinder, D. (2005). Arts of urban exploration. *Cultural Geographies*, *12*(4), 383–411.

Pinder, D. (2008). Urban interventions: Art, politics and pedagogy. *International Journal of Urban and Regional Research*, *32*, 730–736.

Purcell, M. (2002). Excavating Lefebvre: The right to the city and its urban politics of the inhabitant. *GeoJournal*, *58* (2–3), 99–108.

Schuermans, N., Loopmans, M. P., & Vandenabeele, J. (2012). Public space, public art and public pedagogy. *Social & Cultural Geography*, *13*(7), 675–682.

Sennett, R. (2017). *The fall of public man, 40th anniversary edition*. New York: WW Norton & Company.

Shirtcliff, B. A. (2014). Sk8ting the sinking city. *Interdisciplinary Environmental Review*, *16*(2–4), 97.

Sho, K. (2018, July 7). *DIY skate park breaks the concrete mould | The Bentway*. Retrieved from https://www.youtube.com/watch?v=WME6DtTGAH0

Silberberg, S., Lorah, K., Disbrow, R., & Muessig, A. (2013). *Places in the making: How placemaking builds places and communities*. Cambridge, MA: Massachusetts Institute of Technology.

Simpson, P. (2011). Street performance and the city: Public space, sociality, and intervening in the everyday. *Space and Culture, 14*(4), 415–430.

Smith, N., & Walters, P. (2018). Desire lines and defensive architecture in modern urban environments. *Urban Studies, 55*(13), 2980–2995.

TAS Design Build. (2018, July 26). On cite at The Bentway. Retrieved from http://www.tasdesignbuild.com/social/on-cite-at-the-bentway/

Taylor, J. (2015). No to protests, yes to festivals: How the creative class organizes in the social movement society. In H. Ramos & K. Rodgers (Eds.), *Protest and politics: The promise of social movement societies* (pp. 173–190). Vancouver: UBC Press.

The Bentway Conservancy. (2018). *CITE – A celebration of skateboard arts and culture: Program recap (June 30th – August 12th, 2018).* Toronto: Bentway Conservancy.

The Bentway Conservancy. (2019a, January 16). About The Bentway. Retrieved from http://www.thebentway.ca/about/.

The Bentway Conservancy. (2019b, January 17). Semblance, build for Bokma. Retrieved from http://www.thebentway.ca/event/semblance-build-for-bokma/.

Vivoni, F. (2009). Spots of spatial desire: Skateparks, skateplazas, and urban politics. *Journal of Sport and Social Issues, 33*(2), 130–149.

Whyte, W. H. (1980). *The social life of small urban spaces.* Washington D.C.: Conservation Foundation.

Wilsey, S. (2015). *More curious.* Austin, TX: University of Texas Press.

Woolley, H., & Johns, R. (2001). Skateboarding: The city as a playground. *Journal of Urban Design, 6*(2), 211–230.

Yin, R. K. (2009). *Design with spirit: Proceedings of the 35th annual conference of the environmental design research association* (Vol. 5). London: Sage.

Zukin, S. (1998). *Politics and aesthetics of public space: The "American" model* (Real city, ideal city: Meaning and function in the modern urban space). "Urbanitats" no. 7. Barcelona: Centre of Contemporary Culture of Barcelona.

The transgressive festival imagination and the idealisation of reversal

Kirstie Jamieson and Louise Todd

ABSTRACT

To consider the festival's potential as an activist tactic may seem naïve and disconnected from the colonising practices of event tourism. However, today's curated immersive experiences are indebted to a wider festival imagination: a spatial imagination suffused with reversal and transgression. In this paper, we trace a transgressive festival imagination through four vectors of reversal that have contributed to how we imagine both festivals and activism: the crowd, play, appropriation and spontaneity. Each point to the significance of festival space as mutable, protean, volatile and transitional. Together, they extend a techne of activist tactics, and contribute to the somatic language of the creative industries' experience economy. By tracing the transgressive festival imagination in this way, we reveal how the contemporary urban festival and the performative tactics of social movements share visions of contingency, playful performance and an aesthetic-political heightened energy.

Introduction

This paper draws from a range of disciplinary perspectives with the aim of contributing a revised view of the festival. We first trace the festival phenomenon through the lens of activism, event tourism, and leisure studies in order to reflect upon the scope and capacity of the festival. By tracing layers of festival meanings through these disciplinary positions, we are then able to consider the festival by way of a *transgressive imagination* that has imbued the festival with the potential for reversal.

While the range of festivals, is vast and beyond the scope of this paper, we recognise that festivals' diverse historical and socio-cultural roles extend beyond 'themed public celebrations' (Getz & Page, 2016, p. 276). Although we consider festivals relatively broadly in this paper as contextually situated cultural celebrations, our specific focus is upon those forms of festival, which since the twentieth-century, have been developed to support cities as destinations through hallmark event tourism (Todd, Leask, & Ensor, 2017). In writing this paper, our aim is to contribute to the current understanding of the festival, beyond that of an instrumental event management view, and in doing so to dilate the leisure studies perspective.

The growth of event management and more recently event studies in the academic literature has led to a more nuanced perspective of festivals and events. Today, we see these as being of particular value, offering an alternative conceptualisation to the festival as an instrument of neoliberal cultural urban planning (Rojek, 2012). Nevertheless, despite an emerging corpus of critical event studies, which 'takes the concept of "event" to be essentially contested' (Lamond & Platt, 2016, p. 5), much of current festival research remains framed by tourism and event management (Laing, 2018).

In contrast to the event management perspective, leisure studies provide a growing body of work that reframes the festival through critical conceptualisations of resistance and social change (Erickson, 2011; Gilchrist & Ravenscroft, 2012; McDonald, 2008; Ravenscroft & Matteucci, 2003; Rojek, 2012; Taylor & Whalley, 2019). Theorists of transgressive spaces of leisure such as Williams (2018) rehabilitate the transformative and cathartic qualities of the festival to make sense of the embodied pursuit of social change.

Still, there remains limited consideration of the relation between those *festive forms of resistance* we see in Critical Mass movements, Occupy or anti-globalisation events and the urban spectacle that revitalises the city as a space of time-based cultural consumption. In her ecological approach to festivals Frost (2016) highlights their paradoxical nature: 'They can make headlines, they can make money, and they can stimulate discussions of identity, politics, art, and more. As sites of cultural practice and experience, they are complex, multiple, and dynamic' (p.569). While it would be pointless to refute festivals' contradictions and incongruous spaces of order and chaos, there is nonetheless more to be said about how reversal is paradoxically figured in both the touristic and activist festival.

In short, we lack a conceptual framework through which to understand the festival as both activist process and event tourism product. Our paper is written in response to the ambiguity of the festival and its capacity to reach across consumerist and activist practices. It is also written in response to our perceived lack of interdisciplinary interpretations of the festival. Importantly for the authors, the paper is also a means to develop a conversation between us as researchers.

Despite a shared interest in festivals, our disciplinary 'homes' are markedly different and as a result our scope and treatment of the festival produces contrasting representations, contexts and relations. Kirstie Jamieson sits between design and urbanism and has approached the urban arts festival critically in relation to the production of space, its role in relation to gentrification and the assemblages of global *Creative City* discourses. Louise Todd's position is as an artist and inter-disciplinary researcher who has lived experiences within festivals and events management; and has approached the urban arts festival as a phenomenon of engagement and relationship building within the *Festival City* discourse across tourism and event studies. While we have studied the urban arts festival from our respective disciplinary positions, we hope this collaborative paper develops previous informal discussions that have taken place between us, while contributing to wider understandings of the festival.

Although our approaches differ, we share the frustration with festivals' naturalised role vis-à-vis the creative and event industries where festivals still remain widely defined by their economic function. We agree that such an instrumental relation to event tourism eclipses more critical and liminal readings. Our emphasis is neither upon the festival as 'deviant leisure' (Rojek, 1999) that transgresses moral norms, nor the festival as a means of conceptualising resistance through leisure. Instead, we are interested in developing an understanding of the ways in which forms of reversal have sustained the festival as *potentially* transgressive. We suggest that distinct modes of reversal have combined to construct a *transgressive festival imagination* that intersects with both revolution and consumerism, where references to freedom, hedonism and transformation are aligned with temporary publics.

Today, the festival prevails as a ubiquitous branded phenomenon that temporalises urban space and showcases the city as a destination. Defined by policy-makers in terms of economic and socio-cultural impact, contemporary festivals must 'earn their keep ... in the age of instrumental art' (Frost, 2016, p. 569) while assuming strategic positions in destinations' event portfolios (Todd et al., 2017; Ziakas, 2019). This distinctly modern idealisation of the festival was first conceived under the auspices of a self-conscious cultural internationalism (Miller, 1993) that produced festival assem-blages and social networks that exceeded the physical delimitation of the city and the nation. During this time, a series of European urban festivals emerged with a view to *staging the international* and hosting cosmopolitan audiences. The cities of Salzburg, Edinburgh and Avignon might be said to have been the destinations of creative tourism *avant la lettre*.

This marked the birth of a self-consciously modern festival identity and paradoxically fuelled a *transgressive festival imagination*; by taking the arts into the streets, appropriating buildings and challenging social and political ideals of urban order (Bakhtin, 1968; Johansson & Kociatkiewicz, 2011; Quinn, 2005). During this period, the festival was re-ontologised 'as a legible sign of temporal urban identity' (Jamieson, 2014, p. 300) and while we do not intend to discuss the international festival in any empirical setting here, it is at this historical juncture that the *festival imagination* was fused as transgressive, disruptive, street-based, and seemingly spontaneous.

Interpretative method: tracing the festival imagination

Our paper and the approach that supports it, argues against reducing the festival to its function in the prevailing context of semiocapitalism (Berardi, 2011), interurban competition and the pervasive development of the experience economy (Pine & Gilmore, 1998). To think in terms of a *festival imagination* rather than festival discourse is to think of today's festival as entangled in a wider frame of cultural knowledge. To consider the festival through the *imagination* of its potential spaces and experiences, is to acknowledge that the festival is 'sustained by often seemingly incongruous elements: facts, fictions, pasts and futures, the cognitive and the somatic, the global and the local (Jamieson, 2014, p. 295).

In their article *Imagination as Method* Hayes, Sameshima, and Watson (2014) argue that to explore lived experience, we must revise our understanding of the relationship between research, society and individual experience. The authors maintain that the imagination furnishes distant communities with a capacity to generate rather than describe societies. The imagination, they argue is a productive force, both psychically and materially. Hayes et al. (2014) present the imagination as having a significant role in cultural and social life, extending as it does a field of possibilities and connections.

In *Modern Social Imaginaries* Taylor (2004) traces ways in which people have imagined their collective social life and explains a crucial relationship between the imagination and ideology. The imagination can be false inasmuch as it is capable of distorting and concealing realities, but our imaginations are never simply a matter of ideology; instead they allow us to construct, challenge and transgress society. We adopt Castoriadis (2005) resistance to the temptation to naturalise cultural meanings, choosing instead to seek out a wider sense of the ideas and ideals that have invested the festival with its transgressive potential.

For Castoriadis (2005) the imagination of society 'creates for each historical period its singular way of living, seeing, and making its own existence' (p. 128). It is this generative capacity of the imagination that Hayes et al. (2014) argue, should not be seen to exist outside of social and cultural inquiry. In the case of the festival, we argue that four elements of reversal are imagined; each of which support both the consensus of the festivalized city and the antagonism of social protest. By privileging the *festival imagination*, we recognise what Hayes et al. (2014) refer to as 'the intensity of differences'; how one thing blends with another and where the intersections might be felt. Moreover, by focusing attention on the qualities of reversal embedded in the crowd, play, spontaneity and appropriation we are able to reveal the capacity of the imagination to generate hopeful futures, tactics of freedom and idealisations of a creative self.

In the paragraphs that follow we explore each of these four elements in turn. We begin by considering how reversal is played out through the invocations of the crowd. It is after all, ultimately the crowd that performatively institutes ideals of freedom through proximate bodies. Secondly, we consider reversal in relation to play and the more insurgent revolutionary forms of reversal associated with the carnival. Thirdly, we turn to appropriation with its tactics of revision to discuss the more structural relations of reversal to the festival. Fourthly, we address spontaneity, to explore whether the prospect of the unplanned and uninvited carries with it a potent currency of reversal. After reflecting on these four elements we discuss ways in which they are mined by creative and event tourism industries and activist assemblages. Finally, we conclude by reflecting on how our attention to the four elements of reversal we identify with a *transgressive festival imagination* might benefit scholars of festivals and protest.

REVERSAL: activism, transgression and the festival crowd

Canetti's Nobel Prize winning contribution to the study of *Crowds and Power* (1962) chronicles the behaviour of the festival crowd and its relation to society. He tells us that 'nothing and no-one threatens and there is nothing to flee from ... Many prohibitions and distinctions are waived ... [but] there is no common identical goal ... The feast *is* the goal ... the equality is in large part an equality simply of indulgence and pleasure' (Canetti, 2000, p. 62).

Unlike the festival crowd, Canetti identifies the reversal crowd as organic and 'open' rather than 'closed' (which he relates to the organised festival crowd). The reversal crowd senses its own collectivity while the festival creates a temporary and delimited space where the extended body of the crowd is temporarily amassed before being emptied back into everyday life. His distinction between the reversal and festival crowd identifies a phenomenological divide: one where the reversal crowd sensing its own modulating vitality seizes the capacity to discharge its power, whereas the festival crowd sensing its contained conditions complies with the spatial order.

Canetti argues that dispersed crowds devoid of touching are most often aligned with an authoritarian spatial configuration. Touch, he argues is fundamental to the crowd's inter-subjective communication and its capacity to act as one. As a spatial and haptic phenomenon, he insists we must understand the crowd relationally and politically. Canetti recognises the untapped potential of the dense crowd as that which is capable of negating and transcending social order. Crowds for Canetti, allow 'individuals to lose themselves, get absorbed, and, in this way, are able (temporarily) to escape commands ... crowds not only negate but also transcend: they pave the ways for new alternatives' (p.5).

Ossewaarde (2012) contends that the fleeting counter-worlds produced by the reversal crowd should not be understood as vying for power over rational structures of democracy. Rather, 'the will of crowds is growth, vitality, density, equality, physical discharge, standing together, body to body, tongues getting together, chanting, clapping, dancing, reciting poems' (Manoukian in Ossewaarde, 2012, p. 14). The crowd and its relation to social order is historically situated and for Khan (2015) it is specifically during the 1960s when the idea of the crowd shifted from that of the undifferentiated mass to that of a diverse and reflective crowd. During the cultural revolution of the 1960s, crowds emerged as both more creative and diverse in age, gender and race. This shift was allied to other changes in the planning and design of urban space that saw an increase in pedestrianised space, amenities and communal space more generally. These concomitant shifts subsequently gave way to new visibilities and inventive ways of occupying and appropriating space.

By tracing these meditations of the crowd, we are able to make connections across periods of technological and social change, and identify a shift towards intentional, collaborative and temporary social groups. These reversal crowds were unified through an intention to *claim* space whether through festivals, protests, sit-ins, or happenings; space became a matter of collective contention. The counter-cultural crowds of the late twentieth century developed a vocabulary of reversal that performed creative and defiant tactics.

Today, the 21st century crowd is often imagined as a *collective* at home amongst the mediated crowds of social media: where networked relationships do not necessarily have boundaries, but cleave to values, identities and experiences. The 21st century crowd is borne of mobilities and formed through global networks. Today, the mediated reversal crowd is brought together by shifting allegiances and practices of sharing, preserving the reversal crowd's affinity with temporary, fluid, immediate and contingent space.

REVERSAL: the transgressive festival imagination and play

Play is fundamental to both the imagination of the urban arts festival and the serious play (Bogad, 2016) that creatively disrupts urban order. Play underwrites the *festival imagination's* capacity to transgress whether through the licenced transgression of the festival, or the contemporary power of creative protest to invert and play with social structures. Play as it is imagined through protesting crowds, jeers and taunts, and mischievously mimics social order. Whereas play as it is imagined through the spectacle of the cultural festival, choreographs an inquisitive audience through the city's temporary spaces.

Critical tourism scholars such as Swain and Hall (2007) consider the festival through its capacity to create playful interactions between spaces and audiences. They identify how the inquisitive crowd is generated through a touristic vocabulary of western embodied gestures. Although useful to the embodied interactions of the *transgressive festival imagination* this kind of critical attention to playful bodies, materials and spaces is not prevalent in tourism literature. Conversely, research around critical play is extensive in leisure studies where it is invoked to describe the tactical performances of critical play; in particular those of culture jamming (Gilchrist and Ravenscroft, 2013, mass bike rides (Williams, 2018) and parkour (Raymen, 2019).

The principal social theorist of play Johan Huizinga (1955), encourages an appreciation of play's space and time as 'imaginative actualisations' that play *with the order of things*. He avoids such binary opposites of play/work, fun/serious, instead suggesting that more consideration is given to the ways in which play's spaces and times 'promote the formation of social groupings' (p.13). Gadamer (1977, 1986) conceives play as a creative experience, which takes place neither *within* the individual nor *to* the individual; but is constituted by two or more subjects in an intersubjective space. These conceptualisations of play endow the festival imagination with a language of ordered disruption; what Dissanayake (1988) refers to as 'the fiction of an alternate life, the excitement lacking in normal experience, and the opportunity to pretend' (p.70). Here, the art of play does not belong to a universal sacred time-zone, but to a horizon of 'still undecided possibilities'.

A further evocation of play that emphasises a temporalised 'potential space' comes from the psychoanalyst D.A. Winnicott (1971) who argues that play functions as a 'third space'. It is beyond the scope of this paper to reflect upon the breadth of influence psychoanalysis has had upon the *festival imagination*, but it is worth identifying the ways in which play has been understood as both liminal and future-making. Firstly, liminality is often understood in relation to the masking of identities and the exaggeration of bodily figures, both of which are common idealisations of reversal in the festival and contemporary protest. These figurations of play celebrate the performing body and its capacities for disruption. Winnicott argues that the body at play makes possible a liminal space wherein the subject is neither 'me' nor 'not me', but exists between that of the individual's own fantasy world and exterior world. Although Winnicott and Lacan are generally thought to occupy opposite poles (Ruti, 2011) of psychanalytic thought Winnicott (1971) develops a structuralist distinction between the Real, Imagination and Symbolic Order, to consider play as a 'potential space' that is, both fluid and peopled by unidentifiable masked subjectivities, each of which are commonly associated with the *festival imagination.*

Winnicott was interested in child development and specifically, the *futurity* of play's potential. The recurrence of the childmotif in Winnicott's psychoanalytic thought signifies the primacy he gives to the power of play in the development of the child's potential future. Play in this formulation, endows the *festival imagination* with a future-giving capacity. We can begin to see the ways in which play provides the *festival imagination* with a time of experimentation, potential and futurity. Through Winnicott's work, play is presented as expressive, embodied and potent with the ability to imagine a more rewarding and authentic future. In this way, play is imagined as a route to self-actualisation, which continuously revises the parameters of possibility by probing, testing and pushing at 'reality'.

Ruti (2011) describes the Winnicottian self as that which is neither passive nor compliant, instead it pursues what both 'Heiddeger and Lacan describe as the subject's poetic relationship to the world' (p.140). For Winnicott, play is a means to confront the monotonous, repetitive and predictable rhythms of life. Play, as it is invoked through Winnicott, provides the tactics to reject a futile compliance with social order and a path to creative living.

In the context of considering the transformative potential of play it would be remiss if we did not introduce the work of Mikhail Bakhtin (1895–1975) whose work is central to theoretical readings of spatial and embodied reinvention and reversal. Bakhtin first conjured the potent force of the carnivalesque in his celebrated *Rabelais and his World* (1968) to describe forms of unofficial culture that use festivity, parody, and grotesque realism as a weapon against official culture and totalitarian order. Bakhtin's original conception of the medieval carnival imagined it (through Rabelais) as a space wherein official divisions of gender, class and social knowledge became the subject of hilarity and ridicule: as masked men dressed up as women and begged for money (an activity known in medieval society as 'mumming') and conventions of class were dramatically inverted through codes of dress and social conventions. Viewed in this way, the carnival is employed to convey playful spaces of dissent.

That Bakhtin's carnival is rooted in a historical context of public community life and a time not wholly given over to industrial clock time provides us with a vocabulary that at once preserves the distinction between spontaneous and institutionalised culture. Igrek (2018) attends to this distinction in her theorisation of festival, laughter and performativity where she considers readings of transgression in relation to excess. For her, 'the affirmation of play is therefore a release of energy which has been masked, veiled, and restricted according to the principles of a utilitarian social organisation" (p.248). For Igrek (ibid.), play as it is formulated in the carnivalesque, imagines the active participant rather than the passive spectator. Similar to Winnicottian play, Bakhtin's play is both future-oriented and a tactic of release if not denial, from an oppressive social order. Both authors present us with forms of critical play that can be seen in the festival tactics of today's performing protestors in *Reclaim the Streets* and *The Rebel Clown Army* where the clowning behaviours of the crowd are transformative, albeit temporarily.

REVERSAL: the transgressive festival imagination and appropriation

The binary between order and chaos is implicit in the paper's title and is germane to the *transgressive festival imagination's* distinction between the festival and more overtly disruptive spaces of protest. This binary reflects its modern origins by acknowledging the design, manipulation, management and engineering (Bauman, 1991, p. 7) of social space. Lefebvre (2003) provides a helpful distinction when he distinguishes between the appropriation of space through festivals and through protest:

> 'The parades, masquerades, balls and folklore festivals authorized by a power structure caricaturize the appropriation and re-appropriation of space. The true appropriation characteristic of effective 'demonstrations' is challenged by the forces of repression, which demand silence and forgetfulness' (p.21).

In leisure studies appropriation is written into the potentiality of reclaiming civic space through the shared pleasure of guerrilla gardening (Reynolds, 2008), the political act of walking and singing (Taylor & Whalley, 2019) and the appropriation of urban infrastructure by *traceurs* (Raymen, 2019). For Taylor and Whalley (2019) these *acts of leisure* appropriation are both artful and critical and are initiated by the community to formulate a 'resistant stance'. Here we identify a propensity to read marginal cultural practices alongside appropriation as acts of reclaiming and celebrating minority space and identity. Through tactics of appropriation these communities re-present themselves as counterpublics (Warner, 2002) whose force lies in their capacity to claim and transform.

Since the postmodern turn, appropriation beyond an aestheticised antagonism is harder to find. Instead, Graw (2004) identifies a surfeit of aesthetic games that engage with playful practices of poaching and revision. Following Crimp's (1980) seminal distinction between critical appropriation (that revises material realities) and a more postmodern form (that appropriates style rather than content) Graw reflects on the persistence of the potency of 'real appropriation' in the arts, at least as an enduring ideal that fuels the festival imagination with the prospect of revision and reclamation.

Within a sliding scale of authentic acts of appropriation Bakhtin's carnivalesque continues to provide a generative framework for understanding the festival as a spatially potent arena: reversal is intrinsic to the blurring of boundaries between spectator and performer, private and public. In this arena, official spaces can be 'turned upside down' by the alternative rhythms of play. St John (2008) identifies what he refers to as an 'explosive resurgence' of the carnivalesque in the 1990's. Citing the *Carnivals Against Capital* (and For Global Justice) and *Global Days of Action* as part of 'massive anti-capitalist and anti-war convergences'. He argues that this period of intensive street protest signalled the emergence of the 'protestival' as 'a variegated complex of action performances enabling exposure and revelation' (p.168).

> "Protestival' is a term coined by radical technician John Jacobs, and offers a useful heuristic for contemporary events simultaneously negative/positive, transgressive/progressive, aesthetic/instrumental. Becoming virulent in a period which has seen an increase in political mobilizations deviating from those conventional to social movements, these events constitute a creative response to the traditional political rituals of the left: those ritual marches from point A to point B' (St John, 2008, p. 168).

The carnival deconstructs and deconsecrates official meanings of spaces and buildings, which Vaneigem (2001) argues is the 'principle of subversion'. Theorist and influential member of the Situationist International (SI), Vaneigem provides us with an enduring conceptualisation of appropriation. He imbues appropriation with powers of reversal, emancipation and the freedom to change that which serves power: 'the freedom, for example, to turn Chartres Cathedral into a funfair, into a labyrinth, into a shooting range, into a dream landscape' (p.259).

The Situationist project argued 'the whole of life experience under capitalism is in some sense alienated from itself' (Plant, 1992, p. 2) and that reality and authenticity lie outside the structures of capitalism. Premised on the separation of art from everyday life (a separation wrought by the powers of the market and commodity fetishism), they urged transgression beyond the confines of capitalism, imperialism and party politics and triumphed through the powers of urban re-coding. The subversive capacity of re-coding is not a given, instead it lies in revealing the contingency of language, materials and space. Its performative act is one of reclaiming (stealing, borrowing, hacking, jamming) language, materials or space: re-inscribing them with meanings or resistance. Today, these feature as prevalent tactics in the aesthetics of protest: for the activists that take to the streets in a theatrical reclamation and appropriation of urban space and for those media activists engaged in hacking and jamming. 'Here, the *hack*, not exclusively a negational practice, is radically creative since it involves the intentional disruption, disorientation and de-programming of "consensus" reality' (St John, 2008, p. 172).

We commonly associate the disruption of the Occupy movement, Global Street Parties and the mass mobilisations of the Arab uprising with make-do grassroots aesthetics and strategies of appropriation. In the hands of protestors, the city is cannibalised in establishing provisional spaces from where protestors can physically disrupt the streets with their bodies by singing, dancing and marching. By appropriating spaces and objects these embodied playful modalities test the limits of their environment countering conformity with improvisation. An improvisational disposition is, as Hanna et al. (2016) argue, crucial to the tactics of appropriation and provides the *transgressive festival imagination* with a vocabulary that yokes appropriation with an imaginative and opportunistic appetite for protean spaces.

REVERSAL: the transgressive festival imagination and spontaneity

Tracing the festival's relation to protest to the mid twentieth century, Bey (1994) like St John identifies an emergent creative force of reversal to an era of happenings, when spontaneity had a less adulterated currency of its own. In the context of the *transgressive festival imagination*, it is important to consider spontaneity as a spatial tactic. As part of the 1960's avant-garde performance art movement, groups such as *Fluxus* explored the potentiality and immanence of spontaneous borrowed spaces and everyday subjectivities. Situationists sought to reclaim the spaces and times of the city that institutionalised time had embezzled from its citizens, regulating, categorising and commodifying how and when the city was used. During this period, performance, theatricality and play became weapons of spatial appropriation.

In its idealisation spontaneity serves as ammunition capable of penetrating the enforced temporality of the city. During the late 60's and 70's, theoretical writing from the Situationist camp and that of Derrida in particular, equated spontaneity with transparency and influenced the trajectory of cultural criticism, the proliferation of spatial metaphors and, a distinctly potent and volatile cultural imagination of festivals.

In his book *The Culture of Spontaneity: Improvisation and the Arts in Post-War America* Belgrad (1998) emphasises the political intent behind spontaneity, arguing that its opposition to imperialism and bureaucratic control was primary. The alternative it promoted, he suggests, was founded on intersubjectivity, 'in which "reality" was understood to emerge through a conversational dynamic' (p.5). Avant-garde spontaneity was intentionally generative of participants rather than spectators. Spontaneity, he argues, was aligned with a certain performative emancipation: an unlocking of the participants' creativity.

In this way, the aesthetic of spontaneity was a phenomenological project that sought to include bodies as part of a *feeling collective*, but as Belgrad (1998) points out, the aim was also to extend the activity and potency of spontaneity beyond the confines of the intellectual cultural sphere. Spontaneity, as a creative idea and socio-political ideal was disseminated through the arts, but its force and application spread through critical platforms emerging as the *techne* (Greek: meaning craft) of carnivalesque protests. As a cornerstone of the *transgressive festival imagination*, spontaneity delivers the promise of unmediated experience. It gives play its immediacy and disruptive force and it is the crowd's spontaneous force that continues to breathe potential into the *transgressive festival imagination*.

In leisure studies, spontaneity is often aligned with an intensity of pleasure, with feeling oneself and with the flow of happiness (Watkins & Bond, 2007). Interestingly, it is also linked with the pursuit of hedonistic pleasures, youth cultures and rebellion (Heath & Potter, 2006). Within the context of late capitalism these are recurrent bedfellows in packaged products and experiences that mine rebellion and resistance; from aged graffiti tagged converse trainers to tattoos and body piercing the aesthetics of nonconformity have become the mainstay of mainstream consumerism. McGuigan's (2006) [1] portrait of 'cool capitalism' remains relevant in 2019 when 'cool' is still 'obliged to act out antibourgeois nonconformity'. McGuigan's criticism of the stylised *acting out* of nonconformity and its seeming spontaneity is set against a more defiant, tactical, authentic and Political resistance *to* power. Spontaneity, like play is subject to commodification, offering as they do the trappings of authenticity.

Despite the fact that spontaneity can readily be incorporated as a strategy to lend flash mobs and pop-up shops authenticity, it continues to provide the *transgressive festival imagination* with a quality that prefixes each of the other four forms of reversal. The crowd, play and appropriation are all augmented by the velocity of spontaneity; it is spontaneity that amplifies their capacity for reversal.

Festival management and the mining of the transgressive festival imagination

Küpers, Sonnenburg, and Zierold (2017) argue that those regimes of knowledge we identify within the *transgressive festival imagination* are both highly mobile and open to multiple readings. In particular the four elements of reversal are prevalent within the experience economy wherein feelings are imagined as intrinsic rather than extrinsic to places and events. The *transgressive festival imagination* in all its capacity for imagining reversal provides festival management with a language of revision: the recipe for endless possible re-inscriptions of festivalized space.

It is important to consider the relation between the ambiance-centric (Thibaud, 2011) *business* of events tourism and the *transgressive festival imagination*: wherein the possibility of embodied transgression and reversal is co-opted by festival management to produce what Raymen (2019) describes as '*symbolic* identities of "cool transgression", effectively displacing the Real by attempting to represent the non-representational through the imagination' (p.149).

In their critical re-thinking of Management Studies in relation to cultural turns in the humanities Küpers et al. (2017) point to the ways in which the cultural imagination permeates disciplines. They discuss the critical potential of cultural theory and its exploitation within what they refer to as the 'dark side of cultural turns in management'. 'Topics and concepts, such as, materiality, embodiment, space, performance, mediality, narration, and sense-making ... have moved more and more into the forefront in the last few decades' (p.22).

They argue that the language of creativity is over-used by the cultural management profession to sell curated experiences of freedom and authenticity. Within this context, the authors identify a 'dark side' of cultural management that exploits the imagination of cultural theory: mining aesthetic experience and cultural practices for consumerist ends. The authors suggest that the seductive appeal of cultural theory lies in the prospect of discursively claiming what Pink (2007) describes as 'the sensory potentials of urban space' (p.66). It is as Frost (2016) insists, important that we consider the disciplinary complicity of event tourism research: 'those studies that embrace the new policy environment are frequently at the same time part of it, producing identikit economic impact assessments to order, without interrogating underlying assumptions' (p.570).

Discussion: the transgressive festival imagination and the four elements of reversal

Our emphasis upon the *transgressive festival imagination* does not fit neatly into conceptualisations of leisure as a context for social change, instead our focus rests upon the predominance of the festival's imagined vectors of reversal. Each of the four elements of reversal discussed above point to the idealisation of a certain kind of festival space, one that is mutable, protean, volatile and transitional.

This mutable spatial quality of the festival crowd is most succinctly captured by Canetti's (2000) politics of touch and related codes of proximity. Such codes of proximity are intrinsic to the experience of both protest space and urban festivals where bodies are choreographed in to produce what Nieland (2008) refers to as, the 'eventfulness of sensation'.

Canetti conjures reversal through the sizeable sensing crowd, which feels its own collectivity and mutable potential. He identifies a phenomenological divide between the reversal and festival crowd, which he argues is rooted in the sensing crowd's reflective capacity to discharge its collective power and feel the force of its action. The reversal crowd performs alternatives through the language of transgression, or what we have called a performative *techne* of resistance. This performative *techne* of resistance associates the protesting crowd with critical play (volatile and oriented to deconstruction and deconsecration). In a similar way, the element of appropriation provides the *transgressive festival imagination* with an opportunistic relation to space. In the act of appropriation, new meanings and new possibilities are made visible. Appropriation in this context belongs to a spatial vocabulary that idealises the protean and the transitional potential of festivals. Appropriation heralds a participative form of urban engagement, one that summons protestors or festival audiences to read urban space as contingent and playful.

Today's playful appropriating crowds of Occupy and Reclaim the Streets are future-oriented and mobilised through creative reality-making activities. Their tactics of spontaneous appropriation reveal the contingency of the city and open up spaces of revision and hope. Spontaneity, in this context provides the prospect of interruption, intervention and emergent forms of being.

Together, crowd, play, appropriation and spontaneity fuse in the *transgressive festival imagination* to extend a 'prefigurative politics' and a performative *techne* of resistance. Each of the four elements of reversal has become operative across the divide of consensus and antagonism. Sharpe's

(2008) prism of 'pleasure-politics' addresses the intersectionality of politics and leisure and allows for a more nuanced understanding of festival beyond merely paradoxical (Frost, 2016). Moreover, echoing the work of Day (2004) Sharpe (2008) identifies a shift in the modalities of protest; from protest politics to prefigurative acts. She argues that in the shift 'from a "politics of demand" to a "politics of the act" … the attempt is to "refuse rather than rearticulate" hegemonic structure' (p.228). We suggest that this shift towards the 'act' of refusal revitalises 'the ephemeral and evanescent, the transformable, the multipurpose and the ambiguous' (Pringle, 2005, p. 145) qualities of the festival.

Because of rather than despite their capacity for reversal, these four elements of the *transgressive festival imagination* are integrated into festival planning and aligned with neoliberal inter-urban competition. In the prevailing context of ambiance-centric urban planning and what Böhme (2016) refers to as *aesthetic economics*, pop-up events, appropriated buildings, flash mobs and temporary publics provide 'something more' to the sensorial experiences of the city.

Conclusion

Our aim in this paper has been to draw upon our previous discussions and interdisciplinary views to consider the *transgressive festival imagination* through four vectors of reversal: the crowd, play, appropriation and spontaneity. We have argued that together these elements have contributed to the idealisations of both festivals and activism. Integral to the experience economy of cultural event tourism, reversal can be mined as both strategic and operable constituents of the somatic economy. We have aimed to re-conceptualise the festival through the prism of the *transgressive festival imagination* moving beyond the event management perspective, to dilate the leisure studies' perspective of the festival.

The *transgressive festival imagination* continues to inform the transformative potential of the festival and the *techne* of resistance. The vibrant crowd offers an aesthetic-political heightened energy to the street that is pursued through urban cultural strategies. Play is both critically potent and embedded within leisure's timescapes. Appropriation offers the promise of a prefigurative politics and the possibility of endless re-inscription of leisure spaces. Spontaneity too, speaks of the possibility of unmediated pleasures and the invisible packaging of curated authenticity.

It is hoped that our desire to understand the *transgressive festival imagination* as it exists at the intersection of politics and leisure might lead to more nuanced understanding of the seemingly incongruous functions of festivals and social protests. We argue that our attention to the imagination is important, revealing an attention to the intensity of differences; how one thing blends with another (Hayes et al., 2014). While our analysis of the *festival imagination* adds to the leisure studies literature, we conclude by suggesting that it may also be of use to scholars of the contemporary festival and culturalised urban policy, and those seeking an understanding of festivals beyond the instrumental logic of tourism and event management.

Note

1. That 'cool' sells everything from Hollywood films to New Labour is not McGuigan's point, instead it is capitalism's appetite of endless appropriation, incorporation and colonisation. For Belgrad (1998) spontaneity continues to embody a cultural stance of refusal, commodified or not, it is read as a symbol of defiance, unpredictability, uncontrollability and disruption. Non-conformity sells and we readily find readings of spontaneity that situate it within a consumerist paradigm. Packaged and sold to youth cultures seeking unmediated authentic cultural experiences Hamilton and Denniss (2005) spontaneity offers the promise of 'performative resistance' (Raymen, 2019) and a more authentic, improvisational and creative self.

Disclosure statement

No potential conflict of interest was reported by the authors.

ORCID

Louise Todd http://orcid.org/0000-0003-1783-0388

References

Bakhtin, M. (1968). Rabelais and his. Trans. Helene Iswolsky. Cambridge, MA: MIT Press.
Bauman, Z. (1991). *Modernity and the holocaust*. Cambridge: Polity Press.
Belgrad, D. (1998). *The culture of spontaneity: Improvisation and the arts in post-war America*. Chicago: The University of Chicago Press.
Berardi, F. (2011). *After the future*. Edinburgh: AK Press.
Bey, H. (1994). *Immediatism*. Edinburgh: AK Press.
Bogad, L. M. (2016). *Tactical performance: The theory and practice of serious play*. New York, NW: Routledge.
Böhme, G. (2016). *Critique of aesthetic capitalism*. Oxford: Mimesis International.
Canetti, E. (2000). *Crowds and power*. London: Weidenfeld and Nicholson.
Castoriadis, C. (2005). *The imagination institution of society*. Cambridge: Polity Press in association with Blackwell Publishers Ltd.
Crimp, D. (1980, October).The photographic activity of postmodernism. *15*(Winter 1980).
Day, R. (2004). From hegemony to affinity: The political logic of the newest social movements. *Cultural Studies*, *18*(5), 716–748.
Dissanayake, E. (1988). *What is art for?* Washington: University of Washington Press.
Erickson, B. (2011). Recreational activism: Politics, nature, and the rise of neoliberalism. *Leisure Studies*, *30*(4), 477–494.
Frost, N. (2016). Anthropology and festivals: Festival ecologies. *Journal of Anthropology*, *81*(4), 569–583.
Gadamer, H. (1977). *Philosophical hermeneutics*. Berkley: University of California Press.
Gadamer, H. (1986). The relevance of the beautiful, art as play, symbol and festival. In H. Gadamer (Ed.), *The relevance of the beautiful and other essays* (pp. 3–53). Cambridge: Cambridge University Press.
Getz, D., & Page, S. (2016). *Event studies: Theory, research and policy for planned events*. London: Routledge.
Gilchrist, P., & Ravenscroft, N. (2012). Paddling, property and piracy: The politics of canoeing in England and Wales. In P. Gilchrist & R. Holden (Eds.), *The politics of sport: Community, mobility, identity* (pp. 25–42). London: Routledge.
Gilchrist, P, & Ravenscroft, N. (2013). Space hijacking and the anarcho-politics of leisure. *Leisure Studies*, *32*(1), 49-68. doi:10.1080/02614367.2012.680069
Graw, I. (2004). Fascination, subversion and dispossession in appropriation art. In D. Evans (Ed.), *Appropriation* (pp. 3–53). Cambridge, MA: MIT.
Hamilton, C., & Denniss, R. (2005). *Affluenza: When too much is never enough*. Sydney: Allen & Unwin.
Hanna, P., Vanclay, F., Langdon, E. J. K., & Arts, J. (2016). Conceptualizing social protest and the significance of protest actions to large projects. *The Extractive Industries and Society*, *3*(1), 217–239.
Hayes, M., Sameshima, P., & Watson, F. (2014). Imagination as method. *International Journal of Qualitative Methods*, *14*(1), 36–52.
Heath, J., & Potter, A. (2006). *The rebel sell: How the counter culture became consumer culture*. Oxford: Capstone.
Huizinga, J. (1955). *HomoLudens, A study of the play element in culture*. Boston: Beacon.
Igrek, A. (2018). The Performative Space of Festival: From Bataille to Butler. *Space and Culture*, *21*(3), 247–258.
Jamieson, K. (2014). Tracing festival imaginaries: Between affective urban idioms and administrative assemblages. *International Journal of Cultural Studies*, *17*(3), 293–303.
Johansson, M., & Kociatkiewicz, J. (2011). City festivals: Creativity and control in staged urban experiences. *European Urban and Regional Studies*, *18*(4), 392–405.

Khan, O. (2015). Crowd choreographies. In J. Geiger (Ed.), *ENTR'ACTE: Performing publics, pervasive media and architecture.* (pp. 127-136). London: Palgrave Macmillan.
Küpers, W., Sonnenburg, S., & Zierold, M. (Eds.). (2017). *ReThinking management: Perspectives and impacts of cultural turns and beyond.* London: Springer.
Laing, J. (2018). Festival and event tourism research: Current and future perspectives. *Tourism Management Perspectives, 25,* 165–168.
Lamond, I. R., & Platt, L. (2016). Introduction. In I. R. Lamond & K. Spracklen (Eds.), *Critical event studies*(pp.1-14). London: Routledge.
Lefebvre, H. (2003). *The urban revolution.* Minneapolis: University of Minnesota Press.
McDonald, M. G. (2008). Rethinking resistance: The queer play of the Women's National Basketball Association, visibility politics and late capitalism. *Leisure Studies, 27*(1), 77–93.
McGuigan, J. (2006). The politics of cultural studies and cool capitalism. *Cultural Politics, 2*(2), 137–158.
Miller, T. (1993). *The well-tempered self, citizenship, culture and the postmodern subject.* London: Johns Hopkins University Press.
Nieland, J. (2008). *Feeling modern: The eccentricities of public life.* Illinois: University of Illinois Press.
Ossewaarde, M. (2012). The crowd in the occupy movement. *Distinktion: Scandinavian Journal of Social Theory, 14* (2), 134–150.
Pine, B. J., & Gilmore, J. H. (1998). Welcome to the experience economy. *Harvard Business Review, 76,* 97–105.
Pink, S. (2007). Sensing Cittàslow: Slow living and the constitution of the sensory city. *Senses and Society, 2*(1), 59–78.
Plant, S. (1992). *The most radical gesture, situationist international in a postmodern age.* London: Routledge.
Pringle, P. (2005). Spatial pleasures. *Space and Culture, 8*(2), 141–159.
Quinn, B. (2005). Arts festivals and the city. *Urban Studies, 42*(5), 927–943.
Ravenscroft, N., & Gilchrist, P. (2009). Spaces of transgression: Governance, discipline and reworking the carnivalesque. *Leisure Studies, 28*(1), 35–49.
Ravenscroft, N., & Matteucci, X. (2003). The festival as carnivalesque: social governance and control at Pamplona's San Fermin Fiesta. *Tourism, Culture and Communication, 4*(1), 1–15.
Raymen, T. (2019). *Parkour, deviance and leisure in the late-capitalist city: An ethnography.* Bingley: Emerald Publishing.
Reynolds, R. (2008). *Guerrilla gardening: A handbook for gardening without boundaries.* London: Bloomsbury.
Rojek, C. (1999). Deviant leisure: The dark side of free-time activity. In E. L. Jackson & T (Eds.). *Leisure studies: Prospects for the twenty-first century,* (pp. 81-96).
Rojek, C. (2012). Global event management: A critique. *Leisure studies.* In L. Burton (Ed.), *Leisure studies: Prospects for the twenty-first century* (pp. 32–47). London: Venture Press.
Ruti, M. (2011). Winnicott with Lacan: Living creatively in a postmodern world. In L. Krishner (Ed.), *Between Winnicott and Lacan: A clinical engagement* (pp. 133–149). London: Routledge.
Sharpe, E. K. (2008). Festivals and social change: Intersections of pleasure and politics at a community music festival. *Leisure Sciences, 30*(3), 217–234.
St John, G. (2008). Protestival: Global days of action and carnivalized politics in the present. *Social Movement Studies, 7*(2), 167–190.
Swain, M., & Hall, D. (2007). Gender analysis in tourism: Personal and global dialectics. In I. Ateljevic, A. Pritchard, & N. Morgan (Eds.), *The critical turn in tourism studies* (pp. 91–104). London: Routledge.
Taylor, C. (2004). *Modern social imaginaries.* Durham: Duke University Press.
Taylor, L., & Whalley, B. (2019). 'Real change comes from below!': Walking and singing about places that matter; the formation of Commoners Choir. *Leisure Studies, 38*(1), 58–73.
Thibaud, J. P. (2011). The sensory fabric of urban ambiances. *The Senses and Society, 6*(2), 203–215.
Todd, L., Leask, A., & Ensor, J. (2017). Understanding primary stakeholders' multiple roles in hallmark event tourism management. *Tourism Management, 59,* 494–509.
Vaneigem, R. (2001). *The Revolution of Everyday Life.* Edinburgh: AK Press.
Warner, M. (2002). *Publics and Counterpublics.* Cambridge, MA.: Zone Books.
Watkins, & Bond. (2007). Ways of experiencing leisure. *Leisure Sciences, 29*(3), 287–307.
Williams, D. (2018). Happiness and freedom in direct action: Critical mass bike rides as ecstatic ritual, play, and temporary autonomous zones. *Leisure Studies, 37*(5), 589–602.
Winnicott, D. (1971). *Playing and reality.* London: Tavistock Publications.
Ziakas, V. (2019). Embracing the event portfolio paradigm in academic discourse and scholarship. *Journal of Policy Research in Tourism, Leisure and Events, 11*(sup1), s27–s33.

Event bidding and new media activism

David McGillivray, John Lauermann and Daniel Turner

ABSTRACT

In this article we draw upon three case studies of American cities bidding to host the Summer Olympic Games to explore the role media, particularly new media, plays in the formation of anti-bid protest movements. Using data gathered from in-depth interviews with leaders of several activist campaigns and a content analysis of related websites and social media accounts, the paper demonstrates the increasing role new media plays in enabling resistant movements to form and articulate messages oppositional to boosterist coverage of mega sport event bids. However, it also highlights the limits of such new media activism in terms of both reach and capacity to effect change in isolation. Rather, the paper demonstrates that new media activitsm is at its most potent when it links and interacts with other actors, including legacy media outlets. The paper therefore concludes by highlighting the need for connectivity to both legacy media and physical acts of resistance and protest in order to generate meaningful impact and generate change.

Introduction

In recent years, public concern over the role played by mega sport events (MSEs) in skewing urban development priorities (Broudehoux & Sanchez, 2015; Müller, 2015), violating human rights (Horne, 2018), and providing the environment for corruption and poor governance to flourish (Hover, Dijk, Breedveld, & van Eekeren, 2016) has increased. This concern has been accompanied by increased evidence of protest and dissent around bidding, planning and delivery processes for the Olympic Games and FIFA World Cup, in particular (Lauermann, 2015; Lauermann & Vogelpohl, 2017; McGillivray & Turner, 2017). Expressions of protest and dissent have gone together with the hosting of MSEs for decades, but these have primarily been concerned with the planning and delivery stages, as opposed to the bid phase itself. However, since the mid-late 2000s, there has been a growth in activist activity around the bid process for MSEs, which has led to a reduction in candidate cities bidding for the Olympic Games between 2022 and 2028 as well as the FIFA World Cup of 2026. The increased visibility of bid activism has coincided with the emergence of new media platforms which have been used successfully to garner support, mobilise opposition and amplify dissent to MSE bids.

In this paper, we draw upon three case studies surrounding bids from American cities for the Summer Olympic games and consider the importance of the media in MSE bid activism, reflecting on the role of 'legacy' media, historically, and the role (and limits) of new media in the professionalisation of opposition that now accompanies these mega spectacles. We also consider the extent to which bid protests interact with more conventional forms of opposition, making use of the urban landscape to express discontent. The paper is guided by a desire to question the role new media plays in protest movements surrounding peripatetic sporting mega-event bids and how such new media interacts with both legacy media and other forms of protest and activism. The paper demonstrates that new media activism plays an increasingly prominent role in the protest movements surrounding sporting mega-events. Increasingly, with each bid cycle, such activism plays a part earlier in the protest movement and has greater reach when employed. However, as the cases examined here also highlight, despite this amplified role and reach, such activism is most effective when integrated with both traditional legacy media and as part of a broader campaign of protest and resistance.

Legacy media, boosterism and bidding

Historically, the mainstream media has played an important role in making the case for a city or nation bidding to host one of the world's MSEs. The broadcast and print media worked closely with the civic boosters responsible for conceiving of the bids to get the message out early, with good news stories focused on the economic benefits of city X hosting the Olympic Games or FIFA World Cup. Walmsley (2008) has suggested that bid committees understand that influencing media coverage is arguably the most effective way to influence public opinion on the value of a bid. Furthermore, Waitt (2001) has suggested that the media played a significant role in the 'propaganda exercise' of the Sydney 2000 Olympic Games bid, seeking to imbue social consensus through the vehicle of spectacle. He highlighted how the promotional campaign accompanying the bid resembled a product launch, backed by mainstream media 'partners'. Lenskyj (2010, 2012), a long-term critic of what she calls the 'Olympic Industry', has also highlighted how the 'terms of the debate' are framed by Olympic boosters and their media partners, leaving those most affected by the proposed bid invisible and powerless. She holds the mainstream media culpable for signing up to support bids, creating friction between two roles:

> as objective reporters of the Olympic Games and as participants in 'Olympic Spirit' promotional events. Similar conflicts existed when major television networks, newspapers and sport magazines paid millions of dollars for the honour of calling themselves Olympic suppliers, donors, sponsors and/or rights holders (Lenskyj, 2010, p. 376).

In signing up to 'back the bid', mainstream media partners have compromised their ability to represent the views of dissenting voices, including activists, human rights defenders, community representatives and critical elected representatives (Shaw, 2008). Securing the rights to exclusive coverage of the MSE itself has led some mainstream media organisations to prioritise potential circulation or viewership increases over scrutiny of bid promotional claims. In a limited-option media environment, securing the support of a national or regional broadcaster or high circulation newspaper provided bid committees with a powerful mechanism to frame the narrative, emphasising opportunities over threats and creating, as McGillivray and Turner (2017) highlight, a near hegemonic narrative that the bid in question is a 'good thing' As Pavoni (2015) has suggested, civic boosters require event-generation to arouse interest in the host locale for having an event, but they also need event-neutralisation to avoid reputationally-damaging expressions of opposition and protest. Managing the message through partnerships with the mainstream media certainly provides an easy route to event generation, represented in the now ubiquitous 'Back the Bid' campaigns. Having media partners contribute to event generation also acts as a neutralising force as fewer column inches, or broadcast minutes are given over to dissenting voices, in what McGillivray and Turner (2017) call a 'denial of discursive space'.

One of the noticeable outcomes of the mainstream media denying discursive space to oppositional interests is that their impact has been limited, in respect of their ability to prevent MSE bids from going ahead. The diverse tapestry of interest groups, including those representing women's rights, anti-poverty movements, disability rights and housing and civil liberties protections has sought to contest MSE bid narratives but with limited success. Watchdogs and anti-Olympics committees have been in existence since at least the 1968 Olympic Games in Mexico, though they have tended to be formed once the bid is won, impacting on their ability to bring about much change. As Shaw (2008) suggests with reference to the unsuccessful No Vancouver 2010 movement, once the bid is successful the space for meaningful opposition is much more constrained. The mainstream media has, at times, provided a space where oppositional voices have been heard in event bidding campaigns – but the time and resources given over to dissenting voices has, historically, been much less.

There are at least two principal reasons why the relationship between oppositional movements and the mainstream media has been unsuccessful. The first relates to the quantity of coverage and the second to the timing of protest movements. In terms of quantity of coverage, in a pre-internet and social media age, there were simply fewer platforms available for oppositional movements to get their message out to a wider public. Control of the news agenda predominantly lay with broadcasters and the print media, who were courted by prospective bid committees from the inception phase. In terms of the temporal dimension, oppositional movements were often simply too late to (oppose) the party, often because those pro-growth coalitions initiating bids developed their thinking and garnered support from business and government away from the public glare. The significant work in establishing a bid committee prior to a mediatised launch and formal statement of the intent to bid itself creates a momentum which then becomes difficult to stop through subsequent protest. This is one of the reasons that Boykoff (2014) calls for oppositional groups to transition from a 'moment of movements' (often post-bid) to a 'movement of movements', where the politics come earlier – at the bid stage – if MSEs boosters are to be effectively held to account for their plans. In the case of the bid process for the 2024 Olympic Games, in particular, it appears that the idea of the politics coming earlier was evident, aided by the emergence of new media platforms that alter the power relations between bid promoter and potential audience. It is to this new trend that the paper now turns.

Changing the modus operandi: locally rooted, globally mediated

Despite the conditions for public protest around MSEs being constrained, historically, since 2008 there has been a noticeable increase in both the number of oppositional campaigns in operation and, crucially, their modus operandi. Additionally, there is both a global and local element to these intimations of opposition that require further consideration. At the macro/global level, the legitimacy of MSEs (the Olympics and the World Cup, in particular) in achieving positive political, economic, social, cultural and environmental impacts has been subject to intense critique, since the 2008 Summer Games were awarded to Beijing (Boykoff, 2014; Coaffee, 2015; Raco, 2014). Central to this trend is a growing body of evidence, in academic, policy and activist/independent media circles, of the adverse effects generated by MSEs for a variety of, often vulnerable, publics (see, for example, O'Bonsawin, 2010).

Of principal concern to those people who oppose event bids is the false premise on which support is secured, the under-estimated costs and over-estimated benefits referred to by Whitson and Horne (2006). Prospective event hosts submit a bid book detailing the outcomes the sanctioning body can expect should they be successful in their application to host. Many commentators have likened the bid book for MSEs, in particular, to be a work of fiction (Müller, 2015), a glossy prospective for what a host might wish to do to transform its urban fabric and economic ambitions. And yet, back the bid campaigns invariably set out to secure public support without providing full information to those who will bear the brunt of the associated costs.

In recent years there has also been a change in the way opposition, dissent or protest towards event bids has been organised and mobilised, which is having some potentially significant impacts on the bidding process itself (what awarding bodies require) and on the practices of prospective host bidding teams, thereafter. No longer is it possible for a potential host (in the advanced liberal democracies, at least) to attract powerful influencers externally with promises of extravagant spectacles without having to account for this investment to an increasingly sceptical, and social media savvy, public.

One important change is in the emergence of what we call a 'new media activism' in relation to MSE bids, seeking to extend the reach and effects of protest or oppositional movements. In terms of reach, the barriers to entry are much lower for campaigners in a new social media-oriented environment than in its legacy media counterpart. While Shaw (2008) bemoaned the power of the Olympic frame to prevent opponents from securing airtime on mainstream media outlets during the Vancouver 2010 bid process, the availability of new media platforms including Facebook and Twitter now provide near barrier-free access to audiences, unimpeded by strict editorial guidelines, political and commercial interests. That said, social media does not sit in a vacuum, separated from its 'mainstream' rival. Rather, broadcast, print and online media outlets and are now deeply entangled with social media, informing and influencing the agenda from within. Bid media partners still, in theory, dilute the effects of new media activism through integrated multi-platform campaigns.

In terms of effects, the influence of new media activism on MSE bid processes stems from several shifts evident in recent years. On the one hand, as legacy media (especially local newspapers) lose market share, MSE boosters have lost what was historically an important bullhorn. On the other hand, new media fosters new kinds of journalistic relationships which activists can exploit, as detailed in the forthcoming case study of Boston. The involvement of non-traditional media outlets like Around the Rings (ATR), GamesBid.com, Games Monitor, and the Counter Olympics Network also contributes to a growing body of critical commentary on bid campaigns that finds its way to mainstream media outlets.

Moreover, the increasing presence of bodies with an interest in human rights and related issues, including Amnesty International, Human Rights Watch, the Centre for Sport and Human Rights, and Transparency International further strengthens the case of oppositional movements and activists in effecting change around the bid process. These actors now frequently combine to draw attention to potential human rights abuses in prospective bid cities or nations and lobby governments, awarding bodies and others to hold bidders to account. Crucially, they have become increasingly effective at media monitoring and applying pressure through concentrated campaigning strategies. Though the influence of these campaigns is difficult to assess, there is already some evidence that the main MSE actors are being forced to adapt their policies and practices because of the pressure exerted by advocacy organisations using a blend of legacy and new media platforms. Part of the bid process for the 2026 World Cup was a requirement to bid nations to include a human rights policy and provide governmental contractual guarantees akin to those related to financial matters. Advocacy organisations have also successfully lobbied FIFA to produce a policy that strengthens the protection of human rights defenders in host nations for the World Cup.

Case study: US new media bid activism

In the remainder of this paper, we assess the growing role of new media activism by analysing the recent history of anti-Olympic activism in the United States. The US has a long Olympic bidding history. Since 1901, American cities have bid on Summer or Winter Games 57 times (and have hosted nine), making the US the most frequent bidder in the history of the modern Olympics. Not surprisingly, there is also a long history of anti-Olympic protest in American cities (Burbank, Heying, & Andranovich, 2000, Cottrell & Nelson, 2011). Lenskyj (2006), in an early piece on 'alternative media' highlights how since the turn of the millenium, such protests have engaged with the web as a tool for holding those in positions of power surrounding the Games to account. However, it is with the most recent American bids in Chicago (failed bid for the 2016 Games), Boston (cancelled bid for the 2024 Games), and Los Angeles (successful bid for the 2028 Games) that new media has played a significant role, making for an interesting case study. This recent activist history has included innovation in protest tactics, in which new media activism has supported new forms of coalition building and new types of relationships between media and civil society.

We analyse this recent history using six in-depth interviews with leaders from activist campaigns in Chicago (No Games Chicago), Boston (No Boston Olympics, No Boston 2024), and Los Angeles (NOlympics LA), asking these representatives questions about their organising and media engagement strategies. We also conducted a qualitative content analysis of websites and social media accounts associated with these same organisations to assess the principal messages and mobilising tactics employed. Specifically, these included the Chicago campaign's website (https://nogames.wordpress.com/), the Boston campaigns' Facebook and Twitter accounts (@NoBosOlympics, @No_Boston2024) and websites (https://www.nobostonolympics.org/; https://www.noboston2024.org/), and the Los Angeles campaign's Twitter account (@NOlympicsLA) and website (https://nolympicsla.com), and the Twitter accounts of 13 individual activists involved in the campaigns. We used these data to assess the role of new media in the professionalisation of opposition movements, focusing on how activists engaged with new and legacy media environments. We also analysed how these media practices facilitated coalition building with broader activist networks (both networks related to MSEs and to other urban political issues).

Chicago

The protests against Chicago's bid for the 2016 Olympics provide an early example of new media activism, occurring in the early years of social media before its political power had been fully demonstrated. Developed between 2007 and 2009, the Chicago bid was relatively conventional by American standards. The bidders proposed a $5.7 billion project involving a variety of new and renovated venues along the city's waterfront, primarily financed by private sector investors (Chicago 2016, 2008, vol. 1, pp. 117–121).[1] The bid promised to produce a number of general economic catalysts and to support sustainable development, in particular in low income neighbourhoods on the south side of the city.

The bid experienced political backlash, however, over the question of whether the mayor should sign the International Olympic Committee's (IOC) standard host city contract. The host city contract is a template document, updated during each bidding cycle, which requires cities to make legal and financial commitments during the bidding and hosting stages. Until recent reforms (International Olympic Committee [IOC], 2018), the mayors of bidding cities were required to pre-emptively sign the contract as a pre-requisite to enter the bidding competition. One of the most contentious clauses in the contract was a commitment by the city to cover future cost overruns – a commitment which will almost certainly be invoked, given that every single Olympics since 1960 has run over budget (Flyvbjerg, Stewart, & Budzier, 2016). Under pressure from activists and members of the city council, Chicago's mayor initially refused to sign the contract, offering instead to purchase an insurance policy against cost overruns. The IOC bluntly rejected that approach, with the organisation's president insisting that 'We have only one host city contract. There is no amendment to the host city contract whatsoever from the IOC.' (Jacques Rogge quoted in Heinzmann & Blake, 2009). The mayor eventually gave in to IOC demands and signed the standard contract, but Chicago's bid ultimately failed in the very first round of IOC voting. This, coupled with significant local concerns regarding the general lack of transparency and opportunity for public participation surrounding the bid (see Mowatt & Travis, 2015), led to the emergence of a sustained protest movement.

The political backlash was inspired in part by a protest organisation called No Games Chicago. In the early years of the bid (2007 and 2008), several small-scale protest campaigns emerged surrounding isolated issues, for instance a neighbourhood campaign to protest impacts against Lincoln Park on the city's north side. These various protests later converged into a more coordinated No Games Chicago campaign, which ultimately asserted itself through a variety of activities up until the failure of the bid in October 2009. The protests encompassed a disparate range of themes, the most prominent of which was concern over municipal spending in the midst of the Great Recession. The anti-Olympic protest was closely linked to a critique of Chicago's uniquely authoritarian brand of municipal politics. The city's mayor at the time – Richard Daley Jr. – inherited control of Chicago's Democratic Party machine from his father, the legendary Richard Daley Sr. These two long-serving mayors consolidated significant urban regime power through 'the Daley machine' (Simpson & Kelly, 2008), creating a tight-knit coalition of civic boosters including much of the city's legacy media. That mayoral coalition strongly backed the bid.

No Games Chicago was able to gain ground in legacy media because they filled a niche within Chicago's political media. After a few months of organising events which received minimal media attention, they abruptly became legacy media's default source for critical commentary, because so few others were willing to challenge the mayor. As one No Games Chicago organiser explained, the bid received broad support from the city's boosters, including from legacy media:

> So originally the whole city is for the bid, all the newspapers were backing it, the media outlets. And it turns out that quite a few media outlets gave money and donated services to the bid, including CBS, Chicago Magazine, ABC and NBC, you know. The Chicago Tribune is owned at the time by a billionaire named Sam Zell, who was listed in the [bid's donor list] at the $100,000 minimum level. So the owner of the Chicago Tribune was giving who knows how much money to the bid . . . The media buckles down and everyone becomes a booster for the bid and it was very common and therefore the opposition – the voice of opposition – has very little space.

However, that monopoly of pro-Olympic voices in legacy media helped to amplify the voices of a relatively small protest campaign, as described in one anecdote from a No Games Chicago organiser:

> We managed to shoe-horn into the media and started putting cracks in the armour. And the more we did it, the more people would come to us [for interviews]. The third time a local television station drove to my house to do a pickup for me in front of my home, I asked the reporter 'Look, I'm flattered that you're seeking us out and you're listening to No Games Chicago, but isn't there anyone else you can go to?' And she said 'No, no there isn't.' I said 'Well why is that?' She looked and me and said 'Well, because the mayor has everyone terrified'. I said, 'Isn't that a story you'd like to cover?' She looked at me, she says, 'Are you kidding me? I want to keep my job.'

The activists thus received a much broader platform than their numbers would have otherwise supported. They did this with relatively little use of new media. They published a blog and maintained a Facebook group, but were not particularly active on social media (which is perhaps unsurprising given the early state of social media platforms at the time).

Instead, No Games Chicago activists used more traditional methods gleaning media attention, by protesting at public events and organising publicity stunts (see Mowatt & Travis, 2015), following an approach similar to that identified by Gerbaudo (2012, p. 5) which understands: 'the crucial element in understanding the role of social media in contemporary social movements is their interaction with and mediation of emerging forms of public gatherings and in particular the mass sit-ins which have become the hallmark of contemporary popular movements'

Two examples of this stand out. The first was a response to a bid initiative called '50 wards in 50 days'. This was a public relations campaign in which the bidders organised a public meeting in each of the city's neighbourhood wards. No Games Chicago sent protestors to each event and made themselves available to any reporters who happened to be in attendance. Their strategy was a simple one – to insert anti-Olympic talking points into the conversation through the public comment session:

> We were able to be at all those meetings and actually help. We had facts, we had people there, supporters who were able to help push the anti-Olympic agenda . . . And they [the bid organisers] ended up hating us so much. We were a real thorn in their side.

A second example was a publicity stunt in which a group of protesters travelled to IOC headquarters in Switzerland and held a press conference while bid officials were meeting with the organisation. In June 2009, three activists used donated airline miles to fly to Switzerland. They printed copies of a 'book of evidence' composed of newspaper clippings and other research, and arrived at the IOC's front gate requesting to distribute the books to IOC members in an effort to dissuade interest in Chicago. As one of the protest participants explained, the spectacle sparked the curiosity of journalists who were already at the location covering the event:

> And nationally it was a sensation. Nothing like this had ever happened before and we spent the next seven hours doing immediate follow up – updating websites, Facebook, answering questions, doing interviews from all over the world *except* Chicago. [original emphasis from the interview]

The Chicago press corps covering the event was less amused, and the activist described being avoided by annoyed Chicago reporters covering the event:

> We had one radio interview with public radio here in Chicago, but we were pretty much blacked out. We were asked to comment by the reporter for the [Chicago] Tribune and the [Chicago] Sun Times, but honestly, when we'd get into a story, it would be like two sentences. I guess it's better than nothing, but I mean, we could never believe there was never any profile on us. If the story had the Olympic bid with 10 paragraphs and we had a sentence in there, that would be a victory for us.

These media strategies continued until the bid failed in October 2009, with Bennett, Bennett, Alexander, and Persky (2013, p. 374) ascribing part of this failure directly to 'the lack of broad support among rank-and-file Chicagoans for the Olympic bid'. After that, however, the activists intentionally disbanded. One of the No Games Chicago founders explained that the campaign was built on an ideologically diverse coalition of activists. They were able to maintain cohesion while focusing on the bid, but once the bid failed the group's raison d'être dissipated. A handful of activists remained loosely engaged in anti-Olympic politics, travelling to Vancouver and Rio de Janeiro to speak at protest events. They have also communicated periodically (in person and online) with activists protesting bids in other cities, but they mostly avoided joining in broader international networks.

Boston

The protests against Boston's bid for the 2024 Olympics offer an example of what is arguably a successful application of new media activism. Developed between 2013 and 2015, the Boston bid aimed to leverage the Olympics to manage the city's historically exceptional growth. The bidders proposed a $8.6 billion project involving a variety of temporary and permanent venues, primarily financed through public-private partnerships (Boston 2024 Partnership, 2015, vol. 6). The bid promised to alleviate some of the pressure on the city's existing residential and commercial real estate markets, by building commercial and residential projects in relatively disadvantaged neighbourhoods on the south side of the city. The bid was also intentionally linked to broader planning initiatives, and was promoted as a rough draft for the city's 2030 master plan.

As in Chicago, the bid experienced political backlash over the question of whether the mayor should sign the IOC's standard host city contract, thereby committing the city to cover cost overruns. In a post-Recession climate of fiscal austerity, the question of public subsidies was a politically toxic one. In an effort to preclude criticism, the bidders repeatedly promised that no public funds would be used to support operational or capital budgets (Kassens-Noor & Lauermann, 2018). This was questionable rhetoric from the start, because the bid plan assumed free or low cost acquisition of public land in inner city Boston (worth tens of billions of dollars if privatised) and relied on $14.6 billion of public transit investments – investments which were approved through separate legislation shortly before the bid (Boston 2024 Partnership, 2015, vol. 6). The public subsidies debate became especially heated when officials from the US Olympic Committee pressured the mayor to sign the host city contract; again, this was a necessary step before the IOC would consider the city's bid. As in Chicago, the mayor sought to avoid signing the contract by instead offering to purchase an insurance policy against future cost overruns. And just as in Chicago, Olympic officials flatly rejected the offer, providing the mayor with an ultimatum to sign the standard contract or cancel the bid. The mayor chose the latter option, withdrawing municipal support – and effectively killing the bid – in August 2015.

The political backlash was coordinated by two protest organisations called No Boston Olympics and No Boston 2024. In the early stages of the bid (2014), No Boston Olympics began organising a handful of activists – many of whom were not previously politically active. The group began to attract public attention when more than a hundred people turned out for its first public meeting in

January 2015. No Boston 2024 emerged in parallel over the early months of 2015, assembling a larger coalition of activists who were already engaged in local social movements pertaining to issues like gentrification and homelessness. The two groups loosely coordinated, though No Boston Olympics presented itself as a coalition of centrist 'establishment' figures while No Boston 2024 adopted a more confrontational and explicitly leftist position. The protests focused on three issues: the potential for cost overruns (and the city's fiscal exposure through the IOC host city contract), a lack of transparency in bid planning, and concerns about the opportunity costs of hosting.

The anti-Olympic campaign relied heavily on new media activism. This stemmed partly from necessity: the city's legacy media – in particular the *Boston Globe* newspaper – were firm supporters of the bid, at least in the beginning. But new media also provided the protesters with a strategic advantage, in the sense that they were better able to respond quickly to events in the news and to generate online outrage. This provided a stark contrast to the public relations team in the bid corporation, which was significantly less nimble when engaging on social media. As one No Boston 2024 organiser put it,

> One thing that helped is social media, which we always used a lot. And it was always interesting to see because Boston 2024 was very bad at it! An example I often like to cite is when they accidentally told people to get inspired by Nazis [by tweeting about the 1936 Olympics]. That was very easy to mock and we were hounding them for the whole afternoon. I think it was something like eight hours afterwards that [a Boston Globe journalist] ended up noticing. And when journalists – actual journalists – noticed, Boston 2024 took it down.

In fact, social media was so central to the anti-Olympic protests that the mayor derisively referred to the protestors as 'ten people on Twitter' (Clauss, 2015), a small but loud cohort of keyboard activists accused of hijacking public debate through the sheer volume of their social media posts. Not surprisingly, a satirical #TenPeopleOnTwitter social media campaign emerged in response. Years later, a number of anti-Olympic activists still reference the hashtag in their social media profiles, and occasionally tweet with it to mock the mayor's office on the anniversary of the bid's cancellation (and in reference to other non-Olympic failures and scandals at City Hall).

Beyond satire, the protesters employed two more serious – and arguably more impactful – forms of new media activism. The first was muckraking: sending out a flurry of FoIA requests for correspondence by public officials related to the bid, forwarding leads to a small group of legacy media journalists, and promoting those journalists' stories on social media when a scandal broke. By providing informal background research for journalists already known to be writing critically about the bid, activists were able to expand the range of critical topics covered in legacy media. One activist explained that his FoIA requests were much broader than that of a typical journalist, for this very reason:

> It's just such a useful strategy, because there's only so much that journalists are going to do. Part of that is because you don't want to use public records across your journalism [when] you can just ask a question. And then part of that is – if you're a journalist and submitting a request – there's normally knowledge of a specific document that you know about. Only one of my requests is targeted at something that I believe exists. Everything else is "I don't know what's there." I don't know what I don't know and that's what I want to find out.

The second form of new media activism was live-tweeting public hearings on the bid. City and bid corporation officials held a number of public hearings in neighbourhoods that would be impacted by the Olympics. The meetings generally followed a standard formula: the meeting would be introduced by a sympathetic local official or celebrity, bid staffers would present the same PowerPoint presentation at each hearing, and then they would answer questions from the general public. Activists discovered a way to commandeer these otherwise staid events, transforming them into virtual and in-person spectacles. Virtually, the activists live-tweeted the events, posting hundreds of tweets per hour while hashtagging topics of local concern and tweeting at journalists in local and national media. In person, activists would place themselves in the queue for the public microphone, asking questions that diverted the hearings towards topics related to anti-Olympic talking points. As one frequent participant in these meeting protests explained, the strategy allowed activists to recruit likeminded citizens from the general public:

> It's also a way of engaging with other people who were at the meetings, as well as dispelling things in real time. It was useful because you can keep records of those comments and then share with people who want to know but weren't there. You also get things trending at times.

Just as importantly, online commentary on real-world hearings was a way to shape media coverage on those events:

> Influencing media coverage is one thing that social media helps to do. We have some connections [to journalists], but social media is one thing that really helps to do that. It helps you actually shape what the press is seeing by being at the community meetings. We never expected the mayor or Boston 2024 to change, but you can make them look bad to the press.

These media strategies continued until the bid was cancelled in August 2015. After that, the activists continued to engage with anti-Olympic protests in other cities. One founder of No Boston Olympics collaborated with a local scholar to write a book on anti-Olympic politics (Dempsey & Zimbalist, 2017). Others met informally with activists in other bidding and hosting cities, for example Hamburg and Rio de Janeiro. Some of the digital resources they created were passed on to other campaigns (e.g. a No Boston Olympics database of Olympic research). But as in Chicago, the national and international reach of the campaign is somewhat unclear.

Los Angeles

The protests against Los Angeles' plans for the 2028 Olympics provide an example of a campaign that did not fully form until after the city won its bid, but which has subsequently amplified to protest the planning process. After Boston cancelled its bid for the 2024 games in 2015, Los Angeles stepped in to become the American bidder. As other bidding cities dropped from the competition due to negative referendums or local protests, Paris and Los Angeles eventually emerged as the sole bidders for the 2024 games. Given the paucity of interest, in September 2017 the IOC made the unprecedented decision to award two Olympics in one bidding cycle: 2024 to Paris, and 2028 to Los Angeles.

Partly due to the complexity of the bidding cycle for the 2024 version, Boston's withdrawal, and successful promotion by city boosters of the Los Angeles 1984 Olympic Games as a commercial success, there was minimal organised protest before the hosting contract was awarded to LA in 2017. The anti-Olympic coalition, NOlympics LA, emerged out of discontent with the US Presidential cycle in 2016. The left and centre left, supporters of Bernie Sanders, felt disenfranchised by the Democratic party. Alongside discontent with the existing party political system, a new political and activist movement, the Democratic Socialists of America (DSA), grew in importance across the US. Tied to the DSA LA chapter, current members of the NOlympics LA coalition had been campaigning since 2014/15 about social issues including gentrification, wealth inequality, militarisation and endemic levels of homelessness in LA. The proposed Olympic bid, supported by the ambitious but controversial Democratic Mayor, Eric Garcetti, became a focal point for DSA activists, radicalising a broad coalition of housing and homelessness organisations, Black Lives Matters activists and other group concerned with racial justice. In early 2017 it became clear that a dual award for the next Olympics was likely and Paris was the favourite to get the 2024 version. As one NOlympics LA activist explained:

> it wasn't really a question that LA would get 2028 so we found ourselves in a very unique situation where we have 11 years to organise against this – which is different to most other places

However, the unique nature of the IOCs decision also meant that the coalition of DSA activists that became NOlympics LA was unable to stop the bid committee from being awarded the 2028 games. There was a recognition that a new organisation was required if the 11 year opportunity to halt the Olympics going ahead was to be a realistic proposition, though maintaining close links to the DSA. As the NOlympics LA coordinator explained:

> It branched out from the (DSA's) homeless and housing committee to be launched on 9 May 2017 – it became kind of its own thing, but still under the umbrella of DSA. We then started going round all these

> groups and officially getting them to sign on to our coalition and starting our press and social media awareness and presence and agitation, and all that stuff. Then we started doing actions in the summer of 2017, elevating our game.

Significantly, politically, NOlympics LA exploited its association with the national DSA movement, which differentiates it from other anti-Olympic organisations. It also recognises that it is part of a long-term political process that relies as much on power shifts within national and local politics as it does on the Olympic bid per se. In contrast to the other cases examined here, the Los Angeles protest therefore demonstrates greater coherence between protest in the spheres of new media, traditional local activism and a broader national movement. So, as the coordinator explains:

> Our approach was that we always thought it would be a several year process – a three to five year process to actually unseat and run out the bid, waiting for some other power shifts to happen. We don't have a lot of official political support though behind closed doors I think there's a lot of doubt and a power shift. Two of the 12 city council members who signed off on this are now out of the picture. And the math says that so many of these people are going to get termed-out and there's going to be an actual power shift dynamic happening in the next couple of years. And what separates us from other anti-Olympic movements is that we're part of a larger movement – we're part of a larger national organisation that consistently funnels new people to our organisation. There's no other anti-Olympic group that's trying to run politicians in three to five years – which is something our group is actively talking about.

In terms of key messages, and narratives, NOlympics LA has focused on reaching local elected officials who originally voted for the bid, despite there being no budget agreed. They believe that the failure to undertake meaningful polling or agree on a budget is the weak spot of the bid committee which can be targeted. As the coordinator explains:

> I'm surprised they signed off on it without a budget which I think ultimately might be the flaw that undoes this whole thing. Because as you know the issue of taxpayer guarantee moves the most people across the political spectrum no matter what city or decade we're talking about ... we've been doing a lot of research – power mapping research across DSA on our locally elected and people hoping to be locally elected and I think we can exert a lot of pressure and way more force on a council member than the Mayor who is a lot more buffered, with more handlers and with more money, so he's insulated.

NOlympics LA generated grassroots funding to undertake polling on LA citizen's attitudes towards the bid in late 2018 and utilised legacy and social media to communicate the results. Their objective was to generate credibility, change the conversation, cast doubt and capture the attention of mainstream media outlets. With only one newspaper, the LA Times, existing in LA, information about the Olympic bid and post-bid planning has been scarce. The bid committee has money, influence and establishment power which enables it to purchase broadcast TV and radio ads but NOlympics LA has been effective at using the strength of its coalition, access to a national organisation and an integrated media strategy to cast doubt on the claims of the bid committee. Their organising has taken physical and online forms, depending heavily on direct action and classical activist tactics, accompanied by creative digital and social media activity. One of the best examples of their direct action was in December 2018, when they ambushed Mayor Garcetti's address at UCLA on the 70th anniversary of the publication of the UN Declaration of Human Rights. As the coordinator explains:

> So we effectively shut his whole speech down in a way that had never happened before. I think that direct action gets the goods. Doing stuff in real life is still the most important thing. And it's the hardest thing to do in a culture and an economy where we're crushed by capital. The LA Times covered our action and bunch of other sites too. I think the press coverage was fair and people online were really excited about it.

Striking a balance between direct action, on the ground, and exploiting the affordances of new media online has been crucial to the activities of NOlympics LA, with the intention of being more nimble, versatile and responsive than the bid committee machine. This strategy was carefully crafted to generate as much attention as possible and be viewed as credible:

> we like to make sure we have a lot of balance to what we're doing. So we never have too much online just being snarky or attacking people, or just agitating. Or just making videos or podcasts. We also have a big teaching and screening series where we're physically in communities – because LA is so sprawled out and dispersed that it's red lined and segregated and it's sprawling and we're organising against that too.

In a similar vein to Boston, social media activity has been deployed to agitate, share information and, perhaps most crucially, garner the attention of other media outlets that can take their messages to new audiences, in and outside of LA. For example, after publishing their citizen poll in late 2018, they successfully generated coverage in New York Times, Deadspin and Sports Illustrated and some other big national media brands. This credibility is also associated with their expertise on the Olympics, transnationally, something the mainstream media struggles to replicate. As the coordinator explains:

> We also found out through that process (the poll) just how uninformed most journalists were – whether on the sport side or sport justice or even on the housing side – how unequipped were to talk about these things or compare these things or deal with these things with nuance and that's because newsrooms have been so drastically underfunded.

Finally, though unsuccessful at stopping the bid from going ahead, NOlympics LA has actively benefitted from collaboration with a broader international anti-Olympic movement and continues to inform other prospective bidders about effective strategies and tactics to contest bid committees. Early on in the process they talked to and visited campaigners in Boston, Tokyo and Paris. They have also participated in discussions about strengthening anti-Olympic solidarity, in person and online. As the coordinator explains:

> They [the Olympics] didn't plan for having a more threaded together, international, transnational movement and I think that's where this is headed and I hope we can put those pieces together. I think in the next year you'll see some more direct actions where we'll be in different parts of the world, shooting some films and doing different actions in addition to strategic meetings. You'll also find other groups covering these issues like Around the Rings, Gamesbids.com. We've even talked about the idea of a shared collective space where oppositional movements to the Olympics, internationally, might host their content, including past bid/host cities. The stories never really end.

In sum, NOlympics LA has a very clear, long term strategy to unsettle the bid committee, cast doubt on their claims and exploit a shift in local and national US politics to suspend LA's Olympic candidacy. Classic direct-action tactics, complemented with online agitation and information circulation, has produced some short-term success but it remains unclear as to whether this activity can be sustained and with what effect on the planning and delivery process itself.

Conclusion

In conclusion, the recent history of anti-Olympic protest in American cities demonstrates the growth – but also the limits – of new media activism for contesting MSEs. In Chicago, activists experimented with new media but largely focused their efforts on gaining a foothold in legacy media otherwise monopolised by Olympic boosters. In Boston, activists aggressively deployed new media to facilitate coalition building and develop mutually-beneficial relationships with the press. In Los Angeles, activists lost the bid but have since sought to use direct action, mediated via new media channels to undermine preparations for the 2028 Olympic Games, on the basis that fact checking, polling and information circulation will pressure city leaders to suspend their hosting plans. Across these recent cases, new media has allowed activists to circumvent the legacy media monopoly over public debate and Olympic boosters' monopoly over local legacy media. It has facilitated the growth of networks of protest and enabled otherwise marginal voices to combine and amplify, countering the boosterist legacy media coverage of bids. However, the case studies above also demonstrate that there are significant limits to the political influence of new media activism. On its own, keyboard activism may generate significant noise but does not necessarily change policy. Instead, it is clear from this analysis, that new media activism is more likely to be successful when combined with a broader urban politics, embedded within existing political parties or social movements, and speaking to broader urban debates (over housing, gentrification, fiscal responsibility, etc.). Similarly, it is most likely to succeed when aligned to more traditional, albeit critical, media outlets which can provide a wider mainstream audience and legitimacy for its critical discourse.

Note

1. All financial figures in the text are inflation adjusted to 2018 USD.

Disclosure statement

No potential conflict of interest was reported by the authors.

ORCID

John Lauermann http://orcid.org/0000-0001-9114-3864

References

Bennett, L., Bennett, M., Alexander, S., & Persky, J. (2013). The political and civic implications of Chicago's unsuccessful bid to host the 2016 Olympic Games. *Journal of Sport and Social Issues*, *37*(4), 364–383.

Boston 2024 Partnership (2015). *Boston 2024 bid to the US Olympic Committee*. Boston, MA: Boston 2024.

Boykoff, J. (2014). *Activism and the Olympics: Dissent at the Games in Vancouver and London*. New Brunswick, NJ: Rutgers University Press.

Broudehoux, A.-M., & Sanchez, F. (2015). The politics of mega event planning in Rio de Janeiro: Contesting the Olympic city of exception. In V. Viehoff & G. Poynter (Eds.), *Mega event cities: Urban legacies of global sport events* (pp. 109–123). London: Routledge.

Burbank, M. J., Heying, C. H., & Andranovich, G. (2000). Antigrowth politics or piecemeal resistance? Citizen opposition to Olympic-related economic growth. *Urban Affairs Review*, *35*(3), 334–357.

Chicago 2016. (2008). *Chicago 2016 candidature city*. Chicago: Author.

Clauss, K. (2015, July 27). Mayor Walsh: Boston 2024 opposition is 'ten people on Twitter'. *Boston Magazine*. Retrieved from www.bostonmagazine.com/

Coaffee, J. (2015). The uneven geographies of the Olympic carceral: From exceptionalism to normalisation. *The Geographical Journal*, *181*(3), 199–211.

Cottrell, M. P., & Nelson, T. (2011). Not just the Games? Power, protest and politics at the Olympics. *European Journal of International Relations*, *17*(4), 729–753.

Dempsey, C., & Zimbalist, A. (2017). *No Boston Olympics: How and why smart cities Are passing on the torch.* Lebanon NH, University Press of New England.

Flyvbjerg, B., Stewart, A., & Budzier, A. (2016). The Oxford Olympics Study 2016: Cost and cost overrun at the games. *Said Business School Working Papers.* University of Oxford.

Gerbaudo, P. (2012). *Tweets and the Streets.* London: Pluto Press.

Heinzmann, D., & Blake, D. (2009, June 28). Daley's verbal gymnastics. *Chicago Tribune.* Retrieved from www.chicagotribune.com/

Horne, J. (2018). Understanding the denial of abuses of human rights connected to sports mega-events. *Leisure Studies, 37*(1), 11–21.

Hover, P., Dijk, B., Breedveld, K., & van Eekeren, F. (2016, January). *Integrity and sport events.* The Netherlands: Muller Institute.

International Olympic Committee. (2018, February). *Olympic Games: the New Norm – Report by the Executive Steering Committee for Olympic Games Delivery.* Retrieved from www.olympic.org/

Kassens-Noor, E., & Lauermann, J. (2018). Mechanisms of policy failure: Boston's 2024 Olympic bid. *Urban Studies, 55*(15), 3369–3384.

Lauermann, J. (2015). Boston's Olympic bid and the evolving urban politics of event-led development. *Urban Geographies, 37*(2), 313–321.

Lauermann, J., & Vogelpohl, A. (2017). Fragile growth coalitions or powerful contestations? Cancelled Olympic bids in Boston and Hamburg. *Environment and Planning A, 49*(8), 1887–1904.

Lenskyj, H. (2010). Olympic impacts on bid and host cities. In V. Girginov (Ed.), *The Olympics: A critical reader*, pp. 373-386. London: Routledge.

Lenskyj, H. (2012). *Best Olympics Ever? The social impacts of Sydney 2000.* New York: Suny Press.

Lenskyj, H. J. (2006). Alternative media versus the Olympic Industry. In *Handbook of sports and media,* (pp. 205–216). New York: Routledge.

McGillivray, D., & Turner, D. (2017). *Event bidding: Politics, persuasion and resistance.* London: Routledge.

Mowatt, R. A., & Travis, J. (2015). Public participation, action, and failure: A case study of the 2016 Olympic bid. *Loisir et Société/Society and Leisure, 38*(2), 249–267.

Müller, M. (2015). The mega-event syndrome: Why so much goes wrong in mega-event planning and what to do about it. *Journal of the American Planning Association, 81*(1), 6–17.

O'Bonsawin, C. M. (2010). 'No Olympics on stolen native land': Contesting Olympic narratives and asserting indigenous rights within the discourse of the 2010 Vancouver Games. *Sport in Society, 13*(1), 143–156.

Pavoni, A. (2015). Resistant legacies. *Annals of Leisure Research, 18*(4), 470–490.

Raco, M. (2014). Delivering flagship projects in an era of regulatory capitalism: State-led privatization and the London Olympics 2012. *International Journal of Urban and Regional Research, 38*(1), 176–197.

Shaw, C. A. (2008). *Five rings circus: Myths and realities of the Olympic Games.* British Colombia, Canada: New Society Publishers.

Simpson, D., & Kelly, T. M. (2008). The new Chicago School of urbanism and the new Daley machine. *Urban Affairs Review, 44*(2), 218–238.

Waitt, G. (2001). The Olympic Spirit and civic boosterism: The Sydney 2000 Olympics. *Tourism Geographies, 3*(3), 249–278.

Walmsley, D. (2008). *Sport event bidding: A strategic guide for bidders and sports property owners.* London: Sport Business Group Limited.

Whitson, D., & Horne, J. (2006). The glocal politics of sports mega events: Underestimated costs and overestimated benefits? Comparing the outcomes of mega sport events in Canada and Japan. *The Sociological Review, 54* (Supplement s2), 71–89.

Experiences of urban cycling: emotional geographies of people and place

Rudy Dunlap, Jeff Rose, Sarah H. Standridge and Courtney L. Pruitt

ABSTRACT

This study explores the experiences and associated contexts of individuals who use a bicycle as their primary means of transportation in a metropolitan city in the United States. Using a qualitative approach, researchers employed semi-structured interviews to explore participants' narratives related to adopting cycling as a means of moving through the urban landscape and as a leisure experience. Findings revealed an evolutionary process whereby participants tested out, experimented with, and sustained various practices of riding a bike in the city. Whereas participants began cycling for a variety of practical, outcome-oriented economic, health, or environmental reasons, the practice was sustained by its often unexpected experiential benefits. When compared to automobile use, urban cycling was also found to foster an enhanced connection to place and a comparitive sense of control and autonomy. Participants articulated pragmatic, physical, restorative, and emotional rationales for initiating and maintaining urban cycling practices. Analyses are developed through emotional geographies that intimately and relationally connect people and place. The study's findings highlight the presence of a political, economic, and spatial regime of auto-centricism against which participants must struggle.

Seen against the backdrop of rush hour gridlock, the urban cyclist is a remarkable phenomenon. Despite a steady increase in the number of individuals commuting by bicycle in urban settings, such riders represent a tiny fraction of the daily trips taken in the United States (McLeod, 2017). Given its exceptionalism, the decision to use bicycles for mobility within the urban landscape is worthy of investigation, even more so as humans have shifted to be an urban dwelling species (Vargo, 2014). As societies have urbanised, the bicycle has occasionally been lauded as an important remedy to the ills of urban life, including gridlock and air pollution, in addition to obesity and physical inactivity (Benjamin, 2010). Untold millions have been spent to coax commuters out of their automobiles and onto their bicycles by renovating transportation infrastructure and educating and encouraging commuters via media campaigns (Transportation Alternatives Data Exchange, 2018). Cycling advocates regularly point to cities such as Portland, Oregon, in the United States and Copenhagen, Denmark, that have made dramatic transformations into 'bike friendly' cities, and in turn have seen their share of trips by bicycle rise to unprecedented levels (Initiative for Bicycle & Pedestrian Innovation, n.d.; Kristensen, 2016). Such cities serve as lauded benchmarks, but hardly represent the state of affairs in most urban centres in North America or around the world. When considered from the standpoint of a cyclist, most urban environments are indifferent, if not hostile, to urban cyclists (League of American Bicyclists, 2018). Despite such antipathy, urban biking has experienced the largest share increase among all transportation modes, rising by 40% between 2000–2014 (Gilderbloom et al., 2016). Such a paradox begs the question, why would anyone take up an activity that, percentage-wise, kills more people annually than driving an automobile (National Highway Traffic Safety Administration, 2017; Pedestrian and Bicycle Information Center, n.d.)? In our view, such a means-end question can hardly be addressed without taking seriously the lived experiences and interpretive processes of individual cyclists. More pointedly, this research sought to contextualise urban cyclists' lived experiences through the emotional and affectual engagement with the very processes that not only functionally move them through the urban landscape, but that speak to their expressions of identity and purpose.

Bicycle riding has been examined variously as a recreational activity that improves health (Kaczynski & Henderson, 2007), a context for serious leisure participation (McCarville, 2007), a source of conflict in outdoor recreation settings (Ramthun, 1994), a behaviour through which individuals might foster place attachment (Moore & Graefe, 1994), and as an activity characterised by specialisation and progression (Shafer & Scott, 2013). Notably, this previous research on cycling has tended to either, 1) treat it as an independent variable in service of an outcome measurement (e.g. time spent in physical activity) or 2) as a context for the elaboration of an existing theoretical framework (e.g. serious leisure). While such approaches have valuable applications, notably absent from the modest scholarship on urban bicycle riding in leisure studies is any thorough attempt to explore the emic perspective of individual cyclists. Thus, the purpose of this study is to describe and inductively analyse the lived experiences and associated contexts of individuals who regularly cycle in urban environments. We then characterise and analyse these experiences through a framework of emotional geographies, which emphasises the affective connections to spaces, places, landscapes, and experiences (Bondi, Davidson, & Smith, 2005; Davidson & Milligan, 2004). A framework of emotional geographies helps not only characterise relational aspects of people and places through a particular activity (cycling), but also helps analyse cyclists experiential ways of knowing the world.

In service of this purpose, we have explored and unpacked the processual, emotional, and affectual experiences of 16 individuals who regularly ride a bicycle to work, school, and/or other daily activities in Nashville, Tennessee, a growing metropolitan city in the southeastern United States. Our focus on *urban* cyclists derives from the fact that regular bicycling is more likely to occur in dense urban areas (National Highway Traffic Safety Administration, 2017), but also because cycling in most American cities is implicitly and often explicitly discouraged by automobile-centric urban design and management (Duany, Plater-Zyberk, & Speck, 2000), in addition to the accompanying physical dangers associated with riding in such environments (Pedestrian and Bicycle Information Center, n.d.). As such, these cyclists' choices 'against the norm' entail a degree of effort and deliberateness that potentially offers much insight into the meaning making processes of individuals and the urban contexts, in addition to the emotional geographies that characterise their mobilities within these contexts.

Nashville's indifference to the bicycle

Nashville, Tennessee's history typifies the brief popularity and then rapid decline of cycling as a form of urban transportation and leisure during the nineteenth and twentieth centuries. Officially chartered in 1784, Nashville's population and footprint remained modest until 1963 when the city and county merged (Buntin, 2018). Accentuated by post-WWII 'white flight', the consolidation created an expansion of Nashville's geographic footprint that accelerated the pace of its sprawling, auto-centric transportation infrastructure (Hale, 2018). Typical of most post-war infrastructure development, Nashville devoted resources to expanding its highway and interstate network (Hale, 2018), thereby hollowing out the downtown business district and destroying many of its adjacent 'streetcar neighborhoods' (Montgomery, 2013). Nashville's sprawled, autocentric development continued until the mayoral election of Phil Bredesen in 1991, who presented an prescient vision of downtown Nashville as both a residential neighbourhood and tourist attraction (Buntin, 2018).

Guided by his vision and two of Bredesen's successors, Nashville has transformed into an exemplar of economic growth (ibid). Predictably and ironically, Nashville's rapid in-migration has created commuting gridlock that the city's legacy of auto-centric development has been unable to accommodate (White, 2014). Successive mayoral administrations have pledged to make 'alternative transportation' a priority, and such efforts have resulted in a standing Bicycle Pedestrian Advisory Committee, a municipal Bike//Ped Coordinator, and more than 150 miles of bicycle lanes and 750 miles of sidwalks constructed (ibid). Despite these gains, safety and connectivity for cyclists continue to be challenges and the city's most recent assessment from the industry group Places for Bikes rated Nashville's infrastructure at 1.5 out 5.0 stars, citing poor connectivity, safety, and reach (Places for Bikes, n.d.). The group's ridership assessment (1.6/5.0) is most revealing in that it represents the likelihood of the average adult feeling comfortable enough to undertake a bike trip to address an activity of daily life in Nashville (e.g. work, school, grocery shopping; ibid).

In summary, Nashville's twentieth and twenty-first century growth has typified broader auto-centric patterns of development in the United States, the result being a thin veneer of bike lanes and 'sharrows' that provides limited connectivity and safety for would-be recreational riders and commuters. Despite this insufficiency, individuals such as our participants continue to take to the streets on two wheels, a phenomenon that begs investigation.

Leisure research on cycling

Within leisure literature, cycling, when examined at all, is overwhelming treated as a type of recreational activity that may be associated with certain desirable outcome variables and/or antecedent conditions that may be used for predictive purposes (e.g. Floyd, Spengler, Maddock, Gobster, & Suau, 2008; Kaczynski & Henderson, 2007). Alternatively, cycling has served as a context for exploring different theoretical constructs, ranging from the theory of planned behaviour (Ajzen & Driver, 1992) to serious leisure (McCarville, 2007) to affect control theory (Lee & Shafer, 2002).

As argued by Parry and Johnson (2007), among others, traditionally positivistic and deductive approaches to inquiry, though useful in their own ways, tend to forego any examination of daily life as a situated and interpretive experience. When attempting to make sense of urban cycling, this neglect of individuals' immediate experiences is troubling because life is not encountered as a series of theoretical constructs or operationalised variables. A few interpretive studies have involved cycling to some degree, though these efforts have been largely tangential to another purpose. These studies include explorations of leisure in an Amish community (Anderson & Autry, 2011), leisure practices among LDS stay-at-home mothers (Freeman, Palmer, & Baker, 2006), intergenerational families as contexts for adoption of leisure practices (Quarmby & Dagkas, 2010), and the gendered construction of risk and identity via mountain biking (Huybers Withers, 2015). Of these studies, Huybers Withers's (2015) exploration of mountain biking is most analogous to the current study. By focusing on the manner in which participants interpret, reproduce, and resist hegemonic norms within a localised mountain biking culture, Huybers Withers targets interpretive practices as the focal point of inquiry. This study also takes the immediate physical and social landscape into its analysis, as cyclists' mobilities throughout particular places is a defining characteristic of urban biking (Aldred & Jungnickel, 2013).

Cycling research in other fields

There is much to the experience of urban cycling that cannot (and arguably should not) be reduced to the functional personal, community, and/or environmental benefits; there are lived, experiential, and socioemotional components to urban biking as well (Fincham, 2006a; Spinney, 2011). The embodied corporeality (Eichler, 2017; Lee, 2016) of moving through the city cannot be adequately captured by analyses of benefits or mappings of geographic space. Fincham (2006a, 2006b, 2008)), uses the experiences of bicycle messengers to consider the roles of urban mobility and the physical and mental consequences associated with this increased freedom, including the likelihood of injury and death. For many people who use bicycles as part of their everyday professional existence, bicycling in the city has blurred a binary distinction between work and leisure (Fincham, 2008). Bike messengers and bicycle-based food deliverers (Lee et al., 2016) both demonstrate the ways in which non-automobile urban mobilities are an integral part of urban labour practices, where cyclists themselves are incorporated into urban economies. Bicycling in the city necessitates skill, freedom, movement, and risk, all of which present both opportunities and tradeoffs for urban cyclists (Fincham, 2006a, 2006b).

From a critical standpoint, urban biking as a process has historically and contemporarily *produced* city life in many urban settings (Spinney, 2016). Cycling through urban spaces is a social process for many (Freudendal-Pedersen, 2015; McIlvenny, 2014), and it is an activity and a way of life that extends social relations across aspects of the urban environment that are rarely conceived through a mobility lens. For many cyclists, moving through the city on a bike is a form of political resistance, as often demonstrated through movements like Critical Mass rides (Blickstein & Hanson, 2001; Morhayim, 2012), even as there is a lack of political and sociodemographic homogeneity within cyclists and cycling communities (e.g. Eichler, 2017). In this way, biking not only serves functional, everyday needs and has durable health and environmental benefits, but also has a political purpose in protesting the lack of investment allocated to alternative forms of transportation in the United States and elsewhere. These bicycle-based 'right to the city' movements both engage and critique the dominance of automobiles in driver-cyclist relationships (Eichler, 2017; Freudendal-Pedersen, 2015; Morhayim, 2012), further supporting more repeated and more defiant insurrections by cycling activists. Such performative protests through lifestyle choices are seen as a necessary response to an unjust system that eliminates or impugns freedom of urban mobility. Bicyclists, then, have been shown to have developed both social connections (McIlvenny, 2014) and communities of solidarity in fighting against existing and future automobile transportation and car-focused infrastructure (Morhayim, 2012). In this way, urban bicyclists form a type of counterhegemonic force in the fabric of the urban city, acting as a visibly subversive force, and creating new visions of the city. It should be noted that despite these efforts by cyclists to reclaim the city and its various non-automotive mobility infrastructures, these efforts are simultaneously governed and developed towards decidedly neoliberal outcomes, including the increased efficiency of circulation of labour (Spinney, 2016).

Methods and participants

With the aim of examining cycling as a situated experience of daily urban life, we employed a broadly interpretive approach to inquiry that relied on semi-structured interviews as the primary means of data generation.

We worked with sixteen participants, all of whom regularly used a bicycle as a mode of transportation to-and-from work, school, and/or other quotidian destinations of daily life, including grocery stores, coffee shops, doctors' offices, friends' houses, etc. Due to a variety of needs and constraints in accessing urban cycling communities, we recruited via a not-for-profit organisation, the mission of which is to advocate for alternatives to auto-centric development, including greater opportunities for walking and bicycling. Beyond posting to this organisation's social media accounts, we used snowball sampling to identify other potential participants. Our interviews were semi-structured, allowing for the exploration of emergent topics, and lasted between forty minutes and two hours. Interviews took place in a variety of locations (e.g. coffee shops, office courtyards, libraries) and asked participants to describe their 'cycling biography' chronologically and then proceeded to explore their current cycling practices and motives. The interviews were recorded and subsequently transcribed to assist in subsequent analyses.

Fourteen of our participants identified as men, two as women, all white, and ranged in age between the mid-twenties to the mid-sixties, demographics that align with many popular perceptions of urban bicyclists (Hoffman, 2016; Lugo, 2016). Every participant had received a bachelor's degree of some sort and many had successfully pursued graduate or professional degrees. They held a range of jobs from lawyer to artist to stay-at-home parent to musical instrument repair technician. Precise data on income levels was not collected, but participants' employment situations and motives for cycling suggested that they lived a relatively secure middle-class lifestyle. Only one of our sixteen participants suggested that riding a bicycle was an economic necessity; the remainder indicated that they did so for a variety of other reasons (e.g. fun, fitness, reducing carbon footprint). The racial, gendered, and economic homogeneity of our participants reflects the broader demographic characteristics of individuals who are involved in alternative transportation advocacy in the United States (ibid.), but is not necessarily indicative of the entirety of individuals who choose to or are in fact forced to ride a bicycle due to the expense of automobility. Despite this demographic homogeneity, our anecdotal observations suggest that there are a substantial number of people riding bicycles who may not fit into our participant profile of white, male, well-educated, and economically secure, and these participants should be pursued in subsequent investigations. Many of our participants also drove and/or rode in automobiles, but more than 25% of their weekly trips were taken by bicycle. For more than half of our participants, a bicycle was their primary means of transportation, i.e. more than 75% of the weekly trips were by bicycle.

Given its exploratory nature, analysis of the data was conducted in a conventionally inductive approach (Charmaz, 2014). After organising and reading the interview transcripts, three of the four authors engaged in successive rounds of open coding after which code lists were compared and consolidated into focused codes. A second round of focused coding facilitated a process of comparing data across all of the interviews and led two of the authors to create graphical representations of the underlying patterns and relationships in the data set (ibid). The graphical illustrations of relationships served as the basis for discussion and debate amongst the authors that ultimately resulted in the analytic categories that follow.

Findings

> Initially I was kind of like doing a moral righteousness thing. It's now almost entirely, just because it's more fun and it makes me feel better and its fairly addictive. So initially I always had to psych myself up to go bike. You know, and lay everything out at night and kind of find motivation and now it's just my default. I have to convince myself to drive. So it's really reduced my tolerance for sitting I traffic. On the few days I do have to drive and sit in traffic I just am always like, you know. I would so much rather be biking in the rain than sitting in traffic.

Kelly's[1] explanation represented a common experience for all of our participants, namely a process of metamorphosis in which one moves through the stages of ideation to experimentation to routinisation of cycling in a city. While participants articulated a variety of pathways in their development as urban cyclists, broad commonalities characterise these experiences. We develop our analyses to describe this process of 'becoming a bike commuter,' and what follows is an empirically-driven elaboration of its stages.

Testing an idea

Participants came to the practice of commuting by bicycle from a variety of experiences and interests. Some decisions to begin riding were slowly and carefully considered, while others were more abrupt responses to opportunity or necessity. In all cases, the idea of riding a bicycle for transportation presented itself as an alternative to the status quo of automobility.

By far the most common reason given was that of solving a transportation challenge in the life of the participant and/or the participant's household. Simon captured his initial motives related to solving transportation challenges in his household.

> Once my son graduated and then was going for job interviews, that kind of opened up that need for a second mode of transportation. And so that was the catalyst. I was not going to purchase another car. The one that we had was going to fit the bill, so even though it was a financial aspect, it was real a logistical one. We have since inherited another vehicle, so we have two vehicles now, but still ... I prefer to use the bike.

The addition of a bicycle to the family's transportation options allowed both Simon and his son to meet their transportation needs while incurring very little expense. As opposed to the necessity of household economy, Kelly's decision to begin cycling resulted from the perceived inconvenience of driving and parking in the city.

> Where I was working when I first moved to town, there wasn't much parking, so the lack of parking certainly made [commuting by bike] much more appealing. Then when I moved to the east side of town, I started biking even more because there are so many more places you can get to [on a bicycle].

Similarly, John explained that he started cycle commuting because no other form of transport was as convenient.

> When I did cycle it was because of the utility of it. Notably when I got a job, I was down across the suburbs. I was going radially, you know how that works, bus routes hardly ever go radially but yes, I cycled ... because I wanted to seek out radial ways and therefore the public transit didn't suit me. Yes, I don't remember thinking about it from an environmental angle. It was yea, it was probably cost and convenience, or the other way around.

For eight of our respondents, cycling solved a transportation challenge by being more convenient and/or cost effective.

If pragmatism was an overriding consideration for participants, it overlapped with concerns about the environmental ills posed by automobile use. 'I come from an environmental background,' explained Mark. 'So there was that focus on that [cycling] is a better way to travel for carbon reduction, and gasoline consumption, but also just kind of felt a like a better way to travel.' Similarly, Kelly was 'interested in urban planning and environmental issues, so I thought I would try [bicycle commuting] out. I was coming at it from "this is the right thing to do" type motivation.' This marriage of practicality and idealism held true for several other participants as well.

Finally, a few participants were drawn to cycling out of a sense of curiosity. Tim explained that he

> ... had a friend that rode purely for transportation, didn't have a car, and it was extremely fascinating ... that he was able to get around Nashville without a car. I thought it would be a cool thing to give a shot because I typically wasn't going further than a few miles on a day-to-day basis.

Similar to other cyclists, Tim was drawn to the idea of commuting by bike simply due to its novelty. The characterisation of urban cycling as a means of operating 'outside the norm' was a theme expressed by virtually every participant related to their initiation of the activity.

Experimentation and expansion

Participants' initial commuting forays tended to function as a 'proof of concept' whereby cycling came to be seen as a viable mode of transportation. Despite an understanding that cycling was possible, every participant proceeded with a period of experimentation during which they tested out the many variables that might contribute to a successful cycling experience.

Most participants developed their commuting habits gradually while also relying on other established modes of transport. Simon exemplified this incremental approach by literally riding further each day before boarding a public bus.

> I started riding toward the nearest bus stop and I extended it to a park and ride and then once I started doing that then I moved a little further and then on this end, on the arrival end, instead of getting off six blocks away which was the nearest point where the bus dropped off I started getting off ten blocks away ... so I just started extending it gradually.

Similarly, others (e.g. John, Mark, Ross, Kelly) began riding one day a week or only when the weather was optimal, thereby not committing fully to this new way of moving about town.

Most crucial to this process of experimentation was a process of searching for the safest, fastest, and most scenic routes. When describing his initial commuting efforts, Tim captured this experimental mindset saying that,

> Finding those new routes was fun for me personally and just testing it out. I am more so a person that if I leave early enough, then I am like 'I never been down that road, I wonder where it takes me.' and then I will go that way. The bike makes it a lot easier for me to enjoy those decisions.

Just as participants experimented with their routes, so too did they experiment with different types of bicycles, cycle-specific clothing, and accessories. 'I think [logistics are] important,' explained Terry. 'If you've got the stuff, it makes commuting so much easier. I started with a bungee cord and a backpack, and it makes such a difference to have the right panier (bag that affixes to a rear bike rack).' The geographic expansion associated with comfort with cycling coincided with an expansion of gear choices; both of these expansions served to further embed urban cycling as part of their lives, to further instantiate 'becoming a bike commuter' as part of their identities.

Related to the search for safe and efficient routes, a unanimous finding was the usefulness of bicycle-specific infrastructure. Some riders explained that cycling infrastructure, such as painted bike lanes, provided actual protection from automobiles. 'When I first got on a bicycle, there was a lot of infrastructure that helped, there was a bike lane my whole way to work.' As Kelly explained, infrastructure in the form of a bike lane facilitated her transition to cycling regularly. Descriptions of infrastructure ranged from 'sharrows' (images of cyclists painted on the roadway) to bike lanes separated by stripes and/or bollards to separated bike paths or greenways. In all cases, participants acknowledged the protection afforded by infrastructure and the instrumentality of such protection in the formation of a cycling practice. Additionally, some participants, such as Steve, explained that infrastructure was also a signal to drivers that cyclists' presence was legitimate. 'I like [infrastructure] in the sense just having the lane signifies to drivers that a bike belongs on the road. A lot of Nashville drivers, Tennessee drivers, don't seem to believe that. It signifies that we belong there.'

Pleasure sustains a practice

Virtually every participant described a process whereby initial interests and motives (e.g. financial, environmental, health) gave way to a set of experiential benefits that sustained their cycling practice. Analysis of the data reveal three related types of experiential benefits that fostered participants' cycling practices: 1) mental and physical enjoyment, 2) enhanced connection to place, and 3) greater sense of control related to transportation.

One the most striking features of participants' descriptions of 'becoming a bike commuter' was the extent to which enjoyment evolved into the dominant characteristic of the riding experience. Terry captured this evolution well: 'It started out seven or eight years ago as "issue biking", for health, environment; and now, it's the best part of my day, the twenty minutes in, the twenty minutes back . . . .I do it for mental health as much as anything.' Mark also highlighted 'the physical feeling. I'm much more alert. When I drive in to work, I'm groggy. If I bike twenty-five minutes up here, then I'm going to be red-faced and sweating, but my mind is [alert].'

Several participants actually pinpointed the biochemical mechanisms and the linkage between physical exertion and mental well-being. Tim explained 'that [flow] is definitely one of the big things for me. It is definitely from releasing endorphins, which generally makes you a lot happier than you would be otherwise. I think that it's a good thing for me. I need that physical release to stay sane.' Similarly, when asked why he continued to commute by bike after so many years, Steve explained, 'it's the endorphins hit from exercising, right? I mean, if I don't ride in for a while I start feeling grumpy and sort of agitated . . . .There is a very clear sort of element feeling peace, feeling good, feeling enjoyment from doing it, that you miss if you don't.'

Despite this sense of enjoyment, almost every participant had fallen while riding and incurred injuries ranging from a skinned knee (Ross) to a broken arm (Walter). Despite injury, every participant, even those who had broken bones, expressed no hesitation to resume their cycling practice. Greg typified this sentiment, saying that 'the exercise and the fun of riding' had him ready to get back on his bike after an accident that left him with a broken hip. Our sample of participants undoubtedly exhibited a 'survivorship bias' (Taleb, 2010) with regard to willingness to continue riding. Nonetheless, our participants clearly demonstrated that the mental and physical pleasure of riding sustained their habits. Summarising this finding, Randy declared, 'I just have gotten to the point where going from a car to commuting [by bicycle] is a pleasurable experience, which you can probably find one percent of people saying is a pleasurable experience, but it's a pleasurable experience to me!'

Another experiential benefit expressed by most participants was the capacity for urban cycling to foster an enhanced connection to the places in which they rode. Lest they be cut off by a driver or ride into a large pothole, cyclists must maintain an intimate awareness of their immediate surroundings, a necessity that opens them to a different experience of place than might be had in an automobile. As described by participants, this enhanced awareness is facilitated by the bicycle's slower average speeds and the lack of physical barriers between the cyclist and the surrounding environment. Our participants relished the opportunity to take in their surroundings and also prided themselves on their intimate knowledge of the places through which they rode. Randy captured this aspect of the experience well:

> If you ever want to know the best way to go anywhere between your house and anything you're asking bicyclists because there's this period of time where you become very curious about how can I get to a point, to home with the least hill or how can I get there with the least stop signs or with the least assholes. I mean you just start going and doing all these things. So then if you're in a car and it's snowing, you know the flattest road. It helps you become aware of things that you never knew existed.

In addition to learning the topography, several participants related the manner in which cycling fostered their knowledge of the social and built environments. On that issue, Mark explained, 'I feel a lot more tied to [places I ride]. I am more appreciative of my place. It is a similar feeling to walking. I don't know if it has to do with the slower speed or not having a physical barrier, but you feel more communal with the actual geography and the people and the building and the roads and everything like that. I feel like that's a very positive feeling to me, and wherever I have lived I have tried to embrace that.' Nearly every participant described similar experiences of having a stronger connection to the environments in which they rode. Ross expressed this dynamic as a piece of advice, 'if you're thinking about buying a house in a neighborhood, get out [of your car] and ride a bike around. You learn a lot more about a place from riding a bike than you ever would just living there.'

Somewhat paradoxically, the final aspect of participants' riding experiences was that of a greater sense of control while riding the city. Though ostensibly at the mercy of cars and their drivers, our participants experience cycling as a means of circumventing the constraints of driving in an urban environment. Tim captured this, saying:

> I love being able to take different routes and go down the alleys or cut through parking lots ... like you can figure out different ways to have a route as the crow flies as opposed to road that were paved for me .... .I get pretty bored in a car driving. You pretty much are going to drive one or two of the same routes wherever you are going, so being able to decide [on a bike] is definitely nice.

In many cases, the ability to avoid congestion was facilitated by bicycle-specific infrastructure that allowed participants to 'slide through' traffic. Mark 'agree[d] that a bike gives a feeling of control. Like the example of events clogging up downtown, you feel completely controlled if you are in a car being told which way to go. Generally on a bike, you can soak it in and go right through .... .It's kind of the best of both worlds: I can ride on the road, I can ride on the paths.'

On its face, a cyclist's greater sense of control makes little sense in an auto-centric city. As Kelly explained,

> A friend ask me once... 'don't you feel like you don't have as much flexibility because you can't get in your car and go somewhere?' And I kind of feel actually the complete opposite because um with a car you have to worry about traffic and other cars and parking and there is always, it kind of feels like more of a trip to go get in your car and go somewhere where as getting on a bike, is more like 'oh I'll just spin around the neighborhood'.

Her observation is grounded in a sense of comfort on a bicycle that is closely tied to the first step of the process in which participants realise that using a bicycle to get around the city is actually a possibility.

Analyses

Processes of 'becoming a cyclist', from ideation to experimentation to routinisation, underscore the emergent nature of leisure in the cycling experience. Indeed, as described by participants, the characteristics of enjoyment, freedom, and competence are all resonant with a conventional conceptualisation of leisure as a state of mind (Kleiber, 1999). And yet, the manner in which individuals came to urban biking, subsequently expanded the scope and scale of urban biking, and sustained urban biking through pleasure, suggests a broader spatio-temporal dimension for our understanding of urban biking; social networks and communities of cyclists developed and complexified; spaces for biking within and beyond the urban environment expanded; and both the amount of time spent biking and the amount of time and resources spent preparing for biking experiences expanded. And these descriptive assessments of people's engagements with urban biking are, in and of themselves, a contribution to the academic understandings of the processes by which cycling is practiced across the urban settings, with the subsequent personal, social, environmental, and health benefits. There are, however, more analytical approaches that help us understand the lived phenomena that constitute the affectual and embodied engagement of biking. Here, we foreground the emotional and affectual relational engagements with space and place to better contextualise these results.

Emotional geographies of cycling

As detailed in our findings, biking within, across, and through urban environments demonstrates an emotional geography (Bondi et al., 2005; Davidson & Milligan, 2004) that emphasises a relational sense of space and place to enrich understandings of this phenomenon. Emotional geographies feature a 'flatter,' more relational ontology (e.g. Rose & Wilson, 2019) that destabilises traditional, hierarchical ways of knowing and being in the world. Further, emotional geographies privilege fluidity between people and place, where humans intimately inform and are informed by the nonhuman worlds in which we exist, while also placing emphasis on the intimacy and proximity in people's engagements with both other people and the nonhuman landscape (Pile, 2010). Places evoke emotions for people, a non-contentious yet largely underrepresented perspective across leisure studies (for exception, see for instance Allen-Collinson & Leledaki, 2015; Evans & Allen-Collinson, 2016; Zajchowski & Rose, online first) and, more broadly, the social sciences (Thrift, 2008), a perspective that emotional geographies have tried to address. In this research, emotions, such as pleasure and freedom, play a crucial role in maintaining cyclists' initiation, expansion, and continuation of this urban practice. Affectual relations between people, place, and community are primary rationales, once the pragmatism of quotidian needs are met. Further, there is emotional labour (e.g. Bosco, 2006) performed through the collective practice of place-based resistance-through-practice urban cycling. This emotional labour and sustained, embodied activism over time and through space demonstrates that a network of social relations transforms a commonly understood leisure activity into a political act of resistance and re-envisioning of urban futures.

As borne out by our results, the experience of cycling in an urban environment is a dynamic one. The testing, experimentation, and sustenance of urban biking was not only a means-end effort to accomplish a particular goal (e.g. commute to work), but was also a social, emotional, and place-based effort towards outreach and connection. For those who persisted (unfortunately, this study did not identify participants who had initiated, but subsequently stopped cycling), an initial venture into urban cycling quickly gave way to a phase of experimentation during which participants gradually solidified the logistics of their commute (routes, times, equipment) and settled into a practice that was sustained by its socioemotional, experiential, and lifestyle benefits. While virtually all recreation activities have spatial dimensions, individuals who regularly ride bikes in urban environments must begin by confronting an environment and discourse that delegitimizes cycling as a form of urban transportation and pleasure (Kunstler, 1993). Most participants experienced an epiphany in which they realised that it is not only possible to cycle to work or the grocery store, but that the experience is enjoyable and rewarding in numerous ways. As described above, these epiphanies related to cycling's feasibility must be understood against the backdrop of the urban landscape's general hostility towards cycling, especially in Nashville.

And yet, experiences of cycling in a city are hardly so simplistic, and these often ebullient facets of cycling can vanish instantly in the face of emotions and materialities associated with hostile drivers, inhospitable roads, an absence of bike parking, or frustrating social stigmatisations, all of which are symptomatic of transportation ideologies and discourses that delegitimize the bicycle as a means of intimately and relationally engaging with the urban environment. The immediate experience of freedom as one glides past rush hour gridlock is bounded by an imminent threat of being 'doored' by a parked car and by the larger realisation that drivers are rarely, if ever, held accountable for damage, injury, or death inflicted on the cycling population. These types of psychological and emotional responses can, in part, be contextualised by cyclists' meaning-making engagements with the experiences of cycling through a city.

Urban bicycling is simultaneously a practice of empowerment, health, and mobility on one hand, and an experience of fear, risk, frustration, and despair on the other hand. As such, when it manifests as leisure, urban cycling must be understood as a form of liminal leisure (Kidder, 2005). As described above, urban cycling was characterised by a sense of freedom for many participants, and yet this freedom is experienced within a spatial, legal, and political framework that largely disavows its existence. In essence, the freedom of urban cycling is stolen spatially and psychologically from the hegemonic regime of automobility. This notion of stealing space is illustrated by the common phrase that one must 'take the lane' when riding on an open roadway, meaning that instead of riding in the gutter next to the curb, a rider should move further into the lane thereby being more visible and assertive towards automobile traffic (Laker, 2011; League of American Bicyclists, n.d.). This practice is a manifestation of re/claiming urban space, and doing so often in an outwardly demonstrable form of emotional place making. Automobile drivers never talk about the need to 'take the lane' that already supposedly belongs to them. Indeed, cyclists are taking not just space to ride their bikes, but also taking back an experience of using the city and its infrastructure from a discourse that portrays automobiles as the only sensible and safe means of transportation (Spinney, 2016), a discourse that is belied by the high rate of death and injury from auto accidents (National Highway Transportation Safety Administration Public Affairs, 2017). Therefore, this urban cycling research also contributes to literature concerning the ways in which leisure interacts and intersects with politics (e.g. Mair, 2002; Rose, Harmon, & Dunlap, 2019), in that power is both an outcome of and an impetus for leisure practices.

Conclusions and recommendations

On the basis of these findings, concrete recommendations to the City of Nashville related to its cycling infrastructure would mirror those of local and national advocacy organisations (www.walkbikenashville.org; www.bikeleague.org/content/making-biking-better). Among other recommendations, these would include creating more miles of protected bikes lanes (i.e. those with a barrier separating bicycles from automobile traffic), creating more connectivity between components of the existing cycling infrastructure, erecting more signage to remind drivers of cyclists' presence, and passage of more stringent laws to protect cyclists from negligent or malicious behaviour on the part of drivers. Such initiatives are being pursued in a piecemeal fashion and incremental improvement to the existing cycling infrastructure will undoubtedly occur. Without disavowing the importance of these initiatives, our findings and those of others suggest the necessity of a more radical approach to infrastructure development and appropriation. The dominance of autocentrism as the organising ideology of Nashville's transportation infrastructure would be more clearly illustrated and remedied by permanently closing some of the city's major thoroughfares to automobile traffic and reserving them exclusively for pedestrian and non-motorised transport. The entrenched nature of autocentrism is illustrated by the city's resistence to closing even a three-mile stretch of city streets for a few hours once a year for the Open Streets Nashville Event (personal communication, N. Kern, 25 January 2019). Despite its perceived radicalness, such an approach has been taken successfully by several munipalities around the globe (Blakemore, 2017).

Future explorations of cycling in urban environments would benefit from a nesting of cyclists' experience inside of a political ecology the urban environment itself. Such an investigation could enlist urban planners, traffic, and/or civil engineers to illuminate the precise ways in which urban planning and design shape the experience of riding and that pose real threats to cyclists' health and safety, while also noting the flows of power and capital that impact experiences of urban cycling mobilities. A further exploration might delve even deeper into the ideology of urban design and its function in the creation of an interpolated subject, the cyclist.

Finally, we acknowledge that our investigation of this topic has been focused on and shaped by individuals who have the privilege to choose to cycle in urban environments. Had we spent time interviewing and even riding with urban residents who more decidedly cycle of out of economic necessity, we would have undoubtedly been given a different illustration of the urban environment. To the extent that movement in urban spaces is shaped by political and economic discourses, that reality is made most clear for individuals on the lower end of the socio-economic perspective.

Note

1. This and all participant names are pseudonyms.

Disclosure statement

No potential conflict of interest was reported by the authors.

ORCID

Jeff Rose http://orcid.org/0000-0003-3171-7242
Sarah H. Standridge http://orcid.org/0000-0002-3734-8460

References

Ajzen, I., & Driver, B. L. (1992). Application of the theory of planned behavior to leisure choice. *Journal of Leisure Research, 24*(3), 207–224.

Aldred, R., & Jungnickel, K. (2013). Matter in or out of place? Bicycle parking strategies and their effects on people, practices and places. *Social & Cultural Geography, 14*(6), 604–624.

Allen-Collinson, J., & Leledaki, A. (2015). Sensing the outdoors: A visual and haptic phenomenology of outdoor exercise embodiment. *Leisure Studies, 34*(4), 457–470.

Anderson, S. C., & Autry, C. E. (2011). Leisure behaviour of the Amish. *World Leisure Journal, 53*(1), 57–66.

Benjamin, R. M. (2010, July-August). The surgeon general's vision for a healthy and fit nation. *Public Health Reports: Surgeon General's Perspectives, 125*, 514–515. doi:10.1177/003335491012500402

Blakemore, E. (2017, March 9). Germans invented the Autobahn. Now they're building a superhighway for bikes. Retrieved from https://www.smithsonianmag.com/smart-news/germans-invented-autobahn-now-theyre-building-superhighway-bikes-180962446/

Blickstein, S., & Hanson, S. (2001). Critical mass: Forging a politics of sustainable mobility in the information age. *Transportation, 28*, 347–362.

Bondi, L., Davidson, J., & Smith, M. (eds.). (2005). *Emotional geographies*. Aldershot, UK: Ashgate.

Bosco, F. (2006). The Madres de Plaza de Mayo and three decades of human rights' activism: Embeddedness, emotions, and social movements. *Annals of the Association of American Geographers, 96*(2), 342–365.

Buntin, J. (2018, July). Amid scandal and explosive growth, Nashville ponders its future. Governing: The States and Localities. Retrieved from https://www.governing.com/topics/urban/gov-nashville.html

Charmaz, K. (2014). *Constructing grounded theory* (2nd ed.). Thousand Oaks, CA: Sage.

Davidson, J., & Milligan, C. (2004). Embodying emotion sensing space: Introducing emotional geographies. *Social & Cultural Geography, 5*(4), 523–532.

Duany, A., Plater-Zyberk, E., & Speck, J. (2000). *Suburban nation: The rise of sprawl and the decline of the American dream*. New York, NY: North Point Press.

Eichler, R. (2017). The resistance of fun: Fixed-gear cycling in urban public spaces. *Space and Culture, 20*(2), 239–254.

Evans, A., & Allen-Collinson, J. (2016). From "just a swimmer" to a "swimming mother": Women's embodied experiences of recreational aquatic activity with pre-school children. *Leisure Studies, 35*(2), 141–156.

Fincham, B. (2006a). Bicycle messengers and the road to freedom. *The Sociological Review, 54*(1), 208–222.

Fincham, B. (2006b). Back to the 'old school': Bicycle messengers, employment and ethnography. *Qualitative Research, 6*(2), 187–205.

Fincham, B. (2008). Balance is everything: Bicycle messengers, work and leisure. *Sociology, 42*(4), 618–634.

Floyd, M. F., Spengler, J. O., Maddock, J. E., Gobster, P. H., & Suau, L. (2008). Environmental and social correlates of physical activity in neighborhood parks: An observational study in Tampa and Chicago. *Leisure Sciences, 30*(4), 360–375.

Freeman, P. A., Palmer, A. A., & Baker, B. L. (2006). Perspectives on leisure of LDS women who are stay-at-home mothers. *Leisure Sciences, 28*(3), 203–221.

Freudendal-Pedersen, M. (2015). Whose commons are mobilities spaces? The case of Copenhagen's cyclists. *ACME: an International E-Journal for Critical Geographies, 14*(2), 598–621.

Gilderbloom, J., Grooms, W., Mog, J., & Meares, W. (2016). The green dividend of urban biking? evidence of improved community and sustainable development. *Local Environment, 21*(8), 991–1008. doi:10.1080/13549839.2015.1060409

Hale, S. (2018, June 7). History repeats itself in North Nashville. *Nashville Scene*. Retrieved from https://www.nashvillescene.com/news/cover-story/article/21007855/history-repeats-itself-in-north-nashville

Hoffmann, M. L. (2016). *Bike lanes are white lanes: Bicycle advocacy and urban planning*. Lincoln, NE: University of Nebraska Press.

Huybers Withers, S. (2015). *An exploration of the gendered culture of mountain biking in Nova Scotia* (Unpublished master's thesis). Dalhousie University, Halifax, Nova Scotia, Canada.

Initiative for Bicycle & Pedestrian Innovation (n.d.). The Portland bicycle story. Retrieved from https://www.pdx.edu/ibpi/sites/www.pdx.edu.ibpi/files/portlandbikestory_1.pdf

Kaczynski, A. T., & Henderson, K. A. (2007). Environmental correlates of physical activity: A review of evidence about parks and recreation. *Leisure Sciences, 29*(4), 315–354.

Kidder, J. L. (2005). Style and action: A decoding of bike messenger symbols. *Journal of Contemporary Ethnography, 34*(2), 344–367.

Kleiber, D. A. (1999). *Leisure experience and human development: a dialectical interpretation*. New York: Basic Books.

Kristensen, M. B. (2016, January 18). *How Denmark became a cycling nation*. Cycling Embassy of Denmark, Copenhagen, Denmark. Retrieved from https://cyclingsolutions.info/embassy/danish-cycling-history/

Laker, L. (August 1, 2011). Is it a cyclist's right to 'take the lane'? *The Guardian*. Retrieved from https://www.theguardian.com/environment/bike-blog/2011/aug/01/cyclist-take-the-lane

League of American Bicyclists. (2018). *2018 state progress reports.* Washington, DC: League of American Wheelmen. Retrieved from https://bikeleague.org/content/progress-reports

League of American Bicyclists. (n.d.). *Ride better tips.* Washington, DC: League of American Wheelmen. Retrieved from https://www.bikeleague.org/content/ride-better-tips

Lee, B., & Shafer, C. S. (2002). The dynamic nature of leisure experience: An application of affect control theory. *Journal of Leisure Research, 34*(3), 290–310.

Lee, D. J., Ho, H., Banks, M., Giampieri, M., Chen, X., & Le, D. (2016). Delivering (in)justice: Food delivery cyclists in New York City. In A. Golub, M. Hoffmann, A. Lugo, & G. Sandoval (Eds.), *Bicycle justice and urban transformation: Biking for all?*. (pp. 114-129) New York, NY: Routledge.

Lee, D. J. (2016). Embodied bicycle commuters in a car world. *Social & Cultural Geography, 17*(3), 401–422.

Lugo, A. (2016). Decentering whiteness in organized bicycling: Notes from inside. In A. Golub, M. Hoffmann, A. Lugo, & G. Sandoval (Eds.), *Bicycle justice and urban transformation: Biking for all?*. (pp. 180-188) New York, NY: Routledge.

Mair, H. (2002). Civil leisure? Exploring the relationship between leisure, activism and social change. *Leisure/Loisir, 27*(3–4), 213–237.

McCarville, R. (2007). From a fall in the mall to a run in the sun: One journey to Ironman triathlon. *Leisure Sciences, 29*(2), 159–173.

McIlvenny, P. (2014). Velomobile formations-in-action: Biking and talking together. *Space and Culture, 17*(2), 137–156.

McLeod, K. (2017). *Where we ride: Analysis of bicycling commuting in American cities.* Washington, DC: The League of American Bicyclists. Retrieved from https://bikeleague.org/sites/default/files/Where_We_Ride_2017_KM_0.pdf

Montgomery, C. (2013). *Happy city: Transforming our lives through urban design.* New York, NY: Farrar, Straus and Giroux.

Moore, R. L., & Graefe, A. R. (1994). Attachments to recreation settings: The case of rail-trail users. *Leisure Sciences, 16*(1), 17–31.

Morhayim, L. (2012). From counterpublics to counterspaces: Bicyclists' efforts to reshape cities. *Justice Spatiale-Spatial Justice, 5*, 1–19.

National Highway Traffic Safety Administration. (2017 February). *Traffic safety facts, 2015.* Washington, DC: NHTSA's National Center for Statistics and Analysis. Retrieved from https://crashstats.nhtsa.dot.gov/Api/Public/ViewPublication/812375

National Highway Transportation Safety Administration Public Affairs (2017, January). USDOT releases 2016 fatal traffic crash data. Retrieved from https://www.nhtsa.gov/press-releases/usdot-releases-2016-fatal-traffic-crash-data

Parry, D. C. & C. W. Johnson. (2007). Contextualizing Leisure Research to Encompass Complexity in Lived Leisure Experience: The Need for Creative Analytic Practice, Leisure Sciences, 29:2, 119–130, doi:10.1080/01490400601160721

Pedestrian and Bicycle Information Center (n.d.). *Pedestrian and bicycle crash statistics.* Federal Highway Administration and National Highway Traffic Safety Administration, Washington, D.C. Retrieved from http://www.pedbikeinfo.org/data/factsheet_crash.cfm

Pile, S. (2010). Emotions and affect in recent human geography. *Transactions of the Institute of British Geographers, 35*(1), 5–20.

Place for Bikes. (n.d.). City ratings. Retrieved on March 29, 2019 at https://cityratings.peopleforbikes.org/all-cities-ratings//

Quarmby, T., & Dagkas, S. (2010). Children's engagement in leisure time physical activity: Exploring family structure as a determinant. *Leisure Studies, 29*(1), 53–66.

Ramthun, R. (1994). Factors in user group conflict between hikers and mountain bikers. *Leisure Sciences, 17*(3), 159–169.

Rose, J., Harmon, J., & Dunlap, R. (2019). Becoming political: An expanding role for critical leisure studies. *Leisure Sciences, 40*(7), 649-662 .

Rose, J., & Wilson, J. (2019). Assembling homelessness: A posthumanist political ecology approach to urban nature, wildlife, and actor-networks. *Leisure Sciences, 41*(5), 402–422.

Shafer, C. S., & Scott, D. (2013). Dynamics of progression in mountain bike racing. *Leisure Sciences, 35*(4), 353–364.

Spinney, J. (2011). A chance to catch a breath: Using mobile video ethnography in cycling research. *Mobilities, 6*(2), 161–182.

Spinney, J. (2016). Fixing mobility in the neoliberal city: Cycling policy and practice in London as a mode of political-economic and biopolitical governance. *Annals of the American Association of Geographers, 106*(2), 450–458.

Taleb, N. N. (2010). *The black swan: The impact of the highly improbable* (2nd ed.). New York, NY: Random House.

Thrift, N. (2008). *Non-representational theory: Space, politics, affect.* London, UK: Routledge.

Transportation Alternatives Data Exchange. (2018). *Transportation alternatives spending report, FY1992-FY2017.* Washington, DC: Rails-to-Trails Conservancy. Retrieved from https://trade.railstotrails.org/action/document/download?document_id=909

Vargo, J. (2014). Metro sapiens: An urban species. *Journal of Environmental Studies and Sciences, 4*(4), 360–363.

White, A. (2014, August 21). Can cars, bikes and pedestrians share Nashville's roadways without someone ending up in the hospital? *Nashville Scene*. Retrieved from https://www.nashvillescene.com/news/article/13055147/can-cars-bikes-and-pedestrians-share-nashvilles-roadways-without-someone-ending-up-in-the-hospital

Zajchowski, C., & Rose, J. (online first). Sensitive leisure: Writing the lived experience of air pollution. *Leisure Sciences*. doi:10.1080/01490400.2018.1448026

Leisure activism and *engaged ethnography*: heterogeneous voices and the urban palimpsest

Ian R. Lamond, Esther Solano and Vitor Blotta

ABSTRACT

Studying the conflictualities between leisure activism, understood as participation in events of dissent as a nonwork-based activity, and those tasked with 'maintaining order', requires techniques that can work with diverse voices and contesting world views. However, many of the methods familiar to us in the social sciences risk reinforcing relationships of power that can undermine such inquiry. Drawing on the conceptual work of scholars from the global south and the global north, we examine approaches to protests as event, the construction of urban space and the performativity of violence, in two democracies: Brazil and the UK. From that we were led to conclude such research requires a less canonical approach. It is through the adoption of a more engaged ethnography, one that establishes horizontal relations between researchers and participants that are drawn from backgrounds reflecting such conflictualities, combined with an understanding of the process of research as more like that of an event, that the diversity of the heterogeneous voices associated with dissent, within an urban palimpsest, can be heard.

Whilst political engagement, through participating in acts of protest, has long been one way people have chosen to use some of their leisure time, this century has seen participation in events of dissent, from online petitions to large scale public demonstrations, emerge as a global phenomenon (Gerbaudo, 2017). Yet, to date, discussion of such *activist leisure* has been limited (Pickard, 2017). In part this reflects the paucity of debate around those methods best suited to investigating both the manifestation and the representation of such events of dissent within leisure and event studies. Consequently, in this paper we seek to address the question; *how are we to assemble a critical framework that can analyse events of dissent and leisure activism* (Mair, 2002) *within a democratic state?* In order to do that, we argue, approaches and methodologies need to be developed that challenge many of the mainstays of traditional social science research.

The manifestations of mass protest, whether localised or as part of a pan-global event of dissent, are commonly mediated through multiple discourses, a plurality of public spheres and a diverse range of information and communications technologies (Habermas, 1992). As such they are not intelligible through the application of a single narrative; consequently, a multidisciplinary approach becomes essential. Familiar, if somewhat safe, social science methods, such as interviews, surveys and questionnaires, are unable to grasp the complexity and nuance of the articulation of such mediated acts of leisure activism, alternatives are required (Lamond, in press). Whilst the emergence of the digital social sciences and humanities attempt to address that complexity (Marres, 2017), the use of big data inclines towards describing networked relationships rather than trying to qualitatively understand the world views that are being contested. In order to develop a richer understanding of leisure activism, and such events, it is essential that we consider alternatives to, and adaptations of, the research toolkit many of us are familiar with.

The aim of this paper is to propose a research plan that could contribute to an inquiry into the multiplicity of narratives (the heterogenous voices of our title) associated with leisure activism, drawing on the experience of two democratic states, both currently experiencing uncertainty and instability; Brazil and the UK. In recent years the political establishment of Brazil has been rocked by a series of scandals around corruption, in part the result of the Lava-Jato investigation into links between governmental officials and several state-wide businesses. Meanwhile, in the UK, uncertainty and divisiveness has followed the 2016 referendum on its membership of the EU; resulting in three different Prime Ministers in three years. We will pursue our aim through two central tasks.

First, we will map out the theoretical landscape required by any methodology that wishes to investigate leisure activism and events of dissent. In that part of the paper we will discuss the relevance of critical event studies (CES) as a conceptual orientation. In addition, it is important to recognise that public protest, demonstrations etc. are comprised of relationships that involve the mobility and immobility of agents (both collective and individual) within spatial imaginaries. Such spatialities can, in Massey's (1991) terms, be ' … imagined as articulated moments in networks of social relations' (p.7). Consequently, we will also reflect on how space is constructed through social relations. Discourses of dissent also evoke conflictualities around those imaginaries of space, our inter-relational connections to each other and our association with the institutions of the state, some of which become mediated as acts of violence (Zizek, 2008). The next step will thus be the conceptualisation of violence. Finally, as such conflictualities are either contested and/or amplified through the relationship between the media and protest, we will spend some time examining the complexity of that relationship.

Our second task will be to consider why tools familiar to social science research, common to many quantitative, qualitative and mixed methods, are ineffective in handling the imaginaries and conflictualities of activist leisure. This leads us to suggest that given the conceptualisation of 'event' within CES, if research is to grasp the complexities of leisure activism (Rose, Harmon, & Dunlap, 2018), public protest, and the mediation of events of dissent, it also needs to take on attributes that are more event-like. In conclusion, through a synthesis drawn from our discussion, we propose a new approach, one that challenges participants, researchers and how we construe research; we refer to this as an *engaged ethnographic approach*.

Mapping the theoretical landscape around dissent

Protest as event

The field of event studies can come across as a somewhat corporatist domain whose principal purpose is to support event-based tourism and the management of what Getz (2016) calls 'planned' events. One of the struggles within the field is an assumption that any answer to the question – To what does the term 'event' refer? – seems to narrowly focus on the economic. Spracklen and Lamond (2016) argue to approach the study of events in this way reinforces its colonisation, along with a concomitant commodification of leisure, by a dominant neo-liberal hegemony. Consequently, such construals of 'event' and 'leisure' can hinder our capacity to challenge dominant relationships of power and oppression. CES construes 'event' differently. In place of the typology of events proposed by Donald Getz (Getz, 2016), it argues that space is relational (as suggested, for example, in Massey, 2004) and that the spatial aspects of 'events' are a palimpsest (Huyssen, 2003), where power inscribes, erases and re-inscribes commodified meaning, producing complex layered relationships of power and manipulation. Within such a field, leisure becomes contested.

So that we can better address the conflictualities in the mediation of the complexity of 'events' we must confront such contestation, and thereby gain a greater insight into how the event is being constructed. To do that, an understanding of the place of disruption/routine in the manifestation of protest, and the discourses of identity and othering, exposed through the manifestation of dissent, becomes a priority (Glynos & Howarth, 2007). We propose to begin this by considering theories of space appropriate to the urban context in which many protests happen. Our focus is on public open space, such as those used in protest marches, occupations, and rallies, which have become closely associated with the imagery and iconography of the mediated manifestation of dissent (Rovisco & Ong, 2016).

Urban space

Over several texts Lefebvre developed a detailed theory of spatiality (for example Lefebvre, 1991, 2004). He contends that there is a continuum of spatial production from simpler, 'natural', spaces to more complex ones that are socially produced and reproduced. In order to analyse any particular historical spatial moment, he argues, we require a three-part dialectic that combines an understanding of everyday practices and perceptions of space (le perçu), its representation (le conçu) and a grasp of the spatial imaginary of the time (le vécu). His philosophy has been highly influential, informing significant contributions to contemporary, critical, human geography. David Harvey, for example, acknowledges Lefebvre's influence on his own perspective (Harvey, 2004, 2012), which focuses on the appropriation of our own spatial imaginary by a dominant political economy; identified as neo-liberal globalised capitalism. Though less extensive in her recognition of Lefebvre's legacy, Doreen Massey (1992, 2004) credits him with bringing to the fore the dynamics of everyday life to our understanding of space. It is worth noting that whilst Lefebvre's earlier work (Lefebvre, 1991) is cognisant of the role of spatial imaginaries, he downplays the palimpsestic significance of inscription, erasure and re-inscription of space. This is, at least partly, addressed in his last work, 'Rhythmanalysis' (Lefebvre, 2004), in which patterns of repetition within social urban space take a higher profile.

In terms of understanding the manifestation and mediation of protest, we can view dissent as inhabiting a complex relational space of repetition and difference, where an event of dissent can highlight the way relationships of power are producing the lived spaces we inhabit (Harvey, 2012). From a Foucauldian perspective, this suggests that what is being highlighted, or exposed, are the discourses and regimes of truth that are constructing the space (Foucault, 2007). Consequently, one could argue, without protest/disruption we may not be able to apprehend those hegemonically constructed discourses of power as clearly.

Violence and performativity

Despite the threat of violence being a recurring theme in much of the literature associated with studies of protest and dissent (Della Porta, 2008, 2015), the linking of that theme to its aesthetic and performative articulation is a relatively recent phenomenon (Zizek, 2008). The characterisation of the strategic use of property damage towards banks and global fast-food outlets by anti-globalisation and Black Bloc groups, has brought consideration of such themes to the fore (Solano, Manso, & Novaes, 2014). Black Bloc refers to groups of protesters, frequently conveying an anti-globalisation/anti capitalism message, who dress completely in black; this includes covering the face with a scarf, or ski mask, and sunglasses. Arguably, such attire combines personal protection with a means of steering the media's gaze towards the message rather than the individuals through which it is being conveyed.

This greater dimension of the aesthetic and performative aspects of violence in protest can be understood in relation to what scholars' call 'expressive violence' (Block, 1977). According to Wieviorka (1997), this kind of violence does not have to do with social or economic deprivation, but with reaction to denied subjectivities, the loss of the subjectivity, and to forms of violence experienced not only in the objective but the subjective world. It can encompass issues of identity construction manifested by and against specific groups and causes, such as ethnic and gender related violence, as well as violence against migrants, the elderly and so forth. 'Expressive violence' has, as its social and historical background, the impact of neoliberalism in contemporary politics (Jinkings, 2007). Jinkings argues that as financial global markets redefine the role of the State, budgets for social expenses are reduced while the control of punitive instruments are extended; effectively criminalising that which seeks to actively defy the logic of neoliberalism (Jinkings, 2007). Even though the impacts may be quite different in Europe and South America, the main traits are similar: growth of social inequalities, violence, and corporate and state surveillance. For this reason, it is important to show what the violence means to all the parties involved.

In Brazil, this is a sensitive issue because greater parts of the population are not equal before the law; in regard to either individual, social or cultural rights (Kowarick et al., 2009). Throughout its history, Brazil's values of joy and miscegenation have naturalised and hidden aspects of violence and authoritarianism that have forged a highly hierarchised society in public and private (Chaui, 2013). In areas such as the Maré Complex in Rio de Janeiro, a State of exception is the public rule. Since the end of the 2018 Carnival, the city has been under a federal intervention decree. This has militarised public security forces and created an Extraordinary Ministry of Public Security. It has centralised power, and relativised individual rights, as a means of dealing with a supposedly 'out of control' situation with regard to crime and violence. However, instead of lowering crime, it has ignited a series of murders involving police officers and residents, including Marielle Franco, a city deputy, and 14-year-old Marcos Vinicius (Smith, 2018).

According to Passos (2018) Brazil is, in effect, in an undeclared war between groups ostensibly funded through a direct or indirect association with organised crime. This creates marked sectors, where life is in a state of exception, producing homo sacer (Agamben, 1998); lives treated as worthless, that are not protected against violence or racism, that then become the main victims of State violence (de Silva, 2014). This kind of violent and performative reaction becomes manifest through the justifications made by those who use 'violent' methods in protests and public demonstrations (Solano et al., 2014). Those who adopt the Black Bloc tactics we mentioned earlier justify their actions by saying that their acts carry a symbolic and political message, one that needs some level of violence for it to reach the public sphere (Ibid). They argue that their acts are symbolically directed towards people through damage to goods and property; as such they should be seen as a means of articulating a protest against a perceived greater injustice (Ibid). Such political violence, they argue, is a way to contest a much more lethal State violence (Dupuis-Déri, 2014). It is a way to contest the State monopoly of violence and claim a legitimacy for smaller-scale and more private violence, in a form that targets an abuse of violence by the State. In these forms of dissent, the object is the message, and the performativity of that message carries a high symbolic value (Ibid).

Such identity driven protests produce a message of 'symbolic-expressive violence' that sets itself against a Capitalist order (Juris, 2008); here we also see a relationship between symbolic and physical violence. There is an element of rage ('raiva' in Brazilian Portuguese) against the system; this is central to understanding this kind of violence. It is the use of force, understood as a response of rage and anger against the oppressions of inequality and exploitation. As Sullivan (2004) puts it – it is a 'right to the rage' that becomes expressed as frustration, as a conscious feeling, integrated in the politicisation process and manifested through violent performances (Solano et al., 2014). Here Juris (2008) suggests how violent personal and identity denials lead to emotions that structure political vision and ways of contestation.

Another relevant aspect of such a theatrification of conflict, that appears as public transgression (Duvignaud, 1974), is the desire to reach public attention through mass media channels. In this sense, violent acts are also a way to 'make the headlines'. The human rights journalist Bruno Paes Manso recognised that the use of Black Bloc tactics were effective in getting media attention during the 2013 protests in Brazil (Solano et al., 2014). However, as the protests went on and the debate on the legitimacy of direct action grew, the insistence on using violence to get attention gradually weakened the protesters' claims in the Brazilian public sphere. As the media scholar Eugênio Bucci (2016) explains, an exaggerated claim for visibility in protests is part of a logic of the 'spectacle' which has taken over the public spheres of western democracies. Following that logic, the visibility of the protesters' claims become somehow more important than the political claims themselves. It is through understanding the relationship between the protesters' claims and their media visibility that 'violence' can become the language and the 'raw form' of protest (Bucci, 2016).

Media, protest and mediation of dissent

Studies of the relationship between media and protest usually construe the media as either a series of technological channels/institutions that are somewhat apart from, whilst affecting, political and social movements, or as intervenient actors, amongst others, who exchange and facilitate the circulation of symbols, narratives and information (Krajina, 2017). Both approaches produce what Barker and Petley (2002) refer to as *media effects*, that are capable of engendering agenda setting. Such a perspective is similar to Strömback's conceptualisation of *mediatisation* (Strömbäck, 2014), which argues that it is through the mediated logics of how power is made visible, resulting in increased fragmentation/polarisation and inequality of political knowledge, that political events are determined.

Reminiscent of Massey's approach to space (1992), Jesus Martin Barbero proposes a focus of attention on the social relations within and around communication channels and industries; this he refers to as *Mediation* (Barbero, 1993). Such a position locates media as one amongst other actors present in political narratives and conflicts, rather than a neutral, manipulative and unidirectional political asset. In this view, the characteristics of the media and protests would be better captured outside the media; in less media-centric perspectives, that reflect and amplify the social relations of the media, and the role communication technology plays in contemporary western societies. Consequently, it can open up fresh opportunities for capturing empirical data. Ryan, Jeffreys, Ellowitz, and Ryczek (2013) push this further; in 'Walk, talk, fax or tweet', they argue that one needs to grasp the deep perceptions of participants through their narratives and storytelling, as it is through these that they will articulate reminiscent views and memories of past events. Following a process of thick description (Geertz, 1973) they believe storytelling can enable us to grasp people's worldviews and thus facilitate experiences of empathy or agonism between participants and researchers.

It is from such foundations that new research strategies can be established. Instead of asking participants directly what they think, or monitoring covertly their behaviour, techniques that build a bridge of shared respect and trust between participants and researchers, as true research collaborators, can enable participants to share their personal narratives and memories, which can then relate back to relevant topics in the research. However, in order to progress and develop new techniques we first need to consider those methods more familiar, if safe, to a leisure studies/sociological study of protest and dissent, evaluate their effectiveness and assess what, if anything, can be drawn from them.

Familiar social science approaches to the study of protest

The more common and familiar approaches used in social science research tend to operate around a binary of qualitative and quantitative methods that functionally connect to construals of subjectivity and objectivity. Even though there is an increased use of methods that combine the poles of that binary, they do not significantly challenge it. Such triangulatory tactics are reliant on an assumption that research findings are grounded in a neutral realism to which participants and researchers have a shared access (Robson & McCartan, 2015). Here we hit a significant difficulty when working with participants who are either engaged in leisure activism or its suppression.

Lamond et al. (2015) suggest activism, as an aspect of serious leisure, is a form of self-othering, one that constitutes a public sphere in contestation to that of the imaginary articulated by a dominant hegemony. It is the differences in world views, and their associated principles of what constitutes truth and evidence, that sustains that contestation (Weible & Sabatier, 2006). What this means, in practice, is that those associated with dissent, whether they be engaged in protest or its suppression, are often embedded in a discourse where the manifestation of power relations can obfuscate their contribution to research. Colloquially, it could be said that their public sphere produces a 'comfort zone' that establishes the boundaries within which participants are or are not prepared to participate. Consequently, while we may obtain some insight into a dissenting worldview, this will either reinforce our own position, because it is a cause with which we are in sympathy, or prove problematic to decode successfully, as it sits in a world-view for which that sympathy is absent. Even potential neutrality on a cause is insufficient, as this may also obscure the researcher's apprehension of the participants' ways of being in, and knowing, their social world.

Such difficulties strike at the heart of what constitutes qualitative and the quantitative data and grasping what objectivity and subjectivity mean, as such binaries obviate an understanding of what it means to protest and what the mediation of dissent is doing to the articulation of the manifestation of protest. Alternative methodologies are required if we want to gain insight into these public spheres and grasp the complexity of activist leisure, events of dissent, and their mediation. In order to do that we must begin by looking beyond the relatively simple frameworks of interview, questionnaire, survey etc.; tools that have become the default for a lot of sociological inquiry. An exhaustive review of alternatives is outside the scope of a research paper. We have thus focused on two promising examples, from which we seek to learn: Group Dialogic Approaches, and Photo/Artefact elicitation techniques. Both have informed the research approach we will go on to propose. However, to demonstrate that connection it will also be important to consider the place of the researcher within them.

- *Group Dialogic Approaches*

One way of addressing the issues we have raised would be to approach the topic polyphonically. By that we mean the use of multiple researchers as well as group-based participation. It could be argued that by having multiple researchers, drawn from diverse cultural-political-economic backgrounds, and groups of participants also pulled from different backgrounds; that the differences could be used to facilitate a heterogeneity of voices contributing to the data. In something approaching more familiar social science language one might argue that the diversity permits some form of neutrality to be realised, thereby allowing objective data to emerge. There are, however, problems with such a proposal. At a practical level, how confident can we realistically be that any mix of people in a group would be sufficient to produce a *neutral* discussion? And, besides, what do we mean by 'neutrality'? If we are seeking some level of conviviality between participants, the heterogeneity we are trying to examine would be undermined, thus jeopardising our capacity to examine how a dominant cultural-political economy mediates the manifestation of protest? In addition, there is a strong tradition in social theory (for example Garfinkel (1967/1999) that would suggest such dialogic approaches always contain performative elements that may alter the interactions between the participants. Thus, whilst some form of group discussion may be advantageous, we must be mindful of its performative characteristics and establish some techniques to mitigate those difficulties.

If we wish to obtain an understanding of the experience of leisure activism and events of dissent that are rooted in the lives of people intimately involved in, and associated with, protest, some of which will involve aspects of violence, one must also account for the manifestation of trauma in its articulation. In such circumstances group storytelling can facilitate the elicitation of elements of the subjective expression of lived experience. As we mentioned earlier, Ryan et al. (2013) argue that such narratives are neither a perfect recollection of the facts nor a dramaturgical/fictional representation of the events. However, they do present a space through which participants, as co-researchers, affectively connect to the past. Liao, in her description of cultural activism in Taiwan (Liao, 2015) describes the process like this:

> During the performance, the spectators are experiencing the process of interpreting and decoding the past with the present historical context. The narrative of the past is no longer simply a story told. It is . . . 'a cult enacted'; the experience of time and space is not unequivocally of the past but of a 'metaphysical present'. (p.43)

In order to develop a research plan that can support an inquiry into the multiplicity of narratives associated with leisure activism, we need to establish strategies that can evoke, these *representations* and *performances* of past events in group dialogue. If the familiar format of a group dialogic approach potentially inhibits our capacity to develop suitable data, something is required to disrupt that research framework. What seems to be required, therefore, is the gap between participant and researcher, within the research process, must be contested; framing the research activity as an *event*. This, however, needs to be handled with considerable care and sensitivity. When people are attempting to articulate root concepts around who they are, how they grapple with their orientation to others, and the articulation of their being-in-the-world, they can be highly vulnerable and potentially volatile. How we address such matters is something we will handle in more detail later. For now, it is important to carry forward the idea that participation in research that is serious about developing a richer understanding of activist leisure and the mediation of protest, needs to be exhibit a more evental character. In the next section we consider how photo and artefact elicitation can carry this evental character.

- *Photo and Artefact-Elicitation*

In recent years use of photo-elicitation and artefact elicitation, where photographic images or objects are used to stimulate a discussion or form part of an interview, have seen substantial growth as qualitative research methodologies. Such approaches have merit and may be of value in protest research, though they do come with concomitant challenges to the researcher.

The first person to propose using photography as a means of eliciting data from interview participants was John Collier (1967). His approach still forms the backbone of most approaches to photo-elicitation. Recently Feigenbaum, McCurdy, and Frenzel (2013) have used analogous techniques as part of protest-camp research. In their study, photographs were gathered by the researchers and used to stimulate otherwise unstructured 'Camp Fire chats' (p25) with protest camp occupants. The only example we found of the use of photographs drawn from participants, within social movement studies, was in Adamoli's study of activist uses of photographs on social media (Adamoli, 2012). However, that research primarily used photographs as a source of secondary data, and although some elements of photo-elicitation were employed, its use was relatively minor.

Passing over the selection and curation of images to be used to the participants requires the researcher to give up a degree of control. It establishes participants as co-researchers in the project. Whilst they may not be engaged in all aspects of the programme, the giving up of a key element of the research activity to participants both enhances trust and raises the possibility that the research may not follow the pre-thought pathway that the lead researcher initially intended. Listening rather than interpreting thus becomes the group lead's primary role. A similar situation can occur with the lesser used approach of artefact elicitation. First developed by Barrett and Smigiel (2003), they used artefacts to stimulate interviews around familial participation in the arts, in Australia. Whilst we found no instances of the use of artefacts in research associated with protest, activism, or events of dissent, it does appear to be an approach that might be fruitful as a supplement to group dialogic approaches, within the field. Lead researcher selection of imagery/objects may skew findings, not simply because of some implicit presupposition that connects them but because it also robs participants of ownership of material that is central to their own connection to the issue being addressed by the research. Trusting the participant, being open to what they bring and the data they generate through discussing their artefact with others, pushes the researcher into a potentially vulnerable position. It is, however, a position that has the potential to produce participant data that is more honest, and closer to the topic under investigation, than could be generated otherwise.

So far, we have placed the participant at the forefront of our discussion, let us now turn to focus on the researcher.

Researcher position

As Jarvie (1969), in his work around participant observation in anthropology, was to note, participant observation always revolves around a clash of roles; friend/stranger, participant/observer, insider/outsider. Whilst Jarvie suggests the researcher can take a unique and enriched space that is neither insider nor outsider, others, such as those developed by disability, feminist, queer, and critical race theorists, have argued there is a central problematic here that needs to be addressed (Toy-Cronin, 2018). Issues around the binary of insider/outsider do, at least anecdotally, seem to resonate with research into protest and social movements. Some of this is understandable. Police and security services have, historically, infiltrated activist groups (Uysal, 2014), so some level of scepticism around those asking a lot of questions is important for activist and social movement survival. The tension between the academic and the activist, however, even within the study of protest and dissent, may be more in the affect of the researcher. Whilst bias towards a position is always likely to be present, the discursive practices of critical scholars can be fluid and flexible enough to accommodate a degree of contestation in the ideas and world-views being investigated (Eschle & Maiguashca, 2006).

- *Autoethnography as a way of accessing experiences of dissent*

Earlier we suggested that working with participants as partners in the development of knowledge formation may be part of a way forward. We suggested that such an approach requires researcher vulnerability; exposing them as present in the research, not just a prospector for new data. Open and honest autoethnographic co-presence may thus provoke more authentic perceptions from participants as it allows them to talk about themselves, and their personal experiences, without artificial rationalisation. In this sense, it has both analytic and evocative potentials. Through the narrative exchange of their diverse personal experiences, the research approach becomes eventalised. It thus permits the transformation of the researcher and participants, throughout the research process, through trust and shared vulnerability. Autoethnography that uses participant-led elicitation tools can result in the researcher relaxing an excessive grip on the research agenda, increasing the potential for participant engagement. That 'relaxation' allows feelings and narratives to surface, with the intention to push beyond easy realities. As an approach it is risky but, arguably, necessary to reach towards an otherwise unidentified unknown.

Goodall (2000) argues autoethnography can enable ' ... the creation of narratives shaped by the writers personal experiences, within a culture' (p.9). According to Lockford (2004), in order to promote an autoethnographic research setting, researchers and participants need to 'strip themselves' (p.9) emotionally and intellectually, opening a way for evocations:

> I attempt to situate my readers in a visceral connection with the experiences I describe. The principle that governs the autoethnography is that evocation leads to deeper comprehensions than traditional research, where one is informed about ideas. Lockford (2004, preface).

Reed-Danahay (1997) suggests the autoethnographic experience transcends the limits between experience, perception and thought, of the individuals. According to Neumann (1996), it ' ... democratizes the representational sphere of culture by situating the experiences of individuals in tension with the dominant expressions of discursive power' (p.189). By confronting the individual's interpretation of their past actions, it becomes a strategy that contests non-hegemonic and hegemonic discourses. As Tierney (1998) states; ' ... autoethnography (confronts) ... dominant forms of representation and power, with the intentions of claiming, through self-reflexive answers, representative spaces that have been marginalized in the frontiers' (p.66).Autoethnography thus allows the researcher to access different levels of consciousness, as one ' ... look[s] more deeply at intersections between self and other' (Ellis, 2004, p. 37). It is a mixture of investigation, literature and method that aims ' ... to connect the autobiographical and personal to the cultural, social and political' (Ibid, p. XIX), which leads us to also think about the importance of the researcher's personal life story and narrative.

However, autoethnography, as a non-canonical approach, is criticised by many ethnographers who argue that it cannot produce more 'authentic' perceptions by the participants (Freeman, 2011). Because of its 'self-referential' character, some ethnographers see it more as way of provoking narcissist and essentialist narratives (Valdez, 2008). To a considerable extent such criticisms are mitigated through the supplementing of autoethnography with the elicitation techniques proposed earlier. Through engaging with participants as co-researchers, within a space where different actors involved or associated with activist leisure can engage in honest and open dialogues, as equals, a quality often missing from developing a richer picture of dissent may be allowed to emerge. We will now consider, in more depth, just what is entailed by such engaged research.

- *Engaged research*

We have established that the role of the researcher interested in activist leisure and protest needs to confront several questions. These include the place she occupies in the research, how to elaborate the knowledge it enables, and the role of that knowledge. Traditionally, the answers to these dilemmas have been that the researcher must differentiate herself from the 'object' researched, using her distance from it to produce intellectualised knowledge. This is different from the engaged research we propose, the purpose of which is to understand other possibilities and, fundamentally, to think of the political commitment of the research activity. As such, it surpasses the classic division between theory and practice and the idea that scientific knowledge is separate from social reality. We can draw lessons here from congruous social scientific research in Latin America.

Since the 1960s, Latin America has faced a debate about the role of engaged research in the social sciences (e.g. militant research by some South American academic/activists: see Solano et al., 2014) . In a continent previously colonised by European standards, politically, economically, and in the production of knowledge, Latin American universities reproduced historical asymmetries between centre and periphery, imposing Eurocentric, capitalist, and rationalist approaches to the scientific domain (Quijano, 2000). However, given its Cartesian separation between knowledge and its objects, such Eurocentric and rationalist approaches have become vehicles for the reproduction of injustice and violence.

Alternatively, the work of Paulo Freire (Freire, 2015) can play a fundamental role in the construction of the theoretical base of engaged/activist research methods, as it proposes a horizontal relationship between researcher and participant; one that is founded on listening and shared learning, rather than the 'researcher' harvesting 'knowledge' from the *other*. As we have shown, traditional approaches place the researcher in a hierarchical position of superiority, smothering their participants by placing them in a position of subalternity which reproduces historically unequal relationships of power. Counter to this, engaged research can be built horizontally, so as to serve the participants involved (Meksenas, 2006). Mexican educators Rodriquez and Hernandez (1994), point out that one of the characteristics of this type of research is that the traditional relation between subject and object must be progressively transformed into a relation between subject and subject. The results can lead to new interactions, partnerships, reciprocal learning processes and friendship.

The Brazilian scholar Breno Bringel (Bringel & Varella, 2016) argues that we must rupture the dichotomy between the subject and the object of research if we are to generate and consolidate networks of trust; creating spaces of permanent convergence between universities and social movements. This allows for the realisation of engaged research as a space of knowledge production where heterogenous voices of public policies and social movements meet. The central debate around engaged research is how such knowledge can serve the communities, groups, mobilisations, studied, and contribute to popular transformation. A Freirean orientation that values participants as co-researchers can produce politically engaged knowledge (Freire, 1973). Whilst it does not reject methodological rigour or intersubjective control and unconstrained openness, it adds a commitment to concrete change, particularly directed towards the researcher/research participant relationship.

An important dimension of engaged research is its focus on the themes/agendas relevant to those drawn into the study. It approaches normative social struggles by highlighting the participant's needs, and considers their centrality throughout the research planning process, rather than framing them only as the object of the researcher's academic gaze (Baptista, 2006). As we saw in our discussion of autoethnography, this can go beyond the interview or focus group to include sharing images, artefacts and literature, the interpretation of results, and supporting the project's final evaluation. Drawing of Freire's work on critical consciousness (Freire, 1973), engaged research need not end with the completion of the study. Communication between researchers and participants can persist, going beyond the study's conclusion as knowledge production. A process of continuous feedback between the 'researcher' and the 'research participant' can continue to provide tools for future dialogue, enabling decision making between the researchers, participants and social groups involved (Barker & Petley, 2002).

Brandão (1983) argues that we only know something about social life, in depth, when there is a straight and direct involvement between the lives of researchers and participants. He goes on to argue that there is a need for an attitude of coexistence and reciprocity. Research around activist leisure and protest events (engaged research) seeks to promote participation through the recognition of the *other* (acknowledging heterogenous voices), supporting interaction with political intentions and the development of proposals, through a commitment to social change. It must aim to produce a transformation in the research participant(s) and the researcher(s) as both are considered political subjects that need to step out of their comfort zones. In Haraway's (1997) words, in order to provoke transformation, knowing must be 'think-with' work and not 'think about' work (p.36). It is *thinking with* the *other*, which denies there can be thought separate from the societal realm.

Concluding remarks

The purpose of our paper was to develop a method that could inquire into the multiplicity of narratives associated with leisure activism, drawing on the experience of two democratic states currently experiencing uncertainty and instability.

We began by problematising the topic, approaching our reflections on protest from a perspective of leisure activism (Mair, 2002; Rose et al., 2018) and CES (Spracklen & Lamond, 2016), progressing from there we addressed the themes of the social construction of urban space; the performativity of violence and, finally, the relationship between media and dissent. We concluded that those research approaches most familiar to us in the social sciences were insufficient when considering the heterogenous voices articulated in the urban palimpsest. To address those concerns, we needed to think about research as a collaborative endeavour between 'researchers' and 'participants', one where respect and trust could be nurtured, and grow; a process that could take on aspects of the *evental*.

In the second part of our paper we considered several prospective candidates that, whilst not as universally approved as those we argued were more familiar approaches, went some way to addressing the requirements we had identified. Elements of a group dialogic approach, and the use of photo/artefact elicitation tools, were found to go a considerable way to confronting the issues we had raised. However, they risked reproducing the power dynamic of those more familiar techniques. To undermine those systemic power relationships the place of the researcher had to be more closely interrogated; this was achieved through a consideration of how autoethnography may give us insight into the experiences of dissent. While we recognised that many in the social sciences did not regard autoethnography as canonical, we argued that combining such an approach with the eventalisation of the research process, with the transfer of key elements of the inquiry to the 'participants', could open up fruitful new pathways which can deepen our understanding of protest, events of dissent, and leisure activism. We called that approach *engaged research*. Whilst we acknowledge a strong debt to the 'militant research' perspective we chose the adjective *engaged* to emphasise the importance of building relationships, even amongst actors traditionally seen as opposed. By eventalising the research, providing a space where openness was welcomed, we were able to encourage greater trust, conversation and connection.

Listening and sharing have been a key part of the growth and evolution of this project and this paper. The authors are drawn from both the global south and the global north. Without the development of friendship, trust, and genuine interest in the thoughts, perspectives, experiences, and ideas of each other, this paper would not have happened. It is a tapestry, woven by our own heterogenous voices.

Disclosure statement

No potential conflict of interest was reported by the authors.

Funding

This work was supported by the Research Cluster Award: Leeds Beckett University.

References

Adamoli, G. C. E. (2012). Social media and social movements: A critical analysis of audience's use of Facebook to advocate food activism offline. Retrieved from https://diginole.lib.fsu.edu

Agamben, G. (1998). *Homo Sacer: Sovereign power and bare life*. Stanford: Stanford University Press.

Baptista, T. (2006). The most Portuguese village in Portugal: Tradition in the age of its technical reproducibility. Retrieved from https://run.unl.pt

Barbero, J. M. (1993). *Communication, culture and hegemony: From the media to mediations*. London: Sage.

Barker, M., & Petley, J. (2002). *Ill effects: The media violence debate*. Abingdon: Routledge.

Barrett, M. S., & Smigiel, H. M. (2003). Awakening the 'Sleeping Giants'?: The arts in the lives of Australian families. *International Journal of Education & the Arts*, *4*(4), 1–9.

Block, R. (1977). *Violent crime: Environment, interaction, and death*. Lexington: D.C. Heath.

Brandão, C. R. (1983). *Os caipiras de São Paulo* (Vol. 75). São Paulo: Editora Brasiliense.

Bringel, B., & Varella, R. V. S. (2016). A pesquisa militante na América Latina hoje: Reflexões sobre as desigualdades e as possibilidades de produção de conhecimentos. *Revista Digital De Direito Administrativo*, *3*(3), 474–489.

Bucci, E. (2016). *A forma bruta dos protestos: Das manifestações de junho de 2013 à queda de Dilma Rousseff em 2016*. São Paulo: Editora Campanhia das Letras.

Chaui, M. (2013). Democracia e Classe Média. *Conferência realizada no Centro Cultural Oscar Niemeyer, Projeto Café de Ideias.*Goias, Brazil.

Collier, J. (1967). *Visual anthropology: Photography as a research method*. New York: Holt, Rinehart and Winston.

de Silva, J. (2014). Valour, violence and the ethics of struggle: Constructing militant masculinities in Sri Lanka. *South Asian History and Culture*, *5*(4), 438–456.

Della Porta, D. (2008). Research on social movements and political violence. *Qualitative Sociology*, *31*(3), 221–230.

Della Porta, D. (2015). *Social movements in times of austerity*. Cambridge: Polity Press.

Dupuis-Déri, F. (2014). *Who's afraid of the Black Blocs? Anarchy in action around the world*. (L. Lederhendler, Trans.). Oakland: PM Press.

Duvignaud, J. (1974) *Sociologia Guia Alfabetico*. (nl),Forense.

Ellis, C. (2004). *The ethnographic I: A methodological novel about autoethnography*. Maryland: AltaMira Press.

Eschle, C., & Maiguashca, B. (2006). Bridging the academic/activist divide: Feminist activism and the teaching of global politics. *Millennium*, *35*(1), 119–137.

Feigenbaum, A., McCurdy, P., & Frenzel, F. (2013). Towards a method for studying affect in (micro) politics: The campfire chats project and the occupy movement. *Parallax*, *19*(2), 21–37.

Foucault, M. (2007). *Security, territory, population. Lectures at the College de France: 1977–1978*. (G. Burchell, Trans.). Basingstoke: Palgrave Macmillan.

Freeman, J. (2011). Solipsism, self-indulgence and circular arguments: Why autoethnography promises much more than it delivers. *Journal of Arts & Communities*, *3*(3), 213–227.

Freire, P. (1973). *Education for critical consciousness*. London: Bloomsbury Publishing.

Freire, P. (2015). *Pedagogy of indignation*. Abingdon: Routledge.

Garfinkel, H. (1967/1999). *Studies in ethnomethodology: Social and political theory)*. Oxford: Blackwell Publishing.

Geertz, C. (1973). The interpretation of cultures. In *Selected essays*. New York: Basic Books.

Gerbaudo, P. (2017). *The mask and the flag: Populism, citizenism and global protest*. London: C Hurst & Co.

Getz, D. (2016). *Event studies: Theory, research and policy for planned events* (3rd ed.). Abingdon: Routledge.

Glynos, J., & Howarth, D. (2007). *Logics of critical explanation in social and political theory*. Abingdon: Routledge.

Goodall, H. L., Jr. (2000). *Writing the new ethnography*. Maryland: AltaMira Press.

Habermas, J. (1992) The Structural Transformation of the Public Sphere. Cambridge. Polity Press.

Haraway, D. J. (1997). *Feminism and the technosphere*. New York: Routledge.

Harvey, D. (2004). The right to the city. In Harvey, D. (ed.), *The right to the city* (pp. 236-239) London: Sage. doi:10.4135/9781446221365

Harvey, D. (2012). *Rebel cities*. London: Verso Books.

Huyssen, A. (2003). *Urban palimpsests and the politics of memory*. Stanford: Stanford University Press.

Jarvie, I. C. (1969). The problem of ethical integrity in participant observation. *Current Anthropology*, *10*(5), 505–508.

Jinkings, I. (2007). Sob o domínio do medo: Controle social e criminalização da miséria no neoliberalismo. Retrieved from http://repositorio.unicamp.br

Juris, J. S. (2008). *Networking futures: The movements against corporate globalization*. Durham: Duke University Press.

Kowarick, L., Gurza Lavalle, A., Marques, E., Moya, M. E., Moura, F., & Gervaiseau, H. (2009). *A cidade de São Paulo sempre foi um tema importante para você*. Como foram ... [Entrevista]. Retrato de grupo: 40 anos do Cebrap.

Krajina, Z. (2017). Media and social solidarity: Assessing Dayan and Katz's 'Media Events'. *Medijske Studije*, *3*(5), 3–17.

Lead author. et al. (2015).

Lead author. (in press).

Lefebvre, H. (1991). *The production of space*. (D. Nicholson-Smith, Trans.). Oxford: Blackwell's.

Lefebvre, H. (2004). *Rhythmanalysis: space, time and everyday life*. London: Continuum.

Liao, D. Y. (2015). Space and memory in the Huashan Event. In I. R. Lamond & L. Platt (Eds.), *Critical event studies: approaches to research* (pp. 109–130). London: Palgrave Macmillan.

Lockford, L. (2004). *Performing femininity: Rewriting gender identity*. Maryland: AltaMira Press.

Mair, H. (2002). Civil leisure? Exploring the relationship between leisure, activism and social change. *Leisure/Loisir*, *27*(3–4), 213–237.

Marres, N. (2017). *Digital sociology: The reinvention of social research*. Cambridge: Polity Press.

Massey, D. (1991). A global sense of place. Published in Marxism Today, June 1991. Online at: http://www.amielandmelburn.org.uk/collections/mt/index_frame.htm. Accessed: 01/02/2020

Massey, D. (1992). Politics and space/time. *New Left Review*, *196*, 65–84.

Massey, D. (2004). Geographies of responsibility. *Geografiska Annaler. Series B. Human Geography*, *86*(1), 5–18.

Meksenas, P. (2006). Sociedade civil estado: Contradicoes do espaco publico e interesses democraticos. *Revista Linhas*, *7*(2). Retrieved from http://revistas.udesc.br

Neumann, M. (1996). Collecting ourselves at the end of the century. In C. Ellis & A. P. Bochner (Eds.), *Composing ethnography: Alternative forms of qualitative writing.*Maryland: AlterMira Press. (Vol. 1, pp. 172–198).

Passos, A.M. (2018). Fighting crime and maintaining order: shared worldviews of civilian and military elites in brazil and mexico. *Third World Quarterly*, *39*(2), 314-330. doi:10.1080/01436597.2017.1374836

Pickard, S. (2017) Politically engaged leisure: The political participation of young people in contemporary Britain beyond the Serious Leisure model. Retrieved from https://angles.saesfrance.org/index.php?id=1083

Quijano, A. (2000). Coloniality of power and Eurocentrism in Latin America. *International Sociology*, *15*(2), 215–232.

Reed-Danahay, D. (1997). *Auto/ethnography*. New York: Berg.

Robson, C., & McCartan, K. (2015). *Real world research* (4th ed.). Chichester: John Wiley & Sons Ltd.

Rodriquez, G. L., & Hernandez, L. (1994). *Investigación participativa*. Madrid: Centro de Investigaciones Sociológicas.

Rose, J., Harmon, J., & Dunlap, R. (2018). Becoming political: An expanding role for critical leisure studies. *Leisure Sciences*, *40*(7), 649–663.

Rovisco, M., & Ong, J. C. (eds.). (2016). *Taking the square: Mediated dissent and occupations of public space*. London: Rowman & Littlefield Int.

Ryan, C., Jeffreys, K., Ellowitz, T., & Ryczek, J. (2013). Walk, talk, fax or tweet: Reconstructing media movement interactions through group history telling. In B. Cammaerts, A. Mattoni, & P. McCurdy (Eds.), *Mediation and protest movements* (pp. 133–158). Bristol: Intellect Books.

Smith, C. (2018). Lingering trauma in Brazil: Police violence against black women. *NACLA Report on the Americas*, *50*(4), 369–376.

Solano, E., Manso, B. P., & Novaes, W. (2014). *Mascarados: A verdadeira história dos adeptos da tática Black Bloc*. Sao Paulo: Geração Editorial.

Spracklen, K., & Lamond, I. R. (2016). *Critical event studies*. Abingdon: Routledge.

Strömbäck, J. (2014). Greater media choice risks creating an information gap between 'news-seekers' and 'news-avoiders'. LSE European Politics and Policy (EUROPP) Blog. Retrieved from http://eprints.lse.ac.uk

Sullivan, S. (2004) *We are the heartbroken and furious! Engaging with violence and the (anti)globalisation movement-(s), University of Warwick Centre for the Study of Globalisation and Regionalisation* (CSGR Working Paper 123/03).

Tierney, W. G. (1998). Life history's history: Subjects foretold. *Qualitative Inquiry*, *4*(1), 49–70.

Toy-Cronin, B. (2018). Ethical issues in insider-outsider research. In R.Iphofen & M. Tolich (Eds.), *The SAGE handbook of qualitative research ethics*. London: Sage. pp.455-469

Uysal, A. (2014). Doctrine du maintien de l'ordre et encadrement policier des manifestations en Turquie. *Revista de Estudios Internacionales Mediterráneos*, 17. http://revistas.uam.es/index.php/reim/article/view/941/929 Accessed: 01/02/2020

Valdez, C. G. (2008). Expresión autoetnográfica: Consciencia de oposición en las literaturas de los Estados Unidos. *Revista de Antropología social*, *17*, 73–94.

Weible, C. M., & Sabatier, P. A. (2006). A guide to the advocacy coalition framework. In F. Fischer & G. J. Miller (Eds.), *Handbook of public policy: Theory, politics, and methods* (pp. 123–136). Florida: CRC Press.

Wieviorka, M. (1997). The new paradigm of violence. *Tempo Social*, *9*(1), 5–41.

Zizek, S. (2008). *Violence*. London: People Books Ltd.

Young activists in political squats. Mixing engagement and leisure

Carlo Genova

ABSTRACT
The aim of the article is to show that youth involvement in political groups is often driven by such multifaceted motivations that it is relegated to the border between engagement and leisure. Focussing on the European context, research about youth and politics often highlights that few young people are personally involved in political forms of action. In most studies, this involvement is interpreted as the actualisation of a set of values, through their translation into specific aims and means, on the basis of correspondent wider worldviews, that is, representations of society and human beings. Such an interpretative approach is challenged on the basis of the results of research conducted in Italy through qualitative interviews with young activists involved in political squats. Through an in-depth analysis of young activists' narratives, it is suggested that youth involvement in political groups often represents partly, or even mainly, a form of leisure connected with variegated sensitivities and tastes at least partially external to perspectives of political engagement, and conversely connected with personal satisfaction and fulfilment.

1. Rethinking the interconnection between leisure and activism

In social sciences, the study of leisure and its activities has been for a long time quite independent of the study of social and political participation. Both topics have a long tradition of studies but, on the one hand, different disciplines have exclusively focussed on one or the other of these two fields; on the other hand, even those disciplines, such as sociology, which have studied both topics, have actually developed separate sub-disciplines, concepts and approaches for the two research streams. Only very recently, therefore, have activism and leisure been explicitly presented as fields with fuzzy boundaries, and even then as concepts in a dialogue (Arora, 2015; Gilchrist & Ravenscroft, 2013; Kjølsrød, 2013; Lamond, 2018; Lamond & Spracklen, 2014).

The main reasons for this situation seem to be rooted more in scholars' perception than in social reality. The historical role of music, and art more generally, in social movements has for example, been clearly highlighted (Bogad, 2016; Eyerman & Jamison, 1998; Friedman, 2013). The point, however, is that very often this research has essentially interpreted artistic practices as instruments of intervention and protest. Somehow the meaning of these practices was reduced to their, more or less direct, contribution to goal-oriented perspectives which characterise, in scholars' eyes, protests and social movements. Consequently, it was taken for granted that the conceptual frames emerging from the study of social and political participation were also sufficient to interpret these forms of action. It is then easy to understand that, partly due to the weaker conceptual structuring of the field of leisure studies, the intersection between leisure and activism has been mainly investigated by trying to interpret 'leisure as activism'.

In the past decade a growing amount of research has explored this intersection from different perspectives. The aim of the article is to contribute to this work, focussing on young activists involved in political squats: the hypothesis is that this involvement can be interpreted as a mix of engagement and leisure. Political squats are particularly interesting because, through the occupation of abandoned public buildings, they conjointly promote explicitly political, ideologically inspired, often radical, forms of action, and a great variety of social and cultural activities which are usually categorised by the research itself as belonging to the leisure field. Moreover, political squats still belong to groups with political connotations where the presence of youth is most relevant.

2. Youth, politics and activism

As Barrett and Pachi (2019) suggest, young people's relations with politics, as well as their different forms of social and political participation, have been widely explored in the last two decades. Focussing on the European context, most of this research is greatly fragmented: there are many qualitative studies dedicated to specific phenomena, in specific territorial areas, and adopting different dimensions of analysis; there are some national surveys with a wider perspective but through a limited number of often very traditional or even outdated items.

It is thus not easy to sketch an updated portrait of youth from this point of view; nevertheless, on the basis of the most recent wide-ranging research, some general distinctive traits can be highlighted. Since the beginning of the 2000s most Europeans, particularly young people, have increasingly lost trust in political systems and taken their distance from institutions of representative democracy, as well as from institutional forms of participation (Dalton, 2004; Franklin, 2004; Pharr & Putnam, 2000; Torcal & Montero, 2006). Today's young people, compared with adults, are less interested in politics and in the political debate; less trusting in political systems, institutions, parties and politicians; less involved in institutionalised forms of political participation, such as voting, activism in political parties and candidacies for formal political positions. Nevertheless, a significant proportion are aware of the main social problems, reflect upon potential solutions, and are more active than adults in non-institutional forms of participation, such as social movements, protests, petitions, digital activism and some forms of social intervention (Andersson et al., 2016; Cammaerts et al., 2016; García-Albacete, 2014; Loncle et al., 2012; Maggini, 2017; Pilkington et al., 2018; Roholt et al., 2014).

In the Italian context the situation is similar but assumes distinctive traits (Alteri et al., 2016; Bichi & Istituto Giuseppe Toniolo, 2013; Bonanomi et al., 2018). A disconnection between youth and institutional politics is evident. Considering first of all political collocation on the left-right scale, 35–40% of youth do not express a position. Moreover, the same percentage does not favour any existent political party or declare any intention to vote. Less than half of young people recognise and adopt basic institutional political landmarks and agree, or are able, to express a personal positioning among these landmarks. And focussing on their attitudes towards politics, the scene is not very different: less than 5% declare themselves to be 'politically engaged' and around 35% declare themselves to be uninterested in, or even disgusted by, politics (Bichi & Istituto Giuseppe Toniolo, 2013). Additionally, trust in political institutions is very weak and decreasing. Political parties, parliament and government obtain the lowest levels of trust, whereas higher levels can be observed only for local or transnational institutions and 'politically neutral' institutions such as schools and police (Bonanomi et al., 2018). Finally, only a few young people in Italy are directly involved in institutionalised forms of political participation or in protest events. Although involvement in associations and groups with social-intervention aims is more common, it concerns a minority of youth (around 15% in the case of social engagement, and around 5% in the case of political engagement). Considering that over 90% of youth claims to discuss politics (although only occasionally), this means that only in a minority of cases does this interest evolve into active participation (Bichi & Istituto Giuseppe Toniolo, 2013).

In short, most Italian young people have little difficulty in defining which socially-relevant goals politics should pursue; they express interest in issues of collective relevance; they declare themselves to be informed about politics; they express keen willingness to engage; they even recognise a relevant role for 'politics' in the improvement of the social context. At the same time, however, few of them have structured collective political worldviews; few of them assign much relevance to politics; few are personally engaged in institutional forms of political intervention or with political groups in general (even if non-institutional, occasional forms of political action and of social intervention are more widespread).

Based on such data, it is often argued (both in research and in public debate) that the weak diffusion among youth of forms of political action can be interpreted in two different ways: either as a consequence of the weak relevance attributed to politics and of the fragmentation of collective political worldviews; or as a consequence of the interaction of these values and worldviews with other factors (such as the lack of trust in political institutions and the costs of participation) which interfere with their translation into forms of action. This means that it is taken for granted that worldviews and values are the fundamental drivers of action in the political field, which is to say that youth forms of action in the political field represent the actualisation of a set of values (concerning 'how reality should be'), through their translation into specific aims and means (concerning 'how reality can be changed'), on the basis of correspondent wider worldviews about society and human beings (concerning 'how reality is'). The problem is that, as previously underlined, a wide range of surveys and of qualitative research about specific phenomena concerning youth, politics and participation shows that there is only partial correspondence among the possession of political worldviews, the attribution of relevance to politics and political action, and the adoption of political aims and personal involvement in political action. Differentiated profiles of the presence and absence of these different elements among young people can be observed (strong values but fuzzy aims, strong values and aims but no action, and even action with weak values and not-so-clear political aims).

3. Methodology

The aim of this paper is to reflect upon possible alternative interpretative models of youth involvement in political groups, in particular based on the hypothesis that, nowadays, it often represents a mix of engagement and leisure. The article focusses on a specific case, political squats; on a specific context, Italy, where this phenomenon is quite widespread; and on a specific sector of young people, the activists, the individuals most involved in these groups.

The article is based on research conducted through qualitative interviews with 27 activists (19 to 29 years old; 12 female and 15 male; from Brescia, Fermo, Florence, Padua, Rome, Turin, Treviso and Venice). Documentary analysis of websites, Facebook pages and flyers produced by the groups has also been conducted. The groups were chosen on the basis both of geographical variability and of contacts resulting from snowball sampling. The interviews were obtained by presenting the research and its aims, depending on the case, either to the interviewees or to the assembly of the group, focussing on those individuals most regularly involved in the activities of the group.

Since the article aims at exploring the 'leisure dimension' of the activists' involvement in their squats, the analytical categories usually adopted in the study of youth political participation (such as ideologies, representations, values, aims, strategies, activities) were not sufficient. Following Rojek (2005; 2010), Best (2010), and Stebbins (2017), the study of leisure with reference to individual drivers of action focusses on personal desires, satisfaction, fulfilment, pleasure (and then on personal sensitivities, interests, tastes), so these categories have been added to the research. Mixing these two sets, differently from the most widespread literature on youth activism, the article examines individual drivers of participation and collective perspectives of action with a wider perspective, going beyond the boundaries of politics; and it takes into consideration all the relevant individual practices and lifestyles which are collectively shared in the groups, even when they are neither formally organised nor presented as official activities by the groups.

More specifically, the analysis focusses on eight main dimensions: individual biographical paths of the activists; individual meanings and motivations of the activists; collective activities and forms of protest; collective issues of intervention and aims; organisational instruments and strategies; collective representations and narratives; distinctive traits, practices and lifestyles of the activists, inside and outside of the squat and its formal activities; and the uses and representations of squat premises and urban space.

The different empirical materials have been coded through a qualitative content analysis approach (Grbich, 2013; Kuckartz, 2014; Schreier, 2012) on the basis of these thematic dimensions. Subsequently three different streams of processing have been adopted conjointly. First, focussing on each dimension separately, the analysis has been oriented towards the individuation of different modalities with the aim of elaborating an internal typology as an instrument of systematisation and synthesis. Second, reading the different modalities with a transversal approach, the analysis has aimed at identifying possible emergent patterns of co-occurrence, and thus of elaborating more general typical profiles. Third, focussing in particular on the ideological matrix of the different squats, the analysis has attempted to observe whether a connection between profiles and matrixes can be found.

4. Results and discussion

4.1. Society

Following a classical approach, the first element in the analysis of youth political action is world-views: representations of society, of its main problems and of their causes and guilty parts.

Most of the young activists' narrations on this topic highlight first of all the difficulty, or even the impossibility, of synthetically describing today's society, and of just identifying some of its distinctive traits.[1] This society is frequently perceived to be so complex and articulated that any comprehensive portrait is felt to be beyond the activists' capabilities; nevertheless, some critical aspects seem to emerge from their words.

Present society is described as capitalist, and consequently as characterised by an excessive focus on economic aims and, in parallel, by strong inequalities of resources and thus of power. In the interviewees' words, 'capitalism', 'fascism', 'racism', and 'sexism', intended as interconnected forms of dominion by powerful minorities, elites, over the population, are the main reasons for the different existing forms of injustice.

Focussing on the economic level, which is often described as the core of the question, elites are accused of pursuing wealth accumulation through exploitation of individuals, both producers and consumers. And since standardisation is a core principle of production because of its advantages with regard to economic production and social control, homogenisation is one of the main traits promoted in consumption, and more in general in society.

At the same time, however, economic production needs competition, so, in tandem, and only apparently in contradiction, individualism is widely glorified and safeguarded. The same elites, through their cultural power, infuse thus in society the celebration of economic success, proposing it as the main goal for individuals. The result of these processes, in the activists' eyes', is the weakening of traditional social ties, in the absence of the emergence of new, different, ones.

Few activists compose all these different elements into a structured, coherent narration; in most cases only some of these traits are highlighted, and only some of their interconnections. It is clear that no collectively shared, pre-defined, structured, 'ideological' narrations circulate in their groups, but rather some only-partially-interconnected coordinates of interpretation. Awareness of the complexity, and also of the rapid mutability, of this society seems to be at the same time the cause and the effect of this weakness of the young activists' worldviews: on the one hand, they cannot find any satisfying grand narrative able, in their eyes, to give an account of today's society and its problems because of their complexity and rapid change. On the other hand, they seem to underline this complexity so explicitly and frequently as to make sense of their lacking a structured narration/interpretation of this society.

> Surely the logic of exploitation and submission to financial capitalism is clear to everybody, and also why one should fight against them ... I mean, I don't know if this is a comprehensive vision of society, I don't think so, partly because society has many facets. (Interview 12)

> Well ... let's say that a shared vision ... we are building it. [...] In broad terms [...] we all envisage a dialectic with institutions ... but it is clear that having, from a political point of view, different positions, one tells you that he is there for social struggle, another one tells you that an alternative political vision is needed. [...] The background vision is more or less the same, we are all against capitalism, [...] [but] it is necessary to clarify the topic of capitalism, I mean ... it is neither simple nor to be taken for granted. (Interview 17)

> [We share the idea that] society doesn't represent us and agree about what its problems are, [...] that we live in a society that is not like the one we would like to live in. That's it. (Interview 7)

4.2. Perspectives of intervention

Once activists' worldviews have been considered, the subsequent elements to be analysed are their representations of the perspectives of intervention of the groups they are involved in, as regards aims, activities and beneficiaries. A great variety of approaches can be observed in interviews and documents; and even if most of them clearly show a political structure, some of them are more-or-less directly connected to a leisure dimension, going beyond political aims and instrumental activities, and being oriented not only to external beneficiaries, or to the entire society, but also to the activists themselves and to the satisfaction of their needs and desires. Four main perspectives can be identified.

The first perspective aims at increasing awareness and education. The target is people in general, or, more realistically, those people with whom the political group has the opportunity to come into contact. The goals are to inform these people about issues and situations the group is trying to act on, and to spread the values and projects of the group through a three-step process: First, disseminating a more critical and independent attitude towards mainstream information and cultural models, propagated primarily by the mass media. Second, increasing attention towards topics and problems, as well as proposals about strategies of intervention which are neglected or criticised by the mass media. Third, diffusing awareness, belief in the possibility of social change in this direction. The main activities consist of cultural ventures, debates, book launches and social networks, as well as concerts, screenings, leaflets and marches.

The second perspective aims at a concrete intervention on specific situations and problems, both through direct action and through pressure on decision makers or other subjects with power of action. In most cases these forms of intervention are in favour of deprived people whose improvement in life conditions is supposed to depend on the choices and decisions of power centres. The approach is not that of acting 'on behalf of others', but rather to conjointly help people in acquiring awareness of their possibilities of action, as well as in organising their action, and to join them in this action. Protests, pickets and fundraising are among the main activities.

At the core of the third perspective is the goal of training for the activists of the group. Instruments employed are activities of internal formation, collective analysis and study, such as meetings, seminars, debates, research and the creation of archives. Improvement of the activists' knowledge aims at greater ability both in analysing reality and in acting to change it. The approach is not that of transmitting a pre-defined set of principles and notions, but rather of promoting the development of individual skills and the collective elaboration of shared frames. The result is never the elaboration of structured analytical and operative models, but the progressive and temporary coordination of fragmented elements.

The fourth perspective concerns the experimentation, here and now, of alternative mindstyles and lifestyles. Besides action for wider change in society, the experimentation of practices and styles alternative to the mainstream, dominant, ones and prefiguring future society, is fundamental in political squats. In this case, not only the official and public activities of the group, but also a wide range of everyday practices (as will be described in the following sections), are developed as forms of experimentation and concretisation of an alternative culture.

The unifying horizon for all these perspectives is a general and radical social change.

> We want a society which is free from work, free from institutional forms of delegation, from psychological and social forms of control. We have a shared idea of freedom, more than a shared idea of society, let's say. [...] We are not reformist, so we don't have short-term goals. [...] We want to be a permanent criticism, a form of alternative organisation which is reproducible and shareable by as many people as possible. (Interview 25)

> There is a set of goals concerning the short-medium term, directly concerning rights, [...] to try to tear away as many pieces as possible from the state, [...] to redistribute them in society. [...] On the one hand there is the desire of looking to a short-medium term to raise issues and try to solve them; about urgent needs, on the other hand, there is anyway ... always that tension [...] to ensure that something changes in this country and also beyond it to really change direction. (Interview 11)

4.3. The place of the squat in urban space

Compared with other radical political groups, the main distinctive traits of squats is their being occupied places. A political squat as a place is a building, almost always public property, with different previous functions, at a certain point neglected, and subsequently occupied to develop public activities and to live in. The choice of occupation is partially connected with the need of a group of people for a place to develop their activities, depending on the lack of places provided by the institutions, but also partially with the desire to highlight the lack of non-commercial places available for human sociality in today's society. Significantly, most political squats' architecture has aesthetic traits which make them very 'different' and very 'visible' against the urban background: this visible alterity aims at expressing their non-visible social and cultural otherness.

This otherness, however, is not a total externality. Political squats often claim in their documents to be «other» and «against» but also «within» this society. In this sense squats as places have porous boundaries (with continuous waves of comings and goings). They represent 'protected' places where mainstream culture, in its material and immaterial dimensions, is, at least partially, substituted by an alternative one, experimented and built mainly through the freedom supplied by the squats to the individuals and through their interaction in the squats. But the squat is also a place where people who do not belong to the political group come and participate in public events, just as it is the place where the activities to be developed 'outside' the squat are organised.

Moreover, political squats are places where explicit reflection about space is developed, in particular about public urban space. Political squats, in Italy, are in most contexts, an urban phenomenon. The city is their field of action, and public urban space is often intended as a battleground. On the one hand, public urban space is one of the contexts where «dominant» social, cultural, economic and political processes become more visible; on the other hand, it is the terrain where political squats mainly develop their action against these processes. For these reasons, «reclaim the city» is one of their most widespread slogans.

The squares and streets of cities are thus core places for the young activists, instruments both to make their presence, their activities and their messages publicly visible and to show the possibility for all the individuals to use those places for their own needs, transgressing the social and legal rules which usually control them, and highlighting the possibility of breaking those rules. Both political activities (such as marches and pickets) and socio-cultural activities (such as concerts, dinners and performances) are developed in public urban places. The relative importance of the squat and of the streets as places of reference depends on the sensitivities, and on the activities, of the different squats and of the different activists.

4.4. Meanings of involvement

In the previous sections, attention has been paid to the different perspectives of intervention characterising political squats as they appear in activists' descriptions and in their public documents. It is now fundamental to move the focus onto the activists' individual motivations, meanings of involvement in squats, on the basis of their narrations. Mixing leisure studies and research on youth political participation, this aspect has been explored by paying attention both to political representations, values and aims and to elements of self-satisfaction and fulfilment. Complex, often fragmented, frames emerged, but it is possible to identify some prevalent drivers, and to organise them into a comprehensive typology of four main sets.

The first set is political, and is linked to explicit dissatisfaction with, and criticism of, today's society on its various levels. This society, coherently with the general worldviews previously presented, is described as characterised by injustice rooted specifically in social inequalities, and a consequent distribution of power, mainly connected with capitalism. One of the reasons for being involved in a political squat is thus acting against both the causes and the effects of this injustice.

The second set of drivers is connected with the artistic and cultural dimension. The squats organise not only protest events such as demonstrations and marches, but also cultural events such as concerts, dances, cinema projections and stage shows. These events have two distinctive traits. First, they are aesthetically different from the mainstream, proposing different styles, having different messages and contents, and being as they are for the most part connected with a critique of the 'dominant mainstream culture' and with the promotion of the issues and the sensitivities shared in the squats. Second, alternative social rules are adopted in the squats during these public events: low prices, different (and somehow more informal and weaker) dress codes, different modes of personal interaction (e.g. macho forms of intersexual approach are strongly condemned), and visible use of soft drugs. Some of the activists get in touch with their squat mainly to participate in these activities and to enjoy a different milieu.

The third set could be defined as 'social'. Albeit with different approaches, all the squats have among their aims the building of social networks. Some activists appreciate the presence in the squat of a dense, tightly-knit group of people characterised by sharing specific values, aims, tastes, styles and practices weakly diffused in the society as a whole; for others the squat is primarily a place to meet an ever-changing set of people sharing a more fuzzy set of sensitivities and tastes; in both cases they participate following a 'social' driver.

Finally, the fourth set of drivers is connected with all the others: the squat, as a place and as a group and network of people, allows them to experience, 'here and now', alternative everyday practices and lifestyles. It supplies spaces, people, events, objects and languages different from dominant mainstream ones, through which to experiment another way of living in this society.

> There was this group of people doing things in an anarchist way, making decisions collectively, and I simply thought it was cool. It was something very naive, everything was overlapping, punk and politics with anarchism and horizontalism, everything mixed. Actually it is in this group that I trained and gained higher awareness ... I felt that it reflected what I was experiencing on my own. (Interview 22)

> What enables you to move on is the fact that inside you truly wish to influence the future of what surrounds you and desire to try to change reality, that is what moves all of us. You are not a militant because it is in fashion, but because you truly desire to change things. Then also a group spirit emerges, and a community. It takes a lot, but it also gives a lot. For me it has been an automatic passage, with no doubts, progressively. (Interview 19)

> What drove me [...] is a discourse of political strategy. [...] Political reasons are a part of what drove me to join this collective, because actually I immediately found [also] a great sync with these people, [...] very, very, friendly, very ... not arrogant, not pretentious. [...] I immediately found a great openness, great friendship, even the possibility of expressing my own weaknesses, my doubts, ... without feeling judged. (Interview 20)

4.5. The choice of squat

After reconstructing these complex portraits of the young activists' drivers of engagement, we can try to deepen our understanding of why they are involved in a squat, instead of adopting other forms of participation, once more paying attention both to political and leisure-oriented drivers. The main difficulty in finding an answer to this question, on the basis of the narrations given by the activists themselves, is that it intersects biographical paths, reflexive choices and more casual events.

Two main different 'drivers' of contact exist, at least on the basis of the young activists' accounts. For some of them the socio-cultural dimension is the main one, so the first contact with the squat occurred by attending a concert, a music night, a film screening, a theatre show or other similar events. For other activists the path was 'political' from the beginning, and in these cases public protests represent the first occasion of contact. In both cases friends and peers are relevant agencies of socialisation, as sources of information and stimuli about political and cultural opportunities in the city; peers in high school in particular very often represent a fundamental source of opportunities. The impact of family and parents is quite variable: in some cases the young activists grew up in contexts with left-wing and social sensitivities, but in other cases the family was rather a neutral, or even hostile, milieu from this point of view.

Concerning this aspect, however, the territorial context has a relevant impact. In the bigger cities, even if at present the number of squats and radical political groups is smaller than in the 1990s, still several projects exist. The first contact with a group on the scene is indeed important, but subsequently individuals have the opportunity to explore other groups, and eventually to choose the one which best fits with their personal sensitivities. But in smaller cities only one squat or radical political group exists, so involvement in the scene implies involvement with that specific group because no alternative exists.

The most interesting aspect is that, in both cases, after the first contact and a period of 'exploration', remaining in a group and direct involvement in its activities depend on the fact that there the individual finds, and continues to find, the satisfaction of different personal needs. As pointed out already, different reasons motivate this involvement, different desires, different needs (not all are political); what is more, these reasons and needs can change over time. The active and involved participation of an individual in the group depends therefore on the fact that it allows him/her to sufficiently satisfy all these different needs.

It is interesting to observe, however, that both in bigger and smaller cities, after the first 'exploratory' period, once the individual has found the group that fits with her/his personal sensitivities, when involvement in a squat is no longer satisfying, the young activists tend either to remain in their group with weaker involvement or to abandon politics as a whole. Moving from one squat to another is more common only among the anarchists, whose squats tend to be evicted more often.

> I grew up hanging out at the oratory of my parish and the local branch of the PCI (ed.: the Italian Communist Party) where my father was a member. [...] Around the last year of junior high school me and my friends heard that [...] near our neighbourhood a big place had been occupied and there were concerts on Saturday afternoons. [...] Me and my friends were immediately attracted by punks, we liked music, we like the style, we made new friends among them. (Interview 8)

> I arrived here, together with other "misfit mates", after four or five years of active political militancy in several groups, both in high school and in university. We matured, first of all intellectually by study because [...] we arrived here first of all as musicians and secondly motivated by a political ethos. [...] My friends and I shared

> political ideas, for example, Che Guevara, peace, … I mean, what a high school student […] can find … the first collectives, the first assemblies, […] and also, at least for me subjectively, the necessity of clearer answers, because I have always been a great devourer of books, so the questions were deeper and deeper and more precise (Interview 3).

4.6. The group

After having considered the narrations of the activists about their motivations, meanings, engagement and perspectives on the intervention of the groups they are involved in, it is fundamental to consider their representation of the people active in these groups, and in particular of their peers, focussing in particular on the traits of reciprocal recognition.

Usually research on youth activism disregards this dimension, or at least takes into consideration only political frames, values, aims and activities. In the following analysis these aspects have of course been monitored, but besides this, following leisure studies, attention has been paid also to clothing and aesthetics, cultural tastes and forms of consumption, as well as spare-time activities.

The first aspect which can be considered is that of political worldviews. In the interviewees' narrations, and in the documents of the groups, a critical description of today's society and an orientation towards a radical transformation are explicit. This general frame is often connected to four main streams of intervention: anti-capitalism, anti-fascism, anti-racism and anti-sexism. A fifth, animalism, is also often present, especially in groups with anarchist sensitivities. However, these elements are rarely inserted by the interviewees into a structured narration with clear and complex coordinates, but rather emerge as quite fragmented: attention to social processes, a general sense of injustice, the will to change reality and distrust of political institutions are very often present and reciprocally connected; but few other transversal components can be identified in their discourses.

The second aspect is that of forms of action: moving from the above-mentioned distrust of political institutions, very often young activists identify occupation and the forms of action described in previous sections as distinctive traits of their group. And it is interesting to highlight that very often these forms of action are narrated as relevant for the group not only, or mainly, because of their efficacy as forms of political action, but as meaningful in themselves, as symbols of the culture of the group.

Concerning these two aspects, however, weak references to wider representations, in particular to ideological frames or even authors and doctrines, as well as to specific symbols and keywords, appeared in the narrations (albeit some keywords and iconic ideological symbols and references are present in documents). Boundaries and cornerstones of collective frames about 'how today's society works', 'how society should work' and 'what we can do about it' are, on the whole, quite blurred. Political frames seem to be weakly defined in the groups through top-down processes, but rather open to the influence of individual sensitivities, mainly resulting from an informal, partial and temporary alignment among the activists' individual sensitivities, even if in a dialogue with some 'official' lines of the group.

Besides these 'political' elements of collective identification, others (more heterogeneous) came out of the narrations and the documents as equally relevant. Clothing styles and aesthetics are one of the main additional elements: even if significant differences exist depending on the group and on the ideological matrix, a sort of shared custom exists. In some cases specific items of clothing are distinctive (examples are black hoodies with connoted drawings, icons or words). In other cases there is a more comprehensive style, such as only black. Piercings, tattoos, metal accessories (in steel, not gold) and further elements recalling the rockabilly, punk, skinhead, Rasta and post-industrial styles can often be seen. Very interesting is that in most cases the individual aesthetic is not so particular as to radically distinguish, in the eyes of an external observer, an activist in the middle of a group of non-activist peers. Nevertheless, the image of a group of young activists all together immediately acquires, in the eyes of the same observer, an undeniably distinctive effect.

Often connected with custom are musical tastes, which represent a further relevant element of identification: some songs, some bands or entire genres can be fundamental traits of collective recognition either for the single group or for an entire area of movement. Even if musical sensitivities have kept on changing among young squat activists, as they have among their peers, during the three or four decades since political squats emerged in Italy, some tastes have continued to be points of reference: punk, rap, reggae and ska are the main styles. Similarly, specific artists and bands, old and new, keep on being considered as benchmarks for the scene or for parts of it.

In parallel, tastes and interests concerning spare time, sport and cultural consumption often represent important points of reference. It is more difficult to identify these traits precisely because they are often totally informal and less visible, and different in different squats. But some points of reference can be found. Connections with groups of football hooligans exist. Boxing is sometimes the main shared sport activity, partly through the organisation of 'popular' gyms in the squats. Soft drugs, in particular cannabis, are widely consumed, whether or not the group campaigns for their liberalisation. Alternative food styles – such as vegetarianism, veganism, fair-trade, organic style and supportive buying groups – are widespread, again with or without an official line. These are often individually adopted practices among the activists rather than formally structured choices organised and promoted by the group. All these different elements can be relevant to collective distinction and mutual recognition among the young activists.

5. Conclusion: young activists between leisure and engagement

The early sections of this paper underlined that, following the traditional analytical approach to youth participation, youth forms of activism ought to be considered as the actualisation of a set of values (concerning 'how reality should be'), through their translation into specific aims and means (concerning 'how reality can be changed'), on the basis of correspondent wider worldviews about society and human beings (concerning 'how reality is') (Andersson et al., 2016; Cammaerts et al., 2016; García-Albacete, 2014; Pilkington et al., 2018).

However, if we apply this model to the findings of the research presented in the previous sections, it only partially fits. Few systematic, consistent narrations about today's society, its main problems, 'guilty parties', and potential solutions emerged in interviews, only fragmented and partial discourses (§ 4). Different perspectives of action were presented, oriented both to an intervention on society and to the activists of the group (§ 5–6). Both self-oriented and hetero-oriented drivers of individual engagement can be observed, very often in the discourse of the same individual. And these findings were confirmed by the reasons for the individual's choice of squat (§ 7–8). Political worldviews and forms of political intervention were described as relevant elements of collective identification and mutual recognition in the groups – but without structured shared narrations – in parallel with relevance to aesthetic styles, consumer practices, interests and both non-political and non-engaged practices (§ 9). The squat itself was seen as a place not only to organise and develop political activities but also to experiment alternative lifestyles.[2]

As a result, it is possible to assert that the structure of shared political worldviews, values, aims and means which, according to the traditional analytical approach, ought to be at the basis of the young activists' engagement in political squats finds only very fragmented and partial correspondence in the research data. So it is not possible to explain and interpret this engagement using that model.

Here is an alternative proposal. The interactions among individual representations, values, aims and actions of the young activists are more complex than expected; the meanings they connect with their actions in the political field are also external to the boundaries of politics, and mix collective aims of social improvement and individual aims of self-satisfaction, socio-cultural positioning, self-expression, experimentation, self-formation and network building. More specifically, youth involvement in political squats has to be interpreted through more complex frames, and cannot be integrally interpreted as a form of political engagement, but rather represents a mix of activism and leisure.

It is not easy to define what leisure is: both in social science encyclopaedias and dictionaries and in dedicated handbooks, definitions of leisure are very different or even absent. But two aspects seem to emerge and are particularly relevant here (see Best, 2010; Rojek, 2005; 2010; Spracklen, 2011; Stebbins, 2017; Veal, 2018). On the one hand, leisure is mainly intended as made up of activities, and in particular of activities chosen by free will, developed in periods of time free from work and other compulsory activities. On the other hand, these activities are described as taste-driven, connected with personal sensitivities, and thus with individuals' attempt to fulfil pleasure and satisfy desire as well as to position themselves in society.

The main point here is the methodological and analytical consequences of interpreting youth involvement in political squats as a mix of activism and leisure. First: instead of focussing only on worldviews, values, aims and formal political activities, research must take into consideration tastes and sensitivities, and more in general the complexity of meanings that individuals connect with their involvement. Second: research cannot investigate only formal political activities developed in political groups. It must also consider formal activities without political connotations, as well as those informal practices adopted by the activists. Such practices represent relevant elements of identification, distinction and recognition within the group, but are at the same time external to the group's set of officially organised and developed activities.

The present article has tried to follow these two directions, which has allowed explaining and interpreting young activists' involvement in political squats despite the weakness of the traditional factors adopted in explaining political activism in their application to the study of this phenomenon.

Notes

1. In the following pages the article will use the expression 'today's society' as an emic concept, in order to describe the accounts in activists' narrations of the social context they feel they act within. Thus, although the boundaries and scale of this context are not objectively or transversally definable, the concept in itself seems to be sufficiently shared among the young activists to be used in the analysis of the interviews.
2. For a comparison between cultural frames and forms of action of Italian activists of political squats and those in other territorial contexts in Europe, see Squatting Europe Kollektive (2013), Cattaneo and Martínez (2014), and Martínez López (2018). Focussing on the Italian context, for a comparison between political squatting and other youth cultures involved in alternative uses of urban space (parkour's *traceurs*, skateboarders, and graffiti writers) see Ferrero Camoletto and Genova (2019).

Disclosure statement

No potential conflict of interest was reported by the author.

References

Alteri, L., Leccardi, C., & Raffini, L. (2016). Youth and the reinvention of politics: New forms of participation in the age of individualization and presentification. *Partecipazione e conflitto*, 9(3), 717–747. DOI:10.1285/i20356609v9i3p717

Andersson, B., Cuconato, M., De Luigi, N., Demozzi, S., Forkby, T., Ilardo, M., Martelli, A., Pitti, I., Tuorto, D., & Zannoni, F. (2016). *National contexts of youth participation* (Comparative report. PARTISPACE deliverable 2.2). https://zenodo.org/record/48113

Arora, P. (2015). Usurping public leisure space for protest: Social activism in the digital and material commons. *Space and Culture, 18*(1), 55–68. https://doi.org/10.1177/1206331213517609

Barrett, M.& Pachi, D. (2019). *Youth civic and political engagement*. Routledge.

Best, S. (2010). *Leisure studies: Themes and perspectives*. Sage.

Bichi, R. (2013). La partecipazione politica. In Istituto Giuseppe Toniolo, *La condizione giovanile in Italia: Rapporto Giovani 2013*. pp. 157-176. Il mulino.

Bogad, L. M. (2016). *Tactical performance: The theory and practice of serious play*. Routledge.

Bonanomi, A., Migliavacca, M., & Rosina, A. (2018). Domanda di rappresentanza e orientamento politico. In Istituto Giuseppe Toniolo, *La condizione giovanile in Italia: Rapporto Giovani 2018*. pp. 109-136. Il mulino.

Cammaerts, B., Bruter, M., Banaji, S., Harrison, S., & Anstead, N. (2016). *Youth participation in democratic life: Stories of hope and disillusion*. Springer.

Cattaneo, C., & Martínez, M. A. (2014). *The squatters' movement in Europe: Commons and autonomy as alternatives to capitalism*. Pluto Press.

Dalton, R. J. (2004). *Democratic challenges, democratic choices*. Oxford University Press.

Eyerman, R., & Jamison, A. (1998). *Music and social movements: Mobilizing traditions in the twentieth century*. Cambridge University Press.

Ferrero Camoletto, R., & Genova, C. (2019). Alternative spatial styles. An exploration of socio-spatial youth cultures in Turin. In J. K. Fisker, L. Chiappini, L. Pugalis, & A. Bruzzese (Eds.), pp. 179-199. *Enabling urban alternatives: Crises, contestation, and cooperation*. Palgrave MacMillan.

Franklin, M. N. (2004). *Voter turnout and the dynamics of electoral competition in established democracies since 1945*. Cambridge University Press.

Friedman, J. C. (Ed.). (2013). *The Routledge history of social protest in popular music*. Routledge.

García-Albacete, G. (2014). *Young people's political participation in Western Europe: Continuity or generational change?* Springer.

Gilchrist, P., & Ravenscroft, N. (2013). Space hijacking and the anarcho-politics of leisure. *Leisure Studies, 32*(1), 49–68. https://doi.org/10.1080/02614367.2012.680069

Grbich, C. (2013). *Qualitative data analysis: An introduction*. Sage.

Kjølsrød, L. (2013). Mediated activism: Contingent democracy in leisure worlds. *Sociology, 47*(6), 1207–1223. https://doi.org/10.1177/0038038512466970

Kuckartz, U. (2014). *Qualitative text analysis: A guide to methods, practice and using software*. Sage.

Lamond, I. R. (2018). The challenge of articulating human rights at an LGBT 'mega-event': A personal reflection on Sao Paulo Pride 2017. *Leisure Studies, 37*(1), 36–48. https://doi.org/10.1080/02614367.2017.1419370

Lamond, I. R., & Spracklen, K. (Eds). (2014). *Protests as events: Politics, activism and leisure*. Rowman & Littlefield.

Loncle, P., Cuconato, M., Muniglia, V., & Walther, A. (2012). *Beyond discourses, practices and realities of youth participation in Europe*. University of Chicago Press.

Maggini, N. (2017). *Young people's voting behaviour in Europe. A comparative perspective*. Palgrave.

Martínez López, M. A. (Ed.). (2018). *The urban politics of squatters' movements*. Palgrave.

Pharr, S. J., & Putnam, R. D. (Eds.). (2000). *Disaffected democracies: What's troubling the trilateral countries?* Princeton University Press.

Pilkington, H., Pollock, G., & Franc, R. (2018). *Understanding youth participation across Europe*. Springer.

Roholt, R. V., Baizerman, M., & Hildreth, R. W. (2014). *Becoming citizens: Deepening the craft of youth civic engagement*. Routledge.

Rojek, C. (2005). *Leisure theory: Principles and practices*. Palgrave.

Rojek, C. (2010). *The labour of leisure: The culture of free time*. Sage.

Schreier, M. (2012). *Qualitative content analysis in practice*. Sage.

Spracklen, K. (2011). *Constructing leisure: Historical and philosophical debates*. Springer.

Squatting Europe Kollektive. (2013). *Squatting in Europe: Radical spaces, urban struggles*. Minor Compositions.

Stebbins, R. A. (2017). *Leisure activities in context: A micro-macro/agency-structure interpretation of leisure*. Transaction.

Torcal, M., & Montero, J. R. (2006). *Political disaffection in contemporary democracies: Social capital, institutions and politics*. Routledge.

Veal, A. J. (2018). *Research methods for leisure and tourism*. Pearson.

The emerging civil society. Governing through leisure activism in Milan

Sebastiano Citroni and Alessandro Coppola

ABSTRACT

The paper discusses the emerging forms of civil society in the NoLo area of Milan that have acquired political relevance by deploying a combination of leisure and activism. The heterogeneous set of initiatives and events that, using the NoLo label, animate the urban space have two distinct traits: firstly, they exert a subtle political action which is played out at a cultural level, in particular in their ability to draw on and influence common sense and taken-for-granted perceptions; and secondly, the chosen initiatives effectively influence local policy-making processes, in line with the neoliberal governance of the city and the authorities' promise to govern not just for the citizens but with them. The case study provides an empirical illustration of an emerging urban civil society, with specific attention on its functioning, how certain situated events were set up and unfolded, and two specific episodes of involvement in local policy-making. The proposed research findings - including the exclusionary/inclusive pattern that shapes citizens' involvement, the consensus-building strategy enacted by the studied civil society and the increasing political relevance of bottom-up urban initiatives - illustrate the meaning of governing through leisure activism in Milan.

Introduction: the emerging civil society, leisure activism and urban government

The increasing relevance of festivals, public performances and other cultural events promoted by civil society actors has attracted widespread attention from scholars of urbanism and leisure (Citroni, 2020; Sampson, 2012, p. 179). Indeed, such initiatives animate and reshape public spaces in ways that call into question the most well-trodden arguments on urban changes, protest and creativity (Grigoleit et al., 2013). In particular, current convivial and cultural initiatives – such as neighbourhood parties (Morelli, 2019) or graffiti (Brighenti, 2020) – are highly relevant in shaping major processes of urban change, such as gentrification (Zukin, 2010).

The connection between protest and leisure has an emerging history (Gilchrist & Ravenscroft, 2013; Lamond, 2018; Lamond & Spracklen, 2015), drawing on events and the animation of public spaces to express dissent and put forward collective actions in a variety of urban contexts. This process gained further momentum with the advent of the so-called 'new social movements, with their spectacular events and other ephemeral, highly symbolic, practices that challenged the dominant codes of action and discourse' (Citroni, 2020, p. 5).

Nowadays, urban events have regained a central role in contemporary public space, by establishing a different connection with collective action and politics. Indeed, the current growth of events animating urban spaces combines forms of action that fall into categories that in the recent history of protest through arts and leisure were traditionally separated: political activism and for-profit events (Lamond, 2018); mainstream urban development and movements embodying a radical critique of it (McLean, 2014); urban diversity and the subtle exertion of power over its definition (Tissot, 2014); the temporary use of public space as a platform for alternative cultures and practices and their appropriation by mainstream urban processes (Boltanski & Chiapello, 1999/2017).

Based on participant observation of events and situations, a set of in-depth interviews with relevant actors and the critical analysis of media and digital sources, this paper addresses the case of what we define as 'NoLo as a civil society' (hereafter, NCS) The label NoLo refers to a small area of Milan where in recent years new forms of neighbourhood-based forms of urban activism, have arisen. We argue that this case offers a particularly striking combination of leisure and politics: an emerging form of urban civil society that draws widely on convivial events, initially aimed at enhancing the local quality of life and eventually coming to enjoy increasing political relevance. In a nutshell, in the selected case study, leisure activism does not refer to the use of events and leisure practices to protest, but rather to their political use within the local governance framework.

Indeed, our analysis of NCS shows how its political relevance corresponds to the expansion and stabilisation of governing through civil society typical of neoliberal societies (Brighenti, 2016; A. Coppola, 2018a; Foucault, 2005) and allows us to further explore this argument that, while widely discussed in theoretical terms, appears to have been seldom addressed empirically. More specifically, we argue that NCS represents a case of animation of urban spaces through an emerging combination of leisure and activism that resonates distinctively with the Gramscian concept of subtle political action, a kind of action that is played out at a cultural level (Citroni, 2019), in particular in its ability to influence common sense and taken-for-granted perceptions (Gramsci, 1975). Based on this assumption, we addressed the case study with questions such as: how does this specific and situated form of urban government through leisure-oriented civil society actually work? What are its main conditions of possibility and the concrete devices through which it is actually produced on the ground by combining leisure, conviviality and activism? And what are mechanisms and processes of inclusion and exclusion that ultimately make it possible?

The paper is organised as follows: we first introduce the case study, paying particular attention to the ways it defines belonging by enforcing strategies of 'exclusion/inclusion' (Citroni, 2015); second, we focus on two specific public policy processes in which NCS played a significant role, in order to investigate the relationship of this civil society with policy-making processes and local politics; third, we discuss the empirical material and finally we move to the conclusions

The context: NoLo as civil society (NCS)

The name 'NoLo' stems from its geographical location *No*rth of Piazzale *Lo*reto, in north-east Milan. NoLo now appears both on Google Maps and in the city's planning documents, as the city council voted in March 2019 to change the area's designation from 'Loreto' to the new name 'Loreto-Casoretto-NoLo'. This move was the outcome of a longer-term campaign launched in 2015, when a group of Milanese creatives coined the acronym 'for fun' (A.Coppola, 2019). Rapidly, news coverage started to associate the new brand with signs of 'urban regeneration' of an area traditionally represented through negative discourses (Sironi, 2016). In particular, the NoLo narrative reversed the territorial stigma attached to two adjacent neighbourhoods: the area around the central station, with its concentration of homeless shelters and petty crime; and the Via Padova area, a neighbourhood with a large migrant population that in the recent past has recurrently been associated with violence and urban insecurity in mainstream national media reports (Verga, 2016).

Besides its strategic role in spreading a 'positive' narrative , more significantly the NoLo label started to be used as a prefix or suffix in the naming of a variety of new urban initiatives, events and social network pages related to the area. These included, to name but a few: the *Nolo Fringe Festival*, which features live shows and performing arts; *Biennolo*, which organises contemporary art shows in a variety of local spaces; *RadioNolo*, a local internet radio station that, apart from broadcasting, also incorporates a variety of initiatives such as *Sannolo*, a neighbourhood music festival; NoLo Social District (n.d.), a Facebook group, currently with over 9,000 participants, that allows neighbours to contact one another and organise a variety of events to animate local public spaces, such as the open-air Saturday morning breakfast, often through specific Facebook sub-pages; *Qulo* (a variant on the Italian word for 'arse'), another Facebook page which publicly contends that the NoLo brand contributes to the area's gentrification; and *Occupy Nolo*, a protest event, including dancing activists, that took place on 1 May 2019 in NoLo's main square and aimed to draw attention to the risk of gentrification.

This heterogeneous set of initiatives together forms NCS: an open field of social formations, subjectivities and relationships that mobilise the NoLo label to animate the local urban space. What qualifies this field as civil society is not the content of the initiatives it includes or the motivations of those who organise them (Biorcio & Vitale, 2016). Instead, NCS is here intended as civil society in the most familiar sense of the expression, in other words the public or potentially public settings in which uncoerced participants engage in ongoing, voluntary associations, outside of the immediate demands of family, work, or government (Walzer, 1992). Liberal political thinking has defined civil society as a sphere of groups carrying out actions outside institutional politics and its formal procedures but nevertheless affecting institutionalised politics (Habermas, 2000). Although this kind of consequence may appear distant from the meanings attached to the aforementioned initiatives by those who set them up, they nevertheless do produce relevant political implications. Before focusing on such implications, and in order to better grasp their essential conditions of possibility, we must first specify how NCS and its initiatives are structured.

Civil society events and their exclusionary/inclusive pattern

A relatively easy entry point to NCS is NoLo Social District (NSD), a Facebook page that acts as the main organising device and reference point for most of the above-mentioned initiatives. NSD, according to the introduction on the page:

> is an extended social street, a group whose goal is to create connections among people who live in NoLo (North Loreto) and want to get to know and help each other: sharing what is going on in the neighbourhood, exchanging advice on services and shops, and launching neighbourhood initiatives.

As is common in the statutes of non-profit associations and other civil society groups, NSD's self-description makes clear its nature as a non-political and non-partisan project, as 'the group is not associated with either political parties or businesses, and is independent'. In particular, its aim to 'contribute to the improvement of the quality of life of those who live in the neighbourhood' marks NSD out as universally oriented, pursuing goals that are so broadly defined they are difficult to either contest or criticise. However, there are some limits to this inclusivity, as while the group is 'open to all neighbours', the guidelines clarify that 'racist, offensive and intolerant comments are not allowed'. The combination of inclusion and exclusion is particularly striking for readers when seen within a single sentence, such as the following: 'NoLo Social District is a space of free speech: political, religious and ideological propaganda in any form is not permitted'. If this understanding of free speech appears universal and not partisan to the reader, it is probably because he/she shares the same viewpoint.

The many thematic sub-pages associated with the main one, each of them devoted to a specific matter, topic or public, epitomise the concrete articulation of NCS's activities and events: 'environmental sustainability' for *Nolo Plastic Free*; swapping second-hand clothes for *Nolo mercatino dell'usato*; children's activities for *Nolo for Kids* and activities for cat-lovers for *Nolo Cats*; and reading together and sharing recommendations for *Nolo Lettura*. Similar to that which emerges in NSD's self-description, the sub-groups also appear universally oriented, pursuing goals and carrying out activities that are difficult to disapprove of or criticise. These activities comprise leisure practices that are similar to most of NCS's initiatives, such as enjoying the music of *Sannolo* or the fringe culture shows of *Nolo Fringe Festival*, spending time in the local night spots or learning about local history in the *GiroNolo* neighbourhood tours. We are not denying the potential 'politicalness' of meanings attached to such initiatives by those setting them up or participating in them. On the contrary, there are reasons to believe that – as clearly outlined with respect to environmental activism (Lichterman, 1996) – involvement in NCS is associated, in participants' actual experience, with both self-expressive and political motives: for example, swapping second-hand clothes at open-air markets is also done with the aim of emptying wardrobes and combatting consumerism, while at the same time being an enjoyable practice directed towards animating and improving the neighbourhood.

Though such instances coexist, their combination in NCS follows a specific pattern that is typical of urban events (Citroni, 2020) and is crucial to account for the rapid growth and political relevance of this local civil society. It is a double pattern which, on the one hand, portrays NCS events as inclusive, associated to concerns that enjoy wide consensus within the new urban middle classes (such as environmental sustainability) and translated into convivial activities that are difficult to criticise in themselves. On the other hand, while reproducing a given discursive order, the NCS events also produce a new order with respect to the local scale to which they refer and which inevitably includes partial versions of the general issues. Only by moving from the events' official communication to an in-depth analysis of their situated taking place can one grasp this discursive order and the subtle ways in which it conveys its messages, thus reinforcing its inevitably exclusionary boundaries. Seemingly trivial, local urban events promote general values (e.g., sociability, public space and sustainability) while enjoying, as both a condition of the development of such events and their outcome, the possibility to control the situated meanings of these values. This was made clear, for example, by Sylvie Tissot (2014) with respect to civic associations that promoted urban diversity in a local area of Boston through events – such as guided tours – that 'controlled' the local meaning of diversity, presenting a version of the local history as the only legitimate one.

The same can be said of the *GiraNolo* free neighbourhood tours, in which the authors took part as participant observers. This kind of initiative is highly valuable as a free opportunity to get to know and deepen one's knowledge of local history, starting from its contemporary traces in the neighbourhood. That said, the local history narrated during the guided tours of NoLo is inevitably partial, as it stresses certain aspects and neglects other, equally legitimate, ones: largely unintentionally, the past is often interpreted in light of the present, with respect to ongoing projects and the current situation, such as the fact that those narrating the local history tend to position themselves as having a legitimate right to do so. In particular, analysing the contents of the NoLo guided tours highlighted three recurrent features of the local area – a place of arrival for migrants, urban blight, and work – that sustain, and certainly do not contradict, the positioning of NoLo as the latest expression of a wider story, well established in the shapes and uses of the local buildings and the biographies of those who inhabited them.

As will be specified in more detail in the discussion section, we are not claiming here that NCS intentionally or strategically appears as universal and open while instead being covertly partial and purposefully exclusive. This is something that to some extent inevitably occurs, but it is also accentuated because of the urban events adopted as NCS's main repertoire of action: events act as effective weapons of cultural power, as they invite participation in pursuit of general goals while at the same time allowing events' organisers to subtly control the specific meanings of the goals they are pursuing, given that the latter are necessarily specified only when the events actually take place, through apparently irrelevant details (Citroni, 2020). Such forms of power, in the case of NCS, do not pertain solely to its urban events, but are also a feature of the functioning of this local civil society, which can be observed in other aspects, such as the process of the proliferation of Facebook sub-pages through which NSD grows with new activities and participants. This process is key to understanding both the dispersed strategy through which NCS manages to develop a variety of initiatives and events and the way in which it builds consensus and supports the organising process, as it facilitates the recruitment of new proactive participants for NCS's development.

The proliferation of NCS sub-pages is a double process, simultaneously light in its organisational logic and powerful in its effects. On the one hand, for the individual, creating a new group or participating in an existing one is a relatively undemanding task (Wuthnow, 1998). On the other hand, joining thematic groups brings with it major repercussions: it works as a powerful mechanism of consensus building, given that the new adherents – while focused, for example, on running, or knitting with others – simultaneously become proactive promoters of the development of NoLo as a civil society. Given its importance, it is therefore not surprising that the process of the proliferation of new interest groups is channelled through a Facebook page that details the instructions to be followed for the creation of a new NSD thematic group. On this page, the word 'INCLUSION', written in large black characters against a background of small coloured hands with smiling faces, is the title of the section dedicated to 'NoLo Interest Groups' and the 'List of thematic sub-groups and rules for opening'. The graphics resemble those seen on flyers, websites and brochures dedicated to volunteering and solidarity projects, in a similar effort to associate captivating images with empowerment and social cohesion programmes. As the introductory text states:

> The important thing is not to segregate people and to ensure that everyone knows about the events and can participate in them; [...] For us, the key word is always the same: inclusion.

To ensure maximum 'inclusion', the text continues, six rules are established to which readers are 'asked to pay attention'. The first of these dictates that the groups created 'must be closed', while the third states that individuals can only be accepted into these groups if they are already members of NSD. As mentioned above, it is not worth giving undue emphasis to the possible contradiction between the inclusion proclaimed by the group and its betrayal in the restrictive access rules. This contradiction would only apply to critical observers with a demystifying intent, not from the point of view of the person who wrote the page, and therefore in the proposal it offers to the reader. It is therefore only an apparent contradiction, which reveals the same exclusionary/inclusive pattern mentioned above with respect to NCS events: the fact that its inclusionary attitude and aims have as a condition of possibility, and at the same time outcome, the ability to control and shape the local meaning of inclusion being pursued. Given its importance, however, it is vital to avoid misunderstandings about this form of 'control' – and therefore power – activated by NCS, to which we will return in the final discussion, having first illustrated NSD's political importance.

Mobilising change: NCS as a critical partner of critical urban policy

As it moves from the characteristics that we mentioned above, the formation and consolidation of NCS can also be observed by looking at its complex, intense relationships with local public policy-making processes. Traditionally, Milan's local governance system has been described as being uniquely oriented towards the mobilisation of a strong civil society and towards its inclusion in public policy-making processes ... This legacy has positioned the city on the leading edge of more recent evolutions in urban governance, with the city government widely relying on social innovation initiatives, co-creation and co-design processes such as urban living labs and other emerging governing technologies (Evans et al., 2015). Although tailored in a variety of ways and associated with different labels and narratives, all these initiatives have allegedly strived to produce a shift from a top-down to a co-production paradigm of public policy design and implementation (Coppola, 2019b) based on the active inclusion of organised, although at times informal, groups of residents (Citroni, 2020).

In many ways, such patterns of local politics/civil society relations can be seen as a highly significant manifestation of the key promises of the increasingly dominant neo-liberal governance of the city, and more specifically the pledge not so much to govern 'for the citizens' but to govern 'with the citizens'.[1] This promise is a major feature of the discourse of the city leadership and other relevant actors involved in the local system of governance and focuses in particular on issues of urban regeneration and related matters such as philanthropic institutions, social cooperatives and other intermediary organisations, academic institutions and knowledge providers (Coppola & Caudo, 2020). NoLo's discursive order has found opportunities for consolidation and expansion through its links to some critical junctures between public policy and the NCS, activated by the city administration. Some of these junctures have proved to be particularly in line with the conditions of possibility of the new forms of urban civil society that are under examination here. The 'call for projects' on one side and the creation of at times informal and rapidly evolving networks and partnerships on the other are the essential devices for the production of these policy arenas, which provide abundant activation and involvement opportunities for people with a high level of cultural and social capital.

In a way, the rise of NCS has become a source of acceleration of these processes at a local level, twisting the trajectory of public policy in a new direction. Until a few years ago, the city had been mostly engaged in a set of initiatives that revolved around 'social cohesion'. These initiatives focused specifically on the most troubled section of the area, advancing a series of actions aimed at strengthening relations in apartment blocks, and improving the perception of safety in certain areas by funding highly professional actors already active in the externalised social care economies. Settings such as the 'cohesion laboratory' funded between 2014 and 2018 and managed by a social cooperative and a new 2017 call 'with the aim of making peripheral areas "beautiful and happy"' (Comune di Milano, 2018) by funding similar actors epitomise this approach. The area was also included in the framework of the 'Città Intorno' initiative promoted by the Cariplo Foundation, a key player in urban policymaking in Milan, and pursuing the betterment of local quality of life through 'a series of engagement devices aimed at involving local communities' (Fondazione Cariplo, n. d.). A goal not so different from that declared by another city-wide call for projects – 'Eventi nei quartieri' – which supported 'social, cultural and sporting initiatives aimed at animating 24 peripheral areas of the city' (Comune di Milano, 2019). All these programmes, albeit in different ways, clearly shared a focus on the promotion of 'events' in the context of a wider set of actions. These events, taking place both in public and semi-public spaces such as neighbourhood courtyards, were seen in the discourse of both policy designers and providers as tools to enhance 'social cohesion' and support 'urban regeneration', 'creating community', and 'improving relations'. NCS has taken the focus on events, sociability and civilities in a new direction, while clearly heightening its political relevance by profoundly altering the traditional set of actors involved in their implementation.

Redesigning public space from below

Two processes based on a variably significant dynamic of civil society mobilisation can be employed to observe how NCS became a critical actor in local policy making while also contributing to its restructuring. In 2018, the city launched a new call in its participatory budgeting programme aimed at funding small physical interventions based on a three-step process: the design of the proposal, an initial round of voting and subsequent technical assessment carried out by the city, and a final popular vote to choose two projects to put into practice for each municipality. A handful of mostly professional members of NSD decided to participate in the call with a project aimed at implementing a 'soft mobility' strategy within the neighbourhood, which involved widening pavements, turning parking spaces into seating areas with vegetation and building cycle paths. The overall idea was to 're-appropriate public space' while enhancing bicycle and pedestrian mobility within the area and across the main thoroughfare, Viale Monza. The project was developed through a series of meetings and also by using a Facebook group – *Nolopartecipa*, presented as a group belonging to NSD – where the promoters exchanged ideas, shared the results of meetings, published case studies and took on tasks regarding both the design and the networking required for the project. The group had 15 to 20 active members at the time of the design of the initiative and once the project was designed, an open Facebook page – now with 877 followers – with the project name 'Mobì' was started. Some introductory events were organised both in the neighbourhood and outside, in part by turning other NoLo events – in particular, the Saturday morning breakfasts – into special events to support the projects throughout the final vote. All these activities were clearly framed as an 'electoral campaign'. On the Facebook page, a series of posters portrayed a diverse set of neighbourhood residents and users conveying a slogan stating why they would support the project.

Despite gaining many votes, the project was not approved, as the municipality in which NoLo is located had four projects ranked in the first four positions city-wide, making the competition particularly challenging. In a post published on the Mobì page, promoters pointed to this very high level of fragmentation as the main reason for their failure and also underlined the very limited ability of the proposal to gather offline votes as opposed to online votes, as people could vote both ways. Months later, and based on an intervention from the city's transport commissioner, a wider network formed incrementally, comprising city-level groups that had already promoted a similar experiment in another area of the city: Genitori anti-smog (2019), a parents' association advocating more effective anti-pollution policies; *Fiab* and *Ciclobby*, two cycling advocacy groups; and finally *CORE-lab*, a group of consultants in a range of matters including urban greening based in the area. A key resource that this sudden 'scale jump' from a local to a city-level set of actors brought about was the inclusion of an activist-cum-professional who specialised in 'soft mobility' projects and had designed an earlier similar intervention in the city. In this new situation, and differently from what would have happened in the context of the Participatory Budget, the implementation regime was a three-month experiment aimed at gathering evidence on how to implement '*Zone 30*' – areas with a speed limit of 30 km per hour – in the city. The initiative was then relaunched with a new and more spatially limited design, in part due to the specialist's intervention, through a series of meetings involving some of the original activists, activists from the newly included actors and the city's transport experts. A new key actor – *CORE-lab* – was also included, which, initially in charge of the greening component of the project, rapidly also engaged in activities related to conflict management and participation. As some residents voiced opposition to the experiment, mostly due to its impact on traffic and parking, *CORE-lab* organised focus groups and public meetings with the project's supporters and detractors. The idea behind the focus groups was that 'the concept of the common good is constantly renegotiated', and that in the context of *TrentaMi in Verde* – the new name of the initiative – 'the root problem is that these people (i.e. the opponents) did not feel [like] participants because they were not involved in what happens in the city and around them (...), so now that they have been involved, even by expressing discontent, they can feel part of a process'.

After the project was approved by the city, the experiment was set up using wide grassroots participation from local activists, some other city-based and external support. While activists belonging to different entities worked on the construction and installation of urban furniture and vegetation and brightening up the pavements, the city provided paint and some furniture, with other private companies and foundations offering small-scale financial support. The setting up of the experiment was organised as a three-day participative, hands-on festival. The three days included events as varied as an open-air breakfast with the inauguration of a book exchange point, site visits for school pupils, a poetry reading, a workshop on natural cosmetics organised by the *Nolo Plastic Free* group, a children's workshop run by the *NoLo4Kids* group, a tour organised by *GiraNolo*, a pillow fight and finally a party held at a local furniture outlet. On one of the days there was also a live broadcast by *RadioNolo*, while on another day an open-air sports event promoted by the school and the parents' committee was taking place as well, and was included in the programme of *TréntaMi in Verde*'s opening event. The focus on fun throughout the entire enterprise, clearly displayed on the project's Facebook page, was also paramount in the self-identification of the activists as, in the words of one of the promoters, 'we do serious things but always with the aim of having fun, and every time we met for the upkeep of the site we also made sure to eat together and to have a good time' (Nolo Partecipa (n.d.) and Progetto Mobì (n.d.) activist, Milan, 2020).

Turning experiments into policy

Once the project had been realised , the issues of managing it and consolidating it as a long-term solution became the top priority. On the first issue, NSD and *CORE-lab* signed a collaboration pact with the city – a device put in place with the aim of involving and increasing residents' responsibilities in the care of public spaces – while activists continued with their maintenance days. On the second issue, the network promoted a petition on change.org and put petition sheets in some bars and shops that had supported the initiative and the development of NSD throughout (A. Coppola, 2019). By the end of 2019, the collaboration pact, and the experiment itself, was over and the network announced on its pages the launch of 'Dismounting 30MI', participative days aimed at removing plants and furniture that were then donated to local schools. Later, right after the end of the most acute phase of the Covid-19 crisis, the city administration announced the long-term consolidation of the project.

Shortly after the implementation of *TrentaMi*, another initiative was launched in the neighbourhood based on a partnership established by the city administration with *Bloomberg Associates (BA)*, a consulting spin-off involving some members of New York City's two Bloomberg administrations from the mid-2000s to the mid-2010s. Along with another partner (National Association of City Transportation Officials, *Natco*), this initiative experimented with fast, temporary redesigns of streets and under-used urban spaces, with the goal of limiting the presence of cars, improving walkability and creating new public spaces by hosting a range of activities and uses. By pushing administration departments to work collaboratively and by relying on a set of newly recruited young consultants, the partnership between the city and BA promoted several projects across Milan, later consolidating the initiative in a new programme – *Piazze Aperte* – based on a call to residents and other actors to present projects for specific sites (Comune di Milano, 2019b). A thoroughfare located in the NoLo area and originally part of the plan proposed by the Mobì project was chosen by the city to be a site for the experiment. While based on Mobì's original ideas, the project was designed within the framework of collaboration between BA and the city departments and was presented publicly.

As it involved creating an entirely new public space in front of a school, with considerable impact on traffic flow and parking, the project rapidly led to polarisation between some residents and the local trade association – supported by the municipality's right-wing administration – opposing it and a sizeable group of school parents and NCS activists advocating it. Eventually, through more meetings, a final project including some changes in response to opponents' complaints was presented and realised. The final implementation of the project involved a company – *Vestre* – as well as interventions from the city and large-scale participation from volunteers from the local groups and a city-wide group, *Retake*, which promotes clean-up campaigns in general. A festive event involving school children, local activists and key figures from the city administration was held to inaugurate the new square. And in this case too, a collaborative pact for the management of the site was set-up with *RadioNolo*, the school parents' committee and *Vestre*. Therefore, finally, as 'there was a push, there were people able to scratch this negativity' and because the project 'had a long gestation process through so many (policy) containers to give it a critical mass' (City consultant, 2020), the city was able to overcome local resistance. And once more, the proactive participation of NCS activists and its ability to bridge to other key groups – school parents in this case – was a critical resource for the success of the initiative.

Discussion: the subtle methods used to gather consensus and exert power

The variety of urban initiatives it produces illustrates how NCS features leisure activism in specific terms, only partially recalling previous discussions of the topic (Lamond et al., 2020). It is not an example of political activism openly adopting leisure to pursue its objectives, but rather a form of animation of and commitment to an urban space that widely relies on leisure initiatives as devices for building and reproducing a sense of local belonging and identity. Urban events are fundamental in shaping NCS, both in terms of its functioning and for the production of its local, social and political outcomes. Open-air markets, children's parties, neighbourhood breakfasts and other similar practices are seemingly trivial occasions, but considered together, concentrated in one neighbourhood, they can contribute to significant urban changes, such as gentrification processes (Gerosa, 2019); and when taken individually – focusing on their details, as in the in-depth analysis proposed above – they reveal an inclusive/exclusionary pattern that is fundamental to account for the type of power exerted by NCS, both through events and through other devices, such as digital communication.

This power reveals two recurrent features. First, it is not an attribute of any of the individual actors involved and its functioning does not result from any strategic intentionality. As shown with respect to the NSD Facebook sub-groups, the rules for fundamental aspects of their development – such as the eligibility requirements – are not imposed but merely asked to be followed in order to guarantee the maximum possible level of inclusiveness. Thus, no one is responsible for the preventive exclusion of people from these groups or from the NSD page, as everyone is simply called upon to implement this rule while taking advantage of the opportunity to engage a large potential audience for their own initiatives.

Furthermore, NCS's leisure activism puts forward and consolidates a discursive order that, while largely drawing on common sense, has its own autonomy and produces its own implications, such as legitimising and sustaining certain uses of public spaces and associated urban transformations (Zukin, 2010). NCS develops its discourse in openly inclusive terms and this makes disentangling its exclusionary effects particularly difficult. Such effects may eventually become apparent in the context of conflicts involving NCS's responsibility for certain, more large-scale outcomes of its own existence, i.e. signs of the overall improvement of the area (Gerosa, 2019).

At the same time, even when the intentions are allegedly apolitical, NCS produces some quite significant political consequences. NCS's aforementioned ways of exerting power are put to work effectively and made visible by the mobilisation of NCS in the context of the two analysed policy design processes where it has played a genuinely disruptive role, including in respect to established forms of civil society. By engaging with and helping to shape these processes, NCS moves away from the traditional models of civil society engagement, both that based on externalisation – such as the aforementioned 'social cohesion' projects managed by third-sector organisations – and the model based on a more adversarial style of local organising, built around demands that the government is expected to satisfy. In so doing, NCS has come to embody a new form of local agency as it represents a 'more proactive bottom-up form' of local engagement that pushes the administration to organise 'more transversal initiatives (...) by creating a critical mass around possible issues through the collaboration of different professions that happen to be in the same neighbourhood' (City councillor, 2019). By relying on the social and professional capital of participants, NCS shows its ability to package policy interventions, moving from the initial conceptualisation of ideas, their structuring across policy opportunities, the articulation of an organisational network and of a social alliance, its local promotion and finally even the mobilisation of consensus-building strategies.

In this way, NCS has proved to be a critical, and in many ways unexpected, resource in *governing* the neighbourhood by considerably lowering the risks of policy action on behalf of the city administration and its political leaders. This has happened through a decisive reconfiguration of the traditional distribution of roles in policy-making processes that to a great extent leverages the production of forms of leisure activism.

As a city consultant stated, the 'bottom-up' nature of the examined interventions – and more specifically of *Trentami in Verde* – that 'the city supports but does not promote' (City consultant, 2020), allows policy 'to become more of a relationship between residents themselves than between the residents and the city experts' (Architect, 2020). In this perspective, NCS's leisure activism has increased the political feasibility of often contested interventions: building the street furniture together in a convivial way and have older women sewing on the temporary tables 'is the real added value that has been instigated by NoLo' (Architect, 2020). As it has pushed residents to take the lead in policy innovation, it has also made them directly responsible for dealing with diverging preferences and outright resistance from other residents. In this sense, the role played by events – and more specifically leisure events – appears to have been transformed and made more effective in comparison to their use by more traditional actors and in previous policies. Events are no longer the outcome of the instrumental logic of specialised and formalised actors often linked to public funding, but rather an essential dimension of social mobilisation *per se* and a condition for the production of immediate and lasting outcomes in the local environment (Citroni, 2020).

Final remarks. Gramsci's civil society in urban contexts

In search of legitimacy in an era of growing instability, where building consensus is increasingly difficult, urban governments are striving to establish collaboration with citizens (McLean, 2014) while mobilising forms of residents' organisations, including informal groupings (Ranci, 2015). In Milan, as in other urban contexts, the transformation of the urban middle classes and the spread of 'networked governance' models (Davies, 2011) have expanded the opportunities and arenas for the growth of a variety of civil society initiatives. More specifically, emerging civil society actors that commit to local leisure activism initiatives (Lamond and Spracklen, 2015) have received growing interest from city governments. Whether apolitical in their declared meanings or openly challenging the dominant norms and ideologies (Gilchrist and Ravenscroft, 2013), current leisure practices and performances are invested with increasing political relevance, such as when co-opted in urban government and its governance arenas.

The analysis of NCS has proved to be an excellent opportunity to look closely at how emerging forms of civil society mobilising leisure activism practices can actually become influential in political processes. Generally considered highly ephemeral and fragmented or important just for their role as side elements in larger processes of social and economic change, the case of NCS' initiatives has shown how practices of leisure activism can prove to be politically relevant in a fairly outright way. We argue that this largely depends on their rooting in wider civil society structuring processes, characterised by a certain ability to pool resources and promote a discursive order around inclusiveness.

In this perspective, a Gramscian approach appears to be particularly compelling, as it is able to illuminate the unique aspects of the ways contemporary, emerging forms of civil society form and function. By rejecting the bourgeois idea of a civil society that is separated from the state (Gramsci, 1997), Gramsci brings these areas together: more precisely, defining the civil society of liberal societies and above all the hegemony that prevails there as the 'ethical content of the state' (Gramsci, 1975, p. 703). As Gramsci's civil society is the field of struggle for hegemony (Gramsci, 1997), it is not the sphere of action of certain, predefined actors (Alexander, 2006) but the domain that includes all the actions through which different worldviews are put forward and – often silently – fight each other for legitimacy, to be accepted as 'natural' and thus taken for granted (Citroni, 2019).

We argue that, as illuminated by this study, by endorsing such an approach we can better investigate and understand the strategic role of urban contexts in the production of forms of government *through* civil society, and in particular *by* leisure activism. As shown here, convivial and cultural events that aim to improve the local quality of life have become constitutive components of urban politics and policy-making processes (Tissot, 2014). These initiatives are clearly and actively involved and mobilised in an ongoing struggle for hegemony, which is facilitated by political actors and operationalised through highly experimental policy-making processes. Leisure activism, in this context, becomes a decisive resource for exerting the subtle arts of power and influence in an ever-changing and hard-to-govern urban environment.

Note

1. All interviewees are cited according to their occupation and the year during which they were interviewed.

Disclosure statement

No potential conflict of interest was reported by the authors.

ORCID

Sebastiano Citroni http://orcid.org/0000-0002-6373-3725
Alessandro Coppola http://orcid.org/0000-0002-6729-7713

References

Alexander, J. (2006). *The civil sphere*. Oxford University Press.

Biorcio, R., & Vitale, T. (2016). *Italia Civile: Associazionismo, partecipazione e politica*. Carocci.

Boltanski, L., & Chiapello, E. (2017[1999]). *The new spirit of capitalism*. Verso.

Brighenti, A. M. (2016). Antonio Gramsci's theory of the civil society. In S. Moebius, F. Nungesser, & K. Scherke (Eds.), *Handbuch Kultursoziologie. Band 1: Begriffe, Kontexte, Perspektiven, Autor_innen* (pp. 143–165). Springer.

Brighenti, A. M. (2020). At the wall: Graffiti writers, urban territoriality, and the public domain. *Space & Culture, 13* (3), 315–332. https://doi.org/10.1177/1206331210365283

Citroni, S. (2015). *Inclusive togetherness: A comparative ethnography of cultural associations making Milan sociable*. La Scuola.

Citroni, S. (2019). Gramsci's civil society and the implicit dimension of politics. A case study. *Partecipazione & Conflitto, 12*(2), 487–512. https://doi.org/10.1285/i20356609v12i2p487

Citroni, S. (2020). Civil society events: Ambiguities and the exertion of cultural power. *European Journal of Cultural and Political Sociology (Onlinefirst), 7*(2), 150–171. https://doi.org/10.1080/23254823.2020.1727349

Comune Di, M. (2018). *Bando alle periferie 2018. Avviso pubblico per l'erogazione di contributi destinati a progetti di sostegno della rigenerazione urbana nell'ambito delle periferie milanesi*. Comune di Milano.

Comune Di, M. (2019). *Avviso pubblico eventi nei quartieri*. Comune di Milano.

Comune di Milano. (2019b). *Piazze aperte in ogni quartiere. Avviso pubblico per la presentazione di proposte di collaborazione*.

Coppola, A. (2018b). *La sfida (rimandata?) delle governance e delle politiche della complessità a Roma Coppola A., Punziano G., Roma in Transizione. Governo, strategie, metabolismi e quadri di vita di una metropoli* (Vol. 1). Planum Publisher.

Coppola, A. (2018a). Politica e politiche di quartiere nella città neo-liberale. *Civismo Proprietario a Baltimora, Etnografia E Ricerca Qualitativa, 11*(3), 449–475. https://doi.org/10.3240/92126

Coppola, A. (2019). The differentiation of the trivial, The bars in NoLo (Milan) as micro-publics in the age of urban super-diversification. *Lo Squaderno, 53, 41-44.*

Coppola, A., & Caudo, G. (2020). Orizzonti di innovazione democratica. In I. Urban (Ed.), *Quinto rapporto sulle città. Politiche urbane per le periferie, Il Mulino,* pp. 69–80.

Evans, J., Ross Jones, A., Karvonen, L. M., & Wendler, J. (2015). Living labs and co-production: University campuses as platforms for sustainability science. *Current Opinion in Environmental Sustainability*, Vol *16*, 1–6. https://doi.org/10.1016/j.cosust.2015.06.005

Fondazione Cariplo. (n. d.) *La città intorno*. Programma e Obiettivi. https://lacittaintorno.fondazionecariplo.it/programma-obiettivi/

Foucault, M. (2005). *Nascita della biopolitica: Corso al College de France 1978-1979*. Feltrinelli.

Genitori Antismog (2019, March, 24), Trentamì Zona 30 Gente contenta, Youtube Retrieved January 15, 2020, from https://www.youtube.com/watch?v=93vtqC2dDwc&t=43s

Gerosa, A. (2019). Alcohol and the city: The logistics of alcoholic flows in urban transformations. *Lo Squaderno, 52*, 33–38. IL DOI NON L'HO TROVATO PER LO SQUADERNO.

Gilchrist, P., & Ravenscroft, N. (2013). Space hijacking and the anarcho-politics of leisure. Leisure Studies, 32(1), 49–68 doi:10.1080/02614367.2012.680069

Gramsci, A. (1975). *Quaderni dal Carcere*. Einaudi.

Gramsci, A. (1997). *[Ed. Montanari, M.]. Pensare la Democrazia: Antologia dai Quaderni dal Carcere*. Einaudi.

Grigoleit, A., Hahn, J., & Brocchi, D. (2013). "And in the end my street will not be the same". The art project 2-3 streets and its link to (un)sustainability, creative urban development and modernization. *City, Culture and Society, 4*(3), 173–185. https://doi.org/10.1016/j.ccs.2013.05.002

Habermas, J. (2000). *Storia e critica dell'opinione pubblica*. Laterza.

Lamond, I. R. (2018). The challenge of articulating human rights at an LGBT 'mega-event': A personal reflection on Sao Paulo Pride 2017. *Leisure Studies, 37*(1), 36–48. https://doi.org/10.1080/02614367.2017.1419370

Lamond, I. R., Solano, E., & Blotta, V. (2020). Leisure activism and engaged ethnography: Heterogeneous voices and the urban palimpsest. *Leisure Studies (Online First)*, 1–13. https://doi.org/10.1080/02614367.2020.1724318

Lamond, I. R., & Spracklen, K. (2015). Protests as Events: Politics, Activism and Leisure. London: Rowman & Littlefield

Lichterman, P. (1996). *The search for political community: American activists reinventing commitment*. Cambridge University Press.

McLean, H. (2014). Cracks in the creative city: The contradictions of community arts practice. *International Journal of Urban and Regional Research, 38*(6), 2156–2173. https://doi.org/10.1111/1468-2427.12168

Morelli, N. (2019). Creating urban sociality in middle-class neighborhoods in Milan and Bologna: A study on the social streets phenomenon. *City & Community, 18*(3), 834–852. https://doi.org/10.1111/cico.12415

Mulino Davies, J. S. (2011). *Challenging governance theory: From networks to hegemony*. Policy Press.

Nolo Partecipa (n. d.), Facebook, Retrived https://www.facebook.com/groups/140635563338078/

Nolo Social District (n. d.), Facebook, Retrieved, January 15, 2020. https://www.facebook.com/groups/NoLoDistrict/

Progetto Mobì (n. d.), Facebook, Retrieved December 21, 2019, from https://www.facebook.com/progettoMobiNoLo/

Ranci, C. (2015). The long-term evolution of the government third sector partnership in Italy: Old wine in a new bottle? *Voluntas: International Journal of Voluntary and Nonprofit Organizations, 26*(6), 2311–2329. https://doi.org/10.1007/s11266-016-9797-x

Sampson, R. (2012). *Great American City: Chicago and the enduring neighborhood effect*. University of Chicago Press.

Sironi, F. (2016, September 2). *North of Loreto, D.La Repubblica delle Donne*.

Tissot, S. (2014). Loving diversity/Controlling diversity: Exploring the ambivalent mobilization of upper-middle-class gentrifiers, South End, Boston. *International Journal of Urban and Regional Studies, 38*(4), 1181–1194. https://doi.org/10.1111/1468-2427.12128

Verga, P. (2016). Rhetoric in the representation of a multi-ethnic neighbourhood: The case of Via Padova, Milan. *Antipode, 48*(4), 1080–1101. https://doi.org/10.1111/anti.12229

Walzer, M. (1992). The civil society argument. In C. Mouffe (Ed.), *Dimensions of radical democracy: Pluralism, citizenship, community* (pp. 90–107). Verso.

Web and Social media sources

Wuthnow, R. (1998). *Loose connections: Joining together in Americas fragmented communities*. Harvard University Press.

Zukin, S. (2010). *Naked city: The death and life of authentic urban places*. Oxford University Press.

Afterword

Pause and breathe: a point of arrival and departure

Ian R. Lamond, Brett Lashua and Chelsea Reid

This book has presented the contents of a special issue of the journal *Leisure Studies*, co-edited by Ian R Lamond, Brett Lashua, and Chelsea Reid. Even though that special issue was published less than two years before this book, the world of which we are now a part feels very different, yet also strangely familiar. Our introductory chapter was written during the first lockdown period in the UK and despite things supposedly returning to some degree of normality, they have not – nor do they feel as though things will ever be as they were before COVID. Given all that, as editors we decided that the conversion of the special issue into a book warranted a point where we should pause and breathe and acknowledge where we were. The conversation that follows is neither a summation of the past, as presented in the work offered in the book, nor is it a call to action for the future; it is a moment of pause, in which we reflect on where we were – a point that is one of arrival and departure. It also took place as a video call, apropos of the times. As well as being a key member of the discussion, Chelsea took on the role of discussant/provocateur – not an easy task given the characters of the other editors.

Chelsea

As co-editors we are writing not so much to summarise this collection but to take a look back at how things have changed, especially since the COVID-19 pandemic, and to consider how we position some of these papers in wider contexts, and also to provide some thoughts as to where things may go in the future.

Ian

This book is very much a work in progress, and this acts more as flagging up a few things we have found interesting, but we do understand that there's so much more that needs to be done.

Brett

It's always a sign of a book worth reading is that it generates more questions and that it prompts or provokes discussions rather than closing things off.

Chelsea

Exactly. Which leads me onto the first of a few questions I have devised for this discussion.

With COVID-19 and the implementation of the social distancing mandates, do we think that we will see a shift in a traditional form that's of mass participation through protest? And if so, do you think that is just a product of the pandemic or do you think other factors come into play here? Considering the social media elephant in the room, could it be an amalgamation of that or do you think it has purely been a pandemic-based shift?

Brett

It is interesting to consider these chapters (first for the special issue, now for this book) from either side of the COVID-19 pandemic. The introduction was written just as we were entering the first UK lockdown, and the papers were written before COVID-19, and here we are, ostensibly now on the other side. It's quite interesting to look back, but I think for me, the shift that you're asking about has already occurred, and that digital activism or online activism has been with us at least since the early 2010s, since, for example, the 'Arab Spring' ignited in Egypt following the death of Khaled Saeed, as well as through online activism, like the #MeToo movement led by Tarana Burke, and other kinds of social justice protests that have emerged online (#OccupyWallStreet) and in cities. Sometimes social media may be used to organise and coordinate street protests, and if we wanted to pick another example, we could look at the January 6th, 2021, Capitol insurrection in the US, part of which appears to have been coordinated through social media. I think it's that kind of fusion that we're seeing more of, rather than a separation of the two. In this book, David McGillivray, John Lauermann, and Daniel Turner's chapter on Olympic protests is a great example that showcases some of the potential and also the limits of online activism.

Ian

I don't see social media activism as replacing mass protest. One of the exciting and interesting things about protest is how it evolves and adapts. As Paolo Gerbaudo (2012) mentions in *Tweets and the Streets* about the Arab Spring uprisings in Egypt, yes, social media did play a really significant part in this, but it's part of it. It's not the only game in town and I think it's always important to bear that in mind. If you think about activism, like the current anti-drink spiking protests that have been taking place around Europe and the UK, then yes, there's been a social media element to that, but there's been a physical participation element as well. Social media enriches rather than replaces street protest.

Chelsea

I agree. I think it was Morozov (2011) who repurposed this idea of 'slacktivism'. So I think it is kind of supplementary; they have to go kind of hand in hand. Having a successful national, even international campaign based solely on social media would probably be an anomaly, an exception as opposed to the rule. It has to be this kind of amalgamation of both; it has to be a hybrid.

Ian

In some situations, in some contexts, digital dissent is the only form of dissent that people can articulate. You have terms like 'slacktivism' as a sort of pejorative term; yet sometimes it's the only form of dissent that is possible for some people, and so we need to see value in it rather than just automatically rule it out as something that's lazy.

Brett

Sure, but for me questions of digital dissent are also questions of where those elements might pierce or puncture urban spaces, if we want to come back to the animation of cities. It's a question of political consequences and how these shape urban spaces. I think we're still talking about where things blur between online and offline worlds, and I guess the even bigger question is what counts as protest?

Ian

Sure. And I think there has historically been a tendency to feel as though protest is not exclusive to, but the main domain of the left. We need to recognise that protest has a much wider spectrum than that, and I think this millennia particularly has brought that to the fore, strongly.

Chelsea

That's a good segue into the next question actually. Do you think those recent protests that have taken place in physical spaces, for example, the anti-racism social justice protests in the wake of George Floyd, are recording an increase in violence as a result of these forced mandates and of us generally being more 'contained' than ever before, or is it the subject matter driving this passion? In direct contradiction with these protests, Mowatt asks 'where the White Nationalists are' in his paper and goes into detail about the concept of ideologically racist movements being very common, as opposed to anomalies. Will this cause more of an issue and a schism in society moving forward?

Ian

That feels like a long question where ultimately my answer is "yes, but" ...

Brett

Rasul Mowatt's chapter is very important because it points out the long-standing historical thread of right-wing activism in the US and the use of urban public spaces and parks for gatherings centred around causes that I think most people would label as extremely hateful.

Ian

That's it. That was where I was trying to get to when I was mentioning and counter democratic movements and movements that present themselves as being a check and balance towards the excesses of democratic power, and actually what they're doing is undermining democratic power.

Brett

Yes, and I think the idea of leisure as protest is really central to that. I can't really think of more important examples of excessive democratic power than people getting together to protest something and having that protest turn into mob violence.

Ian

We do need to be mindful of what we mean by violence. This depends on the perspective that you're starting from. I mean, I remember, in Brazil, a pro junta demonstration where it seemed so nice, you know, looking from the outside. There were concession stands there, selling food. There were families having picnics. It was really friendly and warm and welcoming, but then you'd see a banner saying, 'Abortion is Murder' and basically 'the only good foreigner is a dead foreigner'. You then have to start thinking, where does violence actually sit? Who's defining what violence is?

Chelsea

Troy Glover, Sarah Munro, Immony Men, Wes Loates, and Ilana Altman's chapter focuses on a 'free' form of participation and leisure in a public space, which is rare in a society so focused on assigning monetary value to activity and interaction. As Glover et al. suggest, is there a need to consciously add these locations into the fabric of mainstream society, or do you believe these activities will remain on the fringe?

Ian

I'm really struggling with this question. I'm thinking about how Pride has been so commercialised and commodified, particularly within the UK and probably the US as well. If you suddenly 'mainstream' these spaces and these forms of activity, they start to become routine, and if they start to become routine, they stop being protest. It's important that urban spaces are animated through dissent, but the more you commodify that and commercialise it then the more you undermine it. It is a tricky balance because you would also want to leave a legacy. You don't want that legacy to be a negative legacy. You don't want to commodify that legacy to such an extent that it stops being impactful or meaningful.

Brett

Yes, most of our contributors wrestled with questions of meaningful impact. Kirsty Jamieson and Louise Todd wrote about cities as playgrounds of dissent against capitalism but argued that urban festivals can be viewed as both consumerist and revolutionary. Skateboarding, as part of Troy Glover et al.'s paper, is another great example of this, where leisure materially transformed the city. Troy and his collaborators wrote about The Bentway, a site underneath a highway overpass that would have traditionally been a space that was not valued. They looked at how it's been repurposed, and the urban and environmental issues that the skateboarders were collectively arguing for and against. I think that's just a really powerful example of how space can be transformed through leisure. Yet, both examples highlight a mix of civic partnerships and civic transformation as well, so it also shows some power through hybrid partnerships between the public, private, and social enterprise, to create a lasting legacy.

Ian

Sebastiano Citroni and Alessandro Coppola's paper echoes that as well, doesn't it? When they write about the "NoLo" district in Milan and how community groups were forming partnerships with others to shape local policy, and how together they have transformed that space. It brings up questions of the 'right to leisure' in cities.

Chelsea

The 'right to leisure' is a key topic, and Harmon goes into detail in his piece on homelessness. Following on from Glover et al.'s idea of free leisure, considered by many to be in direct opposition to a capitalist society, Harmon's 'right to leisure' pushes this even further and presents homelessness not only as devoid of leisure but also as devoid of any real place in society. How closely linked can the broad terms of 'leisure' and 'a sense of place/belonging' be not only in this scenario, but also in wider society?

Brett

A 'sense of place' is certainly part of leisure and the animation of urban environments. In their chapter, Rudy Dunlap, Jeff Rose, Sarah Standridge, and Courtney Pruitt focus on bicycling as a form of everyday practice to develop a sense of place and reclaim urban spaces. In a more overtly political context, Carlo Genova discusses leisure and a sense of place in his chapter on youth and "political squats" – intentional occupations of abandoned buildings, which become, in effect, sites of leisure lifestyles. While these are politically minded chapters, one question that Justin Harmon has raised – do people who are homeless have leisure at all? – is vital when we think about leisure activism as a privilege. But I'm also thinking of questions of what makes a good life, where is a good life, and how can people work individually or collectively toward that? Genova wrote about that in terms of leisure, protest and engaging with some sense of a civil society in cities. That brings us back to the three key lenses of the special issue: leisure, activism, and animation of urban environments. It shows you the difficulty of juggling those three conceptual areas.

Ian

In their presence, and in their absence.

Chelsea

On to the final question: obviously you did mention this in the introduction, but if you can expand on this idea that would be great. What sort of chapter would you have liked to have seen that fills the gap for LGBTQ+ representation? Or is there something else that you would have liked to see in this book that hasn't been covered?

Ian

The issue of LGBT activism, particularly in the Affluent West, is interesting. This links back to a point raised earlier, around the commodification of dissent. Where the event of dissent becomes routine and commodified it risks becoming, effectively, siloed – parked into a neat and manageable niche where it remains important and significant for its community, but outside that silo any expression of activism is only permitted within an implicit socio-cultural frame of reference. The "other" is permitted a voice but only at key points in the calendar. Such a perspective resonates with Bakhtin's conception of the carnivalesque (Bakhtin, 2009). Misrule is permitted, but only within certain prescribed boundaries.

Brett

How do you mean?

Ian

Those boundaries are a manifestation of a discourse of domination and repression that, fundamentally, says – 'OK, right, we've done your LGBT stuff, that's the end of it; you're gonna have to wait until LGBT History Month or Aids Awareness Week. Hey, you're Bi, you're Lesbian, etc. – we've got a visibility week just for you!' We get our dedicated time slot in which we can manifest some form of dissent, in which we can articulate an "othered" message in the public realm – and we are expected to be grateful for that sliver of freedom, despite the persistence of bullying and victimisation in the workplace, in schools, on the street, and aggression at all levels – we have got to remember that hate crime, as a result of someone's sexual identity and/or gender orientation, is rising at an eye-watering rate in many countries.

Brett

So what does this mean in terms of leisure activism?

Ian

There are real conflictualities between what is considered legitimate dissent and what is not. The boundary between what is considered acceptable/legitimate activism and what is not is not clear cut, it's messy. Sure, observance days are important, but observance days alone are not activism. They are permitted misrule in a Bakhtian sense. LGBT concerns and issues still need to be addressed. The juridical freedom and equality that has been granted is not the end of the matter. While there is hate, and heteronormative values are encoded in the fabric and structures of our institutions and societal relations, the discourse of being queer remains on the outside – we remain "other". But it is messy. It's messy because what passes for acceptance is actually a form of invisibility. Queer narratives drown in the ocean of a supposed acceptance that bleaches them of their richness and colour. This is an example of what Escobar refers to when he discusses the importance of a pluriversal politics (Escobar, 2020), a politics that isn't about finding the right narrative but that is accommodating of multiplicity and complexity across multiple narratives. Sure, it is messy – and it is a shame we didn't get any papers that tried to confront that messiness.

Chelsea

So how do we confront that?

Ian

Well, it would have been good to see something that looks at more underground leisure/activism. I'm currently working on something with my good friend, the poet, novelist, musician, Rosie Garland. We are editing a collection that discusses deviant leisure and events of deviance and looking at activism that is being articulated through deviant leisure practice, as framed by mainstream heteronormative society. The multiplicity that can be approached under the umbrella of deviant leisure is interesting because such activity can present ongoing subversive forms of activism that don't fit into any nice, commodified, frame of reference. Observance days and observance weeks, within a political framework when one narrative dominates, carry the risk of creating or sustaining conflictualities. Multiplicity becomes settled and routine – you can be other now because it is your time for being other – we've not accepted you and we are just going to give this special time when you can be different. In the UK, the recently passed Police and Crime Bill seems to echo this regularisation, commodification, siloing, and – ultimately – invisibilising of dissent in urban space. Invisibilising because only events of dissent that don't disrupt, that can pass by, effectively unnoticed, will be considered legitimate. Anyway, I've rambled on too much.

Chelsea

As a member of the LGBT+ community, it is something we do have to navigate on a daily basis. There's an unfortunate unspoken rule that there's a time and a place to be ourselves, and that in other moments we are often relegated to 'other'. Similarly, commodifying our struggles, with an overpriced light stick or a rainbow flag, is something that is hard to adjust to.

Brett

You should write a paper on that, Chelsea! As with all academic publishing, there's a limit on how much content and how many papers are included in any special issue. I was surprised we didn't receive any submissions on leisure, protest, and nationalism, especially in terms of border towns and the migration and movements of people. I suppose I'd have liked to see papers about anti-war protests as leisure, too.

Ian

For sure – it would have been good to see some anti-war protest as leisure in there. Your point about migration and war has also got me thinking. The issue of migrant mobilities raises some important points on which it is worth reflecting. With the current war in the Ukraine, there has been a substantial amount of media coverage around the willingness for people to open their homes to provide space for Ukrainians fleeing the war. Now, I take such action to be morally right. It is something, I believe, should be done. The narrative is that of a willingness to open one's arms to *the other* who is fleeing a war zone. But that narrative, in very recent times, is in stark opposition to that used when referring to people fleeing some other war zones. The willingness to embrace migrants from other areas of conflict, not exclusively but most notably from predominantly Arab states, has not been forthcoming. In fact, we tend to find an oppositional narrative – one of hostility that places the lives of those seeking sanctuary at risk of exploitation and much, much, worse. Families separated; people thrown into large holding camps; and those desperate to find security violently held back. In that situation, migrant mobility is considered a threat and not an opportunity to welcome and support those in need, as a result of war.

Chelsea

I have observed that, while there seems to be an element of almost tokenistic engagement with the war in Ukraine within my small 'bubble' on social media, the vast majority of said engagement has been overwhelmingly positive. This mirrors Ian's observation that we appear to be more tolerant of certain warzones, and of certain migrants, and do tend to favour public declarations of support for those 'closer to home'.

We aren't seeing the sheer volume of 'boots on the ground', as we did with the anti-Iraq war, which could be down to the evolution of how members of society choose to protest and get their voice across. Could it be that we are simply finding new outlets for dissent, for example, using a very popular "colour chart" meme detailing the issues we have with Black and Brown migrants, or that we do have to adopt a 'hybrid' approach to protest in order for it to be at its most effective?

Brett

Well, that's a good ending point for this conversation, I suppose. In that shift towards "meme activism" and online dissent: what are the horizons of how far it goes and what sorts of impact does it have?

Chelsea

There needs to be a volume 2 of this project!

Ian

There's so much more work that needs to be going on out there. And if this volume kickstarts anyone to think about things a little bit differently or to explore ideas and questions that we've raised then that would be brilliant.

Brett

I agree. A major point for me is that it shows in all sorts of ways once again that leisure matters. It's really vital. The pandemic has highlighted that in many ways, but questions around protest and animating urban environments continue to vividly illustrate why leisure deserves to be valued and warrants more attention.

References

Bakhtin, M. (2009). *Rabelais and His World.* Trans. Iswolsky, H. Bloomington: Indiana University Press.
Escobar, A. (2020). *Pluriversal Politics: The Real and the Possible.* Durham, NC: Duke University Press.
Gerbaudo, P. (2012). *Tweets and the Streets: Social Media and Contemporary Activism.* New York: Pluto Press.
Morozov, E. (2011). *The Net Delusion: The Dark Side of Internet Freedom.* New York: Public Affairs.

Index

Note: page numbers followed by "n" denote endnotes.